Jossey-Bass Teacher

Jossey-Bass Teacher provides K–12 teachers with essential knowledge and tools to create a positive and lifelong impact on student learning. Trusted and experienced educational mentors offer practical classroom-tested and theory-based teaching resources for improving teaching practice in a broad range of grade levels and subject areas. From one educator to another, we want to be your first source to make every day your best day in teaching. *Jossey-Bass Teacher* resources serve two types of informational needs—essential knowledge and essential tools.

Essential knowledge resources provide the foundation, strategies, and methods from which teachers may design curriculum and instruction to challenge and excite their students. Connecting theory to practice, essential knowledge books rely on a solid research base and time-tested methods, offering the best ideas and guidance from many of the most experienced and well-respected experts in the field.

Essential tools save teachers time and effort by offering proven, ready-to-use materials for in-class use. Our publications include activities, assessments, exercises, instruments, games, ready reference, and more. They enhance an entire course of study, a weekly lesson, or a daily plan. These essential tools provide insightful, practical, and comprehensive materials on topics that matter most to K–12 teachers.

How to Use the DVD

System Requirements

PC with Microsoft Windows 98 or later
Mac with Apple OS version 10 or later

You will also need:

Quicktime 7.0 or later (available at www.apple.com)
Adobe Acrobat Reader 8.0 or later (available at www.adobe.com)

Using the DVD

1. Insert the DVD into your computer's DVD drive. (Note: this DVD is NOT designed to work in a DVD player, such as the one that hooks up to your television.)

2. If you are using a PC, the DVD should automatically begin to run and give you the options of viewing the videos or the PDFs. You MUST have Quicktime to view the videos, and you MUST have Adobe Acrobat Reader to use the PDFs. If the DVD does not immediately begin to run, go to "My Computer" and double-click on your computer's DVD drive. The DVD should begin to run.

3. If you are working on a Mac, click the DVD icon that appears on your desktop. Then click the "JB" icon that appears in the window that opens. The DVD should begin to run and give you the options of viewing the videos or the PDFs.

4. The PDF forms cannot be saved to the DVD. Save them onto your hard drive.

In Case of Trouble

If you experience difficulty using the DVD, please follow these steps:

1. Make sure your hardware and systems configurations conform to the systems requirements noted under "System Requirements" above.

2. Review the installation procedure for your type of hardware and operating system.

To speak with someone in Product Technical Support, call 800–762–2974 or 317–572–3994 M–F 8:30 a.m.–5:00 p.m. EST. You can also get support and contact Product Technical Support through our website at www.wiley.com/techsupport.
Before calling or writing, please have the following information available:

Type of computer and operating system
Any error messages displayed
Complete description of the problem

It is best if you are sitting at your computer when making the call.

DISCIPLINE

— IN THE —

SECONDARY CLASSROOM

A POSITIVE APPROACH TO BEHAVIOR MANAGEMENT

SECOND EDITION

RANDALL S. SPRICK, PH.D.

JOSSEY-BASS
A Wiley Imprint
www.josseybass.com

Published by Jossey-Bass
A Wiley Imprint
989 Market Street, San Francisco, CA 94103-1741   www.josseybass.com

Jossey-Bass books and products are available through most bookstores. To contact Jossey-Bass directly call our Customer Care Department within the U.S. at 800-956-7739, outside the U.S. at 317-572-3986, or fax 317-572-4002.

Jossey-Bass also publishes its books in a variety of electronic formats. Some content that appears in print may not be available in electronic books.

Library of Congress Cataloging-in-Publication Data
Sprick, Randall S.
 Discipline in the secondary classroom / Randall S. Sprick.— 2nd ed with DVD.
     p. cm.
 Includes bibliographical references and index.
 ISBN: 978-0-470-42226-7
 1. Classroom management. 2. High school students—Discipline. 3. Problem children—Discipline. I. Title.
 LB3013.S64 2006
 373.1102'4—dc22
                    2005032571

Printed in the United States of America
SECOND EDITION
PB Printing   10 9 8 7 6 5 4

The Author

Randall Sprick has an undergraduate degree in general education, a master's degree in special education, and a doctorate in curriculum and supervision. He has taught students with emotional and behavioral problems and trained and supervised teachers at elementary and secondary levels. He has taught postgraduate courses on behavior management and behavioral consultation at the University of Oregon.

Dr. Sprick has written numerous articles and books, as well as developed audio and video in-service programs addressing topics such as classroom management, schoolwide discipline policies, playground discipline, and bus behavior. Among the widely used books he has written are:

- *START on Time! Safe Transitions and Reduced Tardiness*
- *Foundations: Establishing Positive Discipline Policies*
- *CHAMPs: A Proactive and Positive Approach to Classroom Management*
- *The Teacher's Encyclopedia of Behavior Management: 100 Problems/500 Plans*
- *The Administrator's Desk Reference of Behavior Management* (3 vols.)
- *Interventions: Collaborative Planning for Students at Risk*
- *ParaPro: Supporting the Instructional Process*
- *The Solution Book: A Guide to Classroom Discipline*

Dr. Sprick is director of Safe & Civil Schools, which provides in-service programs throughout the country. Each year, he and his training staff conduct workshops and classes for more than thirty thousand teachers. His positive and practical approach is helping schools increase safety, reduce classroom disruption, and improve school climate.

Acknowledgments

I acknowledge the content suggestions and editorial assistance of Beau Prichard, Natalie Conaway, Rohanna Buchanan, Susan Isaacs, Laura Hamilton, Jim Whitaker, and Laura Matson. Thanks to the staffs of Pacific Northwest Publishing and Jossey-Bass Publishing for their willingness to link the approach of this book with the Safe & Civil Schools materials. Finally, I thank Steve Thompson and Kate Gagnon at Jossey-Bass for their gracious professionalism and support throughout the revision of this book.

How to Use
This Book

This book leaves decisions to you. There is no part of the book that is a canned program of specific procedures you must implement. Instead, it is more of a toolshed filled with classroom-tested tools and techniques that are made available to you. As you work through the book, read each task and think about whether your current classroom management plan addresses the issues it addresses. Consider whether implementing some or all of the suggestions within the task would have a positive benefit on behavior and motivation for your students.

The best way to use this book will vary depending on when you choose to implement it. The early chapters are more for preplanning, that is, determining your teaching plan in advance of the school year. All the tasks in this book can be implemented in any classroom at any time, but coming in fully prepared and with a concrete plan is obviously the ideal situation. Because ideal situations are so rare, this book also describes ways to implement your new skills at any time of the year, or even gradually throughout the year:

Beginning in the spring or summer. Ideally, you will have plenty of time to work through Chapters One through Seven in sequence before the school year begins. By working through each task, and deciding which steps to implement and how, you will build the components of your management plan. Chapter Seven in particular will help you pull all these details together for the first day of school. As the school year approaches, you should also review Chapters Eight and Nine to completely prepare yourself to take full advantage of the tools offered in this book.

In some cases, teachers will be given a copy of this book as part of teacher induction to a new district. If that is the case and you have only a little time before the students arrive, you can cover the most vital information first. With limited time, work through Chapters Four and Seven. Also, skim Chapter Eight, putting prompts in your planning calendar about using the tools in this book to monitor and revise your management plan throughout the school year.

Beginning in the fall. The best time to have an impact on student behavior is on the first day of school. Short of that, the first day of second semester is a good time to make some changes if they are needed. Skim through Chapters One through Six to identify any suggestions that you think might be of immediate benefit to your classes; then work through the chapters again in more detail, preparing for the next semester. As you have time, work through Chapters Eight and Nine. During the next summer, work more thoroughly through Chapters One through Seven to revise your plan and fully prepare for the first day of school.

Beginning in winter. Use the Contents to identify tasks and suggestions that might help address specific problems. Then in late spring, follow the suggestions in the section above regarding how to prepare for the new school year.

Motivating students is part art and part science. So, too, is classroom management. And both are lifelong learning tasks. When you use the research-based techniques set out in this book, you will reach and teach students who would otherwise be doomed to school failure and a life emptied of much of the promise of a successful education. Never doubt that an effective teacher can be the defining difference in a child's life.

Randall S. Sprick

Dedication

This book would never have been possible if it were not for the excellent ideas of hundreds of high school teachers from around North America. During in-service sessions over the past twenty-five years, numerous teachers have openly shared their successful techniques with me. Their ideas and methods have helped me formulate the procedures included in these pages. And so I dedicate this book to these competent and caring professionals, who serve such an important role in shaping the future.

Contents

Foreword

About five years ago, I was part of a project designed to improve the academic outcomes for struggling adolescent learners in some inner-city high schools. Great planning went into the selection of the instructional programs for improving their reading and math performance. We instituted a carefully orchestrated professional development effort to make certain that each of the teachers involved was well prepared to teach the targeted interventions. As the program was launched, we were confident that things were going to go well because of our careful planning and attention to the necessary details.

How wrong we were!

Although some successes in student outcomes were seen, they fell far short of our expectations. Puzzled, we visited with teachers and observed what was happening in many of the classrooms. It soon became clear that many of the classes were out of control: large numbers of students were tardy for class, student behavior during classes was often inappropriate, and the amount of time spent teaching the targeted interventions was limited. In short, when instruction did take place, it didn't reach all of the students and was often compromised because of the poor work environment; teachers were frequently interrupting their lesson to regain control of their class.

In light of the problems that we were facing, I called Randy Sprick to see if he would be willing to problem-solve with us. I knew Randy and had carefully followed his work for over two decades. Over the years, I have talked to countless teachers and administrators throughout North America who implemented his student motivation and classroom management programs, programs grounded in proactive, positive, and instructional principles. Randy agreed to analyze what was happening in our schools. As a result of that conversation and the programs described in this book that our team subsequently implemented, we experienced a dramatic change in how business was done in those schools. We witnessed firsthand the dramatic effects these methods can have in transforming secondary schools that were once places of chaos and disengaged students to settings of order and safety, where interactions among students and teachers are respectful, and students are eagerly and productively involved in the learning process.

Discipline in the Secondary Classroom: A Positive Approach to Behavior Management addresses one of the most pressing needs faced by secondary teachers in today's schools: how to effectively motivate and manage adolescent learners so their classrooms can be stimulating, engaging learning environments.

I am convinced that secondary teachers will find this book to be one of the most valuable resources in their teaching toolbox for the following reasons:

- It is grounded in an extensive research base.
- It is hands-on, providing clear, step-by-step instructions for how to implement each procedure.
- It supplies specific examples from actual classroom situations to illustrate each procedure.
- It is principle-based.
- It is comprehensive in scope, including all of the necessary components (and accompanying forms and support mechanisms) to be a self-contained management and motivation system.
- It spells out clearly how to introduce and implement the program throughout the school year.
- It is carefully coordinated with a companion volume designed for elementary students: *CHAMPs: A Proactive Approach to Positive Classroom Management* (Sprick, Garrison, & Howard, 1998), thus enabling school districts to implement a systematic approach to student motivation and classroom management across the entire K–12 grade continuum.

This book is the extraordinary resource that it is because of its author, Randy Sprick. Randy has had extensive experience as a teacher, program developer, researcher, writer, and staff developer. One of the most sought-after teachers in the country, he has a deep understanding of the complexities of secondary schools, the needs of adolescents and teachers, and the dynamic that exists among them. The program outlined in this book has been successfully adopted by hundreds of schools throughout North America. I consider Randy Sprick to be one of the brightest and most insightful educators of our time. His mission has been to improve the quality of environments in schools and enable teachers and students alike to thrive. I believe that he has been extraordinarily successful in that quest.

Achieving successful academic outcomes for students is certainly important, but their overall growth, development, and well-being involve much more than academic success. While teachers understand this, they now find themselves in an educational dynamic that does not encourage (and in some cases does not even permit) an emphasis on the nonacademic dimensions of schooling. This book underscores the fact that understanding and addressing factors beyond academics is not only important, it is essential.

Since the passage of the No Child Left Behind Act, schools have focused almost entirely on increasing the academic performance of students. This book provides one of the foundational cornerstones for enabling teachers to be successful in the academic instruction that they provide. It will empower secondary teachers to create the kind of environment and culture in their classroom that will ultimately promote optimal academic outcomes.

This readable book is written with passion, vivid examples, and countless practical suggestions that can be readily implemented. In my more than thirty-five years as an educator, I have relied on the insights and work of many talented educators. This book will add greatly to my abilities as an educator in secondary schools, and it will be a resource I turn to frequently.

Donald D. Deshler
Director,
University of Kansas Center for Research on Learning

Preface

The first edition of this book was published in 1985. Since that time, research continues to confirm that the proactive, positive, and instructional approaches it advocated are far more effective in managing and motivating students than traditional, authoritarian, and punitive approaches. Teacher effectiveness literature has identified that teachers who are highly successful have classroom management plans that:

- Include high expectations for student success.
- Build positive relationships with students.
- Create consistent, predictable classroom routines.
- Teach students how to behave successfully.
- Provide frequent positive feedback.
- Correct misbehavior in a calm, consistent, logical manner.

This revised edition is designed to translate those broad ideas into specific actions you can take to improve your ability to maintain an orderly and respectful classroom in which students are focused and engaged in meaningful instructional activities.

This book fits in with a larger body of work: the Safe & Civil Schools series from Pacific Northwest Publishing. This series is designed to help school personnel make all settings physically and emotionally safe for all students. Within the series is a book for the elementary and middle school levels: *CHAMPs: A Proactive and Positive Approach to Classroom Management.* The CHAMPs acronym stands for the expectations for behavior that teachers must clarify for students: Conversation, Help, Activity, Movement, and Participation. This book for high school teachers is philosophically and procedurally aligned with CHAMPs and the other Safe & Civil Schools materials.

In implementation projects throughout the country, my colleagues and I have learned that when clear expectations are directly taught to students, the vast majority of students will strive to be cooperative and do their best to meet those expectations. By implementing the procedures in this book, you will spend less time dealing with disruption and resistance and more time teaching.

Introduction

Discipline problems in school have always been and continue to be a leading frustration for teachers and, more and more often, a high-level concern for the public. Currently, half of new teachers will leave the profession within a few years. Two of the most common reasons given for leaving teaching are discipline problems and lack of administrative support for dealing with discipline. Without foreknowledge of variables that can be manipulated to positively influence student behavior, inexperienced and unskilled teachers are often frustrated, and sometimes even terrified, by students who misbehave and challenge authority.

This book is designed to help you manage student behavior and increase student motivation so that you can focus your time and energy on instruction and student success. This approach is proactive, positive, and instructional:

Proactive means that effective teachers focus on preventing problems instead of constantly dealing with them. Through classroom organization and collecting and using meaningful data, a teacher can modify his or her classroom management plan to make it even more effective.

Positive means that effective teachers build collaborative relationships with students and provide them with meaningful, positive feedback to enhance motivation and performance.

Instructional means that effective teachers directly teach expectations at the beginning of the year, review expectations as necessary throughout the year, and treat misbehavior as an opportunity to teach replacement behavior.

There are many obvious and direct links between academic achievement and student behavior. If one student is severely disruptive, the other students in the class will learn less than if all students were behaving responsibly. If students are actively or passively resistant, a seemingly simple transition like moving to lab stations, which should take no more than two minutes, can take as long as ten, wasting large amounts of instructional time. A student who is unmotivated will be less engaged in her work and learn less than if she is excited about the

[handwritten margin note:] Prevent instead of deal w/ later

content. If all of these examples and more occur every day in every class, you are losing huge amounts of instructional time. By implementing effective management techniques, you can simultaneously increase student engagement and improve academic achievement.

Strategies and procedures you will learn in this book hinge on the STOIC model.

STOIC: One who demonstrates patience and endurance in the face of adversity.

S tructure/organize all settings for student success.

T each students how to behave responsibly in every setting.

O bserve student behavior in all school settings. (Supervise!)

I nteract positively with students—build relationships.

C orrect irresponsible behavior fluently—calmly, consistently, immediately, briefly, respectfully.

By manipulating these five variables, you can put an effective behavior management system in place, thereby creating a classroom climate that encourages students to be orderly, responsive, engaged, and motivated.

This book contains nine chapters, each with suggested tasks for building or revising your classroom management plan.

Chapter One, "Vision," presents six tasks that will help you understand the basic principles of behavior and motivation, and set the stage for the remainder of this book. After working through it, you should have a clear understanding of how behavior is learned and the role that you (and your management plan) can play in shaping student behavior in positive and successful directions.

Chapter Two, "Grading," guides you in four tasks through the development of a grading system that will help you teach students that success is an achievable goal. More than a simple evaluation tool, an effective grading system should be a motivational tool. Many of the students who seem not to care about their grades have never been taught that their behavior directly affects their grades, and if they change their behavior, they can move from failure to success.

Chapter Three, "Organization," has five tasks that show how you can manipulate variables such as schedule, physical setting, using an attention signal, beginning and ending routines, and procedures for managing student work. By manipulating these variables, you can create momentum that draws students into mature, responsible, unified, and productive patterns of behavior.

Chapter Four, "Expectations," offers three tasks to help you clarify and then directly teach your expectations for all classroom activities and transitions. The CHAMPs acronym stands for the things that you will need to teach your students for each major instructional activity and transition: Conversation, Help, Activity, Movement, and Participation. When you directly teach these expectations, you are functioning like an effective athletics coach who, before teaching the team content (the plays and patterns of the game), begins the first practice by teaching expectations for how players are to behave during practice and games, on the field and off. An alternative acronym, ACHIEVE, is provided for teachers who prefer a more grown-up-sounding acronym.

Chapter Five, "Rules and Consequences," sets out three tasks that will help you develop a set of classroom rules to address the most likely misbehaviors you will deal with. Once you develop the rules, either on your own or with help from your students, you will determine a system of appropriate consequences. Included are examples of different types of corrective consequences that can be implemented in a high school classroom.

Chapter Six, "Motivation," provides five tasks you can manipulate to increase student motivation, including presentation, implementation, building relationships, providing feedback, and monitoring students. Understanding and acting on what motivates your students will enable you to help them succeed.

Chapter Seven, "Preparation and Launch," has three tasks designed to pull everything from the first six chapters together. You will form a concise plan that you can easily communicate to your students. Included are suggestions for and an example of a comprehensive course syllabus. Steps and suggestions for how to run the first day of school are also provided.

Chapter Eight, "Implementation," describes three tasks to help you implement your management plan throughout the year and monitor the plan's effectiveness, modifying it when necessary. Continually improving and refining your management plan will help you continue to encourage your students' success throughout the year.

Chapter Nine, "Proactive Planning for Chronic Misbehavior," acknowledges that no matter how well you plan and implement, chronic behavior problems will still emerge. This chapter goes in-depth with a task that details how to try an easy intervention first, then leads you through a step-by-step process for dealing with more difficult chronic behaviors. You will learn how misbehaviors may function for the student and how this understanding can help you end them. Four major types of misbehaviors are addressed in the tasks that follow: awareness, ability, attention seeking, and purposeful or habitual. Sample intervention plans are suggested for each.

Following the chapters is a set of appendixes, each with procedures for collecting data on some aspect of student behavior and instructions on how to analyze those data to decide whether and how to revise your management plan to reduce misbehavior and increase motivation. The appendixes are described in Chapter Eight, along with a calendar plan to help identify when during the school year might be best to utilize these data collection tools.

Chapter One

Vision

Understand key concepts about managing student behavior

Four concepts form the framework for this chapter. It is essential to understand these concepts because they also form the framework on which you will build your own classroom management plan. Familiarity with these core concepts will make it easier for you to understand the methods outlined in this book and then adapt them to fit your own teaching style and the specific needs of your students.

These core concepts are laid out as tasks you must understand in order to envision your role as a manager of student behavior and motivation. The fifth and sixth tasks, like the remainder of this book, provide specific actions you can take to prepare and implement an effective classroom management plan. Task 5 will assist you in clarifying your vision of student behavior and motivation for yourself, your students, and their families. Task 6 will help you understand that the degree to which you structure your own classroom will depend on your personal style and the needs of your students. This task also includes a worksheet that you can complete during the summer to help prepare your management plan in advance, based on what you know of your student population.

The six tasks are as follows:

Task 1: Understand the basic principles of behavior modification and your role in that process.

Task 2: Understand motivation and the variables that can be manipulated to increase it.

Task 3: Understand the importance of maintaining high expectations for students' academic and behavioral performance.

Task 4: Understand the importance of building personal relationships with students.

Task 5: Develop and implement Guidelines for Success.

Task 6: Adjust the structure of your management plan based on the needs of your students.

The Self-Assessment Checklist at the end of this chapter will help you determine which tasks you will need to work on as you build or revise your management plan. The Peer Study Worksheet that follows the checklist has a series of discussion questions you can use with one or more of your fellow teachers to share information on how they have improved their own teaching practices. The worksheet also presents a series of activities that can be used by two or more teachers who want to share information and peer support as they work to improve together.

Task 1: Understand the Basic Principles of Behavior Modification and Your Role in That Process

In order to manage student behavior, you need a solid understanding of how behavior is learned and how it can be changed. This knowledge will allow you to help students become progressively more responsible. If you already have an understanding of behavior analysis, you can simply skim this task for a brief review.

Behavior is learned. We are constantly engaged in learning that affects our future behavior. For example, if you purchase a car and you like the way it handles, it rarely needs repairs, and you think it was a good value, you are more likely to buy that brand of car in the future. But if the car needs constant repairs, develops annoying rattles, and you feel that you paid too much for it, you are unlikely to buy this brand in the future. (You may even be driven to take up cycling!) Or if you go to a movie based on a friend's recommendation but find it to be a waste of time and therefore a waste of money, you are less likely to trust that friend's movie recommendations in the future. Scenarios such as these are repeated in each individual's life in uncountable, interwoven combinations that create a rich fabric of experience and learning. Simply put, our behavior is influenced by events and conditions we experience, some of which encourage certain behaviors and others of which discourage certain behaviors (Chance, 1998; Iwata, Smith, & Michael, 2000). Figure 1.1 shows the three main variables that affect behavior.

If you have studied behavioral analysis, you will recognize Figure 1.1 as a simple example of behavioral theory. It is important to understand this model if you are going to manage student behavior successfully. This model suggests that changing behaviors requires focusing on (1) what is prompting a behavior, (2) what is encouraging or sustaining that behavior, and (3) what might discourage that behavior from occurring in the future.

The other important idea to keep in mind as you consider this model is that what may be pleasant consequences for one person could be unpleasant consequences for another. For example, getting a smiley-face sticker for having done good work is likely to

> **Note**
> The technical language of behavior analysis is based on precise definitions of terms such as *reinforcing consequences, positive reinforcers, negative reinforcers, punishing consequences,* and so on. This book avoids this vocabulary because it is not universally used and understood. Instead, throughout this book, the term *encouragement procedure* will be used as a label for any procedure that is used in an attempt to increase desirable student behaviors and the term *corrective consequence* for any procedure that is used in an attempt to decrease misbehavior.

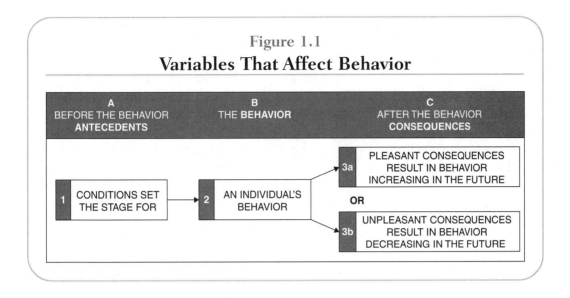

Figure 1.1
Variables That Affect Behavior

A BEFORE THE BEHAVIOR **ANTECEDENTS**	B THE **BEHAVIOR**	C AFTER THE BEHAVIOR **CONSEQUENCES**

1 CONDITIONS SET THE STAGE FOR → **2** AN INDIVIDUAL'S BEHAVIOR

3a PLEASANT CONSEQUENCES RESULT IN BEHAVIOR INCREASING IN THE FUTURE

OR

3b UNPLEASANT CONSEQUENCES RESULT IN BEHAVIOR DECREASING IN THE FUTURE

be a pleasant consequence for most first graders, and something that will encourage them to work hard in the future. However, the same sticker may very well have the opposite effect on most tenth-grade students. Getting a sticker for having done a good job may be so embarrassing to a tenth-grade student that he or she would be *less* likely to work hard in the future. In this case, the teacher's attempt to reinforce the positive behavior with a sticker actually decreases the future probability of that behavior's occurring. In behavior analysis, one would say that the sticker actually served as a punishment consequence.

Any behavior that occurs repeatedly is serving some function for the individual exhibiting the behavior. As you strive to help students behave responsibly, it is essential to keep in mind the idea that chronic behavior serves a function (Chance, 1998). Students who consistently behave responsibly have learned that this behavior leads to things they value, such as parental approval, good grades, teacher attention, a sense of pride and accomplishment, increased opportunity, and so on. Their responsible behavior serves a specific function.

This concept applies equally to behaviors that are negative or destructive as it does to behaviors that are positive and productive—which helps explain an individual student's misbehavior when the consequences of that misbehavior seem so unpleasant. Rex is a student in the tenth grade, and his teachers find his disruptive behavior frustrating. A look at his file shows that he has been exhibiting this behavior since middle school. He is frequently thrown out of class and assigned detention; his parents are called regularly, and school staff are continually angry and frustrated with him. Yet as unpleasant as these consequences appear to be, Rex is clearly getting some benefit from his irresponsible behavior or he would change it.

In this case, Rex's misbehavior results in immediate consequences that are pleasant for him. That is, when he argues, he gets lots of attention from adults, which gives him a sense of power. In addition, he gets lots of attention from peers for appearing strong and powerful enough to "fight" with his teachers. Rex's irresponsible behavior also allows him to avoid the unpleasant consequences that result when he attempts to exhibit responsible behavior. Rex has academic problems, and when he tries to be compliant and do his work, he usually finds that he can't, which frustrates and discourages him. Rex has discovered that if, instead of doing his work, he argues and gets thrown out of class, he not only gets adult and peer attention, but also avoids having to demonstrate in public his lack of academic ability.

When a student frequently behaves irresponsibly, it's likely the student hasn't experienced the benefits of responsible behavior enough, or even at all. It's also likely that this student has learned that irresponsible behavior is a more effective or efficient way of getting his needs met. For example, he gets power, control, and perhaps even admiration from peers (Horner, Vaughn, Day, & Ard, 1996; Lalli et al., 1999).

Student behavior can be changed. Although there are some tendencies and personality traits that seem to be present from birth, most behavior is learned—which means it can also be unlearned (Chance, 1998; Biglan, 1995). Consider the following rather exaggerated example.

Picture Dana: a responsible and successful ninth-grade student. Imagine that as of today, Dana stops getting any positive benefits for behaving responsibly. She does her best work, but always gets failing grades and critical comments; sometimes other students laugh at her work and class participation and either ridicule her as stupid or ignore her altogether. She tries to be nice to adults and other students, but they are no longer nice in return. She stays on task, but no one ever notices. Her parents show no interest in the fact that she is failing. Adults at school and at home never notice or comment about her independence, her cooperation, or her effort, but they are constantly demanding more and more and pouncing on every opportunity to scold and criticize her. If this were to continue day after day, at home and at school, Dana would probably stop trying, and she might even respond with anger and hostility. If she found that this was a way to get people to notice her, she might develop a sense of satisfaction or self-preservation in acting in an antagonistic and aggressive manner. If this were to continue for months or years, Dana would seem like a very different young woman from the one described at the beginning of the paragraph.

Now think back to Rex who is always argumentative, angry, and getting thrown out of class. Imagine that school personnel can create a setting in which he starts experiencing success and good grades, he receives peer recognition for his positive behavior, and he no longer gets so much attention or status for his anger and hostility. If done well, such an environment can create a powerful positive change in Rex (in the opposite way of our example with Dana). Behavior *can* be taught and changed (Langland, Lewis-Palmer, & Sugai, 1998).

To cement the importance of your ability to teach and change behavior, think about a highly motivational sports coach. He will begin the first day of the season by laying out behavioral expectations for the team, and then spend the entire season teaching and having the team practice those same behaviors that will lead to the success he wants. A major part of any management plan involves direct teaching of those behaviors and routines that will lead to your student's success.

Task 2: Understand Motivation and the Variables That Can Be Manipulated to Increase It

To *motivate* can be defined as "to provide an incentive, to move to action, to drive forward." Understanding motivation will enhance your efforts to implement effective motivational procedures with your students (that is, to move them to do their best academically and encourage them to exhibit responsible and successful behavior). The concepts presented here can help you maintain the motivation of students who already follow the rules and do their best on assignments, increase the motivation of students who do nothing or only enough to get by, and motivate responsibility in students who tend to misbehave.

The first concept to understand is this: <u>behavior that is repeated is motivated; behavior does not reoccur if there is no motivation</u>. This concept is always true, regardless of what an individual may think or say about her own behavior. For example, a person may repeatedly complain about his job and even say that he is unmotivated to work, but if he goes to work regularly, he shows that he is in fact motivated in some way to work. Similarly, a person may say she is motivated to paint as a hobby, but if she never gets out her paints and brushes, she is not truly motivated to paint. This does not mean that the man will never lose his motivation to go to work or that the woman will never regain her motivation to paint, but that their current behavior indicates otherwise.

The importance of this concept is that teachers must realize that <u>the student who repeatedly misbehaves is, at the moment, more motivated to misbehave than to behave</u> and that the student who does nothing is more motivated to do nothing than to work. It means that you, as the teacher, will need to increase these students' motivation to behave responsibly and complete assignments. This book is designed to help you do that.

Motivated to misbehave

A second important concept is this. <u>Most people are motivated to engage in a particular behavior by a complex mix of intrinsic and extrinsic factors.</u> A person is intrinsically motivated when the pleasant consequences of a behavior are related to the essential nature of that behavior. Thus, a person who is intrinsically motivated to read, reads because he likes to learn new things, enjoys a good story,

> ## Note
> If your efforts to increase students' motivation to engage in desired behaviors are ineffective, you will also need to work at decreasing their motivation to engage in undesired behaviors. For specific suggestions, see Chapter Nine.

and finds curling up with a book relaxing. The person who is intrinsically motivated to ski does so because she finds the speed exhilarating, the fresh air pleasant, and the feeling of exhaustion at the end of a challenging day gratifying.

Extrinsic motivation occurs when someone engages in a behavior due to pleasant consequences that are not directly related to the essential nature of the behavior. For example, babies tend to utter "mama" and "dada" more frequently than other sounds because of the reactions (for example, smiles, tickles, and praise) these sounds elicit in the most significant people in their lives. A college student will continue to attend and write papers for a class that she does not like because she wants a certain grade and because doing well in the class will move her toward her desired goal of a degree. A six-year-old child will make his bed to get lavish praise from his mom and dad regarding how responsible, hardworking, and helpful he is.

While some people believe that the only valid kind of motivation is intrinsic motivation and that teachers should not give students praise and rewards of any kind, this book does not adhere to this principle (Cameron, Banko, & Pierce, 2001). This mistaken belief will be addressed in more detail in Chapter Six, but it is enough to say that the line between intrinsic and extrinsic motivation is not as distinct as it may seem. Motivation for most behaviors is usually a mix of intrinsic and extrinsic factors. Although the person who reads a lot may do so for the intrinsic rewards of the task, he may also enjoy the compliments he gets for his wide knowledge. The frequent skier may find that in addition to the exhilaration of skiing itself, she also enjoys having others comment on her skill. The baby learning to talk makes "mama" and "dada" sounds because he enjoys making noise, not just because of the reactions of his parents. The college student who attends class and writes papers does so not only because of the grades but also because sometimes the class is genuinely interesting.

This means that when you have students who are unmotivated to work or to behave responsibly, you need to try to enhance both their intrinsic (for example, make a science lesson more engaging) and extrinsic (for example, write an encouraging note on returned homework) motivation. You will find suggestions for both in this chapter and Chapter Six.

A third important concept has to do with the relationship between one's intrinsic motivation to engage in a task and one's proficiency at that task. A skilled woodworker is more likely to find spending time in a workshop rewarding than the person who has never learned to use tools. Similarly, the skilled musician is more likely to find daily practice intrinsically reinforcing than the person who has played for only three weeks. In addition, an individual who has experienced success at learning many different skills in the past is more likely to be motivated to try learning something new in the future than someone who has experienced repeated failure. The student who has had a lot of academic success is more likely to feel excited about the challenge of a tough course than the student who has failed at academic pursuits in the past.

The key implication of this concept is that in the early stages of learning something new or when learning something difficult, some students (particularly those who have experienced frequent past failure) are not likely to be intrinsically motivated to engage in the behaviors necessary to learn.

A further refinement of the concept is the Expectancy × Value theory of motivation. First used by Feather (1982), this theory explains a person's motivation on any given task as a function of this formula:

$$\text{Expectancy} \times \text{Value} = \text{Motivation}$$

In this formula, *expectancy* is defined as "the degree to which an individual expects to be successful at the task" and *value* is "the degree to which an individual values the rewards that accompany that success." The power of this theory is its recognition that a person's level of motivation on any given task is a function of both how much the person wants the rewards that accompany success on the task *and* how much he or she expects to be successful at the task.

Many teachers, when trying to ascertain why a student is unmotivated to behave responsibly or complete assignments, tend to ascribe the lack of motivation to issues involving the value component of the formula only: "Nothing seems to motivate him. He doesn't care about getting good grades. He takes no pride in his accomplishments. He doesn't care about free time or positive notes home. I even tried to put him on a point contract where he could earn time on the computer, but he just said he didn't really care about computers. I guess there isn't anything else I can do." What these explanations fail to take into account is that if the student thinks he will not succeed at behaving responsibly or completing assignments (expectancy), his motivation will be very low or nonexistent.

With this equation, both expectancy and value can be calibrated on a scale of 0 to 10,

> **Note**
> The value factor in the formula can include extrinsic rewards (for example, money, awards, grades) or intrinsic rewards (for example, sense of accomplishment, enjoyment of the task, pride in a job will done), or both. Regardless of the type of "value" involved, if the expectancy of success is low, motivation will be low.

with 0 representing the lowest possible rate and 10 representing the highest possible rate of each. When the value rate and an expectancy rate are multiplied together, they will equal a number between 0 and 100, which would represent the percentage of motivation a person has for that task. The *key implication* is that if the rate for either one of the factors is zero, the other factor won't matter; motivation rate will still be zero (Table 1.1).

Another applied aspect of the theory is that the rates for expectancy and value are defined by what a student believes, not what *you*, the teacher, believe. You may know that the student is perfectly capable of being successful if he would simply try. However, if the student believes he cannot be successful (making his expectancy rate low), his motivation will be low to non-existent (Laraway, Snycerski, Michael, & Poling, 2003).

Whenever a student is not motivated to do something (complete work, participate in class discussions, or behave more responsibly), try to determine whether the lack of motivation stems from a lack of value (intrinsic and extrinsic), a lack of expectancy, or both. To see if you need to increase a student's motivation to complete academic tasks, one of the things you should check is whether the student is capable of being successful at them. If the student is not, you may need to modify the tasks so that the student will be able to succeed. *How* you can modify academic tasks is outside the scope of this program, but there are people in your district who can help with strategies in modifying instruction to bring success within your student's reach. Don Deshler and his colleagues at the University of Kansas have spent many years building a variety of resources for improving instruction and increasing the academic success of struggling learners (see Exhibit 1.1). For more information on the Center for Research on Learning, go to www.ku-crl.org, or read the following:

Schumaker, J. B., Deshler, D. D., & McKnight, P. (2002). In M. A. Shinn, H. M. Walker, & G. Stoner (Eds.), *Interventions for academic and behavior problems II: Preventive and remedial approaches* (pp. 791–823). Bethesda, MD: National Association of School Psychologists. This chapter summarizes key components of an innovative model for providing services to students in general education classes. It includes descriptions of learning strategies and content enhancement routines.

Deshler, D. D., Schumaker, J. B., Lenz, B. K., Bulgren, J. A., Hock, M. F., Knight, J., & Ehren, B. J. (2001). Ensuring content-area learning by secondary students with learning disabilities. *Learning Disabilities Research and Practice, 16*(2), 96–108. This article describes the broad array of services that must be available to students with learning disabilities so they can succeed in learning subject area content. It includes a summary of how the Strategic Instruction Model components relate to these requirements.

Table 1.1

Motivation Formula

Expectancy Rate	× Value Rate	= Motivation
10	× 10	= 100%
10	× 0	= 0%
0	× 10	= 0%

Exhibit 1.1
The Strategic Instruction Model

Drawing on more than twenty-five years of research, the Center for Research on Learning at the University of Kansas has developed the Strategic Instruction Model (SIM), a comprehensive approach to adolescent literacy that addresses the need of students to be able to read and understand large volumes of complex reading materials as well as to be able to express themselves effectively in writing. SIM—used by many state special education departments, thousands of school districts, and four hundred colleges and universities—achieves measurable results by reversing the downward spiral through which so many at-risk and special education students plummet.

SIM integrates two kinds of interventions designed to address the gap between what students are expected to do and what students are able to do. Using a "how-to-learn" approach, SIM's student-focused interventions, including specific learning strategies, enable students to generalize from one task and situation to others. SIM includes tactics and skills that can be used to gain information from texts efficiently, perform more accurately on tests, write more clearly, present written work more attractively, spell more accurately, and perform math operations more efficiently. In short, SIM enables students to deal more effectively with the process of learning.

SIM's teacher-focused interventions, called ***content enhancement routines,*** encourage teachers to teach more effectively by helping them think about, adapt, and present their most important content in learner-friendly fashion. Recognizing that academic interventions alone are not sufficient for student success, SIM also includes components that help students create and participate in productive learning communities, develop strong and appropriate social skills, advocate for themselves and their needs in education conferences, envision positive futures for themselves, and plan how to reach their goals.

To date, more than forty instructional programs have been validated through numerous research studies and developed into instructional materials appropriate for teacher use in the classroom.

A schoolwide approach for integrating SIM and other validated literacy programs can be accomplished through a school-reform model developed by the University of Kansas Center for Research on Learning called the Content Literacy Continuum. This model defines a continuum of instructional intensity that serves as a framework for guiding school improvement and professional development.

A network of certified SIM instructors is available to work with teachers and schools to implement SIM programs. SIM is most effective when teachers are afforded sufficient time to plan what and how they are going to teach in a strategic fashion. Teachers must have an opportunity to work with other teachers to coordinate instruction across classes and settings to ensure that critical strategies and behaviors are prompted and reinforced. SIM holds that highly significant change for students or schools occurs only when teachers are armed with numerous interventions to meet students' diverse needs.

The Expectancy × Value theory can be a particularly useful way of thinking about behavior and motivation for teachers. To develop your understanding of this theory, periodically take the time to analyze activities you personally are motivated and unmotivated to do. When thinking about something you are highly motivated to do, identify the value you place on engaging in and completing the activity and the expectancy of success you have before engaging in it. When you think about an activity that you are not motivated to do, see if you can determine what is low: the expectancy rate, the value rate, or both. Try to identify any activities for which you value the rewards but avoid doing because your expectancy of success is low. Analyzing your own motivation or lack of it will help you develop a deeper understanding of your students' motivations.

As you work through subsequent chapters and analyze your students' motivations, keep the following concepts in mind:

- Your students' behavior will let you know what they are motivated and not motivated to do. You will have to work on increasing their motivation to engage in positive behavior, and possibly on decreasing their negative motivation.

- Use procedures that address both intrinsic and extrinsic motivations when trying to increase positive student behavior.

- Students' motivation to engage in any behavior is related to the degree to which they value the rewards of engaging in that behavior *and* their expectation of succeeding at it.

Task 3: Understand the Importance of Maintaining High Expectations for Students' Academic and Behavioral Performance

For all your students to succeed, it is essential that you maintain *and* communicate high and positive expectations. Research has repeatedly demonstrated what we know from common sense: low expectations predict low achievement (Scarborough & Parker, 2003). Your vision of student achievement and performance has an immeasurable impact on your students. It is crucial for you to convey your high expectations for all your students both in academics and in personal responsibility.

This is not to suggest that you ignore any problems or difficulties your students may have. Against that, you must still maintain high yet realistic expectations for your students if they are to succeed. The difference is best demonstrated through an example. A student who is confined to a wheelchair would not be able to do some of the activities required of the other students in gym. It is reasonable to adapt some of the gym activities so that she can participate. Similarly, simply because she is in a wheelchair does not mean that her classroom expectations are any different from those of her peers.

A less obvious example is a student with chronic behavioral and discipline problems in class. If such a student is in a class you teach, it would be naive to think that he will never misbehave, but you must still *expect* that he can learn to behave responsibly in your class. The goal of this task is forming a belief in the potential success of *every* student.

EVERY STUDENT CAN SUCCEED.

Before putting any work into your students, however, you must first evaluate yourself. You must look objectively at your behavior and make sure that the comments you make to your students and the comments you make to others about your students do not single any of them out or put them down. Even when you make critical comments about a student to another teacher, you are communicating low expectations, and they will come out in other ways. Statements like the following communicate your low expectations for students:

"What can you expect from a kid like that?"

"You can't expect any better from a student with that kind of home life."

"They have ADHD, so what can you do?"

"I wish he weren't in my class."

If you find that you have such thoughts or are making such statements, stopping them is the first step to encouraging success in your students. *You* must believe in their success before expecting it. Try to identify specific negative phrases you may be using, and make an effort to stop. Then think of phrases you can use that embrace positive qualities about your students instead of negative ones. Try to use positive phrasing in circumstances where previously you would have used negative phrasing.

Even when you start the year with strong, positive expectations for your students, it can be difficult to sustain them. It's easy to get so busy that you don't notice negative thoughts creeping back in. It may be that a particularly trying student or class wears you out, and without realizing it, you lower your expectations. To protect against this, you must check in with yourself regularly, evaluating where you are emotionally with your classes and students. It may help to mark a calendar at intervals to remind yourself to examine your attitude periodically. (There are more specific guidelines for this in Chapter Eight.)

In addition, once school is in session, make a point of monitoring the kind of statements you use with your students. Be aware and honestly critical of yourself regarding the kind of language you use with your students, whether it is positive or negative. Watch for statements like the following:

"Here, let me give you something easier."

"Grow up!"

"This group will work with me because they've proven they can't work alone."

"What's the matter with you? Use your head."

When one professor was asked, "What do you do with the kid you just don't like?" he wisely responded, "You can't dislike kids on company time." Although you don't have to personally enjoy every student, you do have to maintain a high expectation for *every* student's success while you're at work.

Implementing some of the following suggestions can help you maintain a positive attitude toward your students:

• *Take care of yourself.* Young people are very quick to see hypocrisy, so make sure you're positive with yourself as well as with them. Look to your own attitudes and health. Design a wellness program for yourself that includes exercise and proper nutrition, and make sure you get enough rest. Make time for activities or interests outside school.

• *Maintain a positive and realistic vision of student success.* When problems occur, as they surely will, remind yourself of the vision you have for your students, the success you want them to have. This is especially important when dealing with students who have chronic problems. If you need it, set aside some time to visualize the student being successful.

• *Be reflective about your plan.* Periodically evaluate your methods to see what is working and what isn't. If you identify something that needs improvement, try something else. Remember that although you may not be able to directly control student behavior, you can control their environment (seating, schedules, interaction) in a way that will positively affect their behavior.

• *Don't take it personally.* If a student misbehaves, try to remain objective. The problem isn't your fault, but you do offer an excellent hope of positively reaching a child. Remind yourself that you're a professional and that eventually every problem can be solved. It may help to remind yourself that the student is likely not singling you out, but treats all adults in her life in a similar manner.

• *Make an overt effort to interact positively with every student.* All students should feel that you notice and care about them. Say hi to them, and show an interest in their activities. When you maintain contact with every student as an individual, they know that you value them, and that will reduce the likelihood that they will misbehave.

• *Consult with colleagues.* If an individual or group becomes particularly challenging, discuss your concerns with fellow staff members. Be careful not to communicate low expectations, but describe the problems the student is having neutrally. Peer problem solving is a powerful tool for getting ideas on helping your students.

> **Note**
> Whether you are starting in the middle of the school year or at the beginning, make sure you spend enough time on this task to ensure that you have high expectations for every student. If you have low expectations for your students' behavior, they will live up (or down) to those expectations. To implement an effective classroom management plan successfully, you must possess *and* communicate high expectations for every student's success.

All of the tasks in this chapter are designed to help you develop and maintain a comprehensive student management program. Throughout this book, you will find guidelines on how to continue communicating high, positive expectations to your students. You will find that some methods will work better than others with different student groups, and using the approach outlined in this book to the fullest means periodically returning to it and evaluating your methods.

Task 4: Understand the Importance of Building Personal Relationships with Students

You will dramatically increase the probability of having cooperative and motivated students if they perceive that you both like and respect them (Hamre & Pianta, 2001; Reddy, Rhodes, & Mulhall, 2003). Think back to your own experience in school, to a particular teacher who made you feel valued and important and how strong an impact that teacher had on you. Many people remember the name of their favorite teacher forever. While you don't have to be every student's favorite teacher, by making an effort to build relationships with students, you are demonstrating to students that you, as a teacher, hope to have a positive influence on their lives. Robert W. Blum, lead researcher of the National Longitudinal Study of Adolescent Health, concluded that making connections with students is more important than organizational variables such as classroom size, rules, and other structural considerations. Blum was at the helm of a study that tracked ninety thousand students in grades 7 to 12 to examine their health choices. He and his colleagues identified that students who had an emotional connection with their school were far less likely to use illegal substances, engage in violence, or initiate sexual activity at an early age than students without an emotional investment in their school. The study further determined that one major factor that affected the emotional connection a student had with the school was positive classroom management (McNeely, Nonnemaker, & Blum, 2002).

The goal of this task is to ensure you build relationships with each of your students. This can be difficult, since you have time limitations and may see up to two hundred students a day. Later sections of this book provide tips on how you can specifically build relationships with your students, but for now, just think about the teacher who affected you. Think about the power of simply using a student's name when you greet him or her. When you address a student by name—"Good morning, Tamisha"—those three words let her know you notice her and therefore value her and are interested in her as a person, not just as a mark in your grade book.

This does not mean you have to be every student's friend. They do not need you to use their slang or follow their trends. They only need you to be their teacher—a teacher with clear expectations, a teacher who is fair and consistent. They need to know you care about them, that you are helping them succeed not only as a student but as a person, and that you accept them for who they are.

Just as maintaining a positive attitude toward your students is essential for their success, so is maintaining a personal connection with them. If they feel you don't really care whether they succeed, they may not work at succeeding. If they feel you want them to succeed but don't feel as if you care about them, they may not work to succeed, no matter how positive you are. Positive attitude and personal connection work as two of the foundation stones of your classroom management plan. If either is lacking, the entire structure will be lacking (Patrick, Turner, Meyer, & Midgley, 2003).

Task 5: Develop and Implement Guidelines for Success

In addition to academics, teachers need to provide their students with specific information about attitudes, traits, and behaviors that will help them succeed in school and throughout their lives. Sadly, there are some students and families who believe that school success is not possible for those who don't come from an educated or a rich family. There are others who believe that school success depends on one's ethnicity. Part of your responsibility as a teacher is to let your students know that everyone can succeed in school and to give them guidelines regarding how.

These Guidelines for Success should reflect broad and noble ideals. They should represent what you really hope students will learn from you—not the content but the attitudes or actions that will help students succeed in your class, the classes they will have in the future, and life in general.

Having these Guidelines for Success is important regardless of the level of structure that may be of most benefit to your students. This can be especially critical if your school or class has a large number of high-needs students. High-needs students often lack the knowledge or motivation to exhibit traits that educators want, need, or expect them to have. Figure 1.2 has an example of schoolwide guidelines for success.

When developing your own Guidelines for Success (or goals to strive toward, or whatever else you choose to call them), frame them as brief phrases that describe the attitudes, traits, and characteristics you hope to instill in your students. Note that these guidelines are different from classroom rules. Rules pertain to specific and observable behaviors, and they generally have consequences associated with failing to follow them, whereas your Guidelines for Success are attitudes or traits that you hope to inspire students to strive toward. Rules are like speed limits that you as the teacher will enforce. Guidelines are values that you hope to instill in your students—values that will help them succeed in your class and in all other aspects of life. You can find information on developing specific classroom rules in Chapter Five.

> ## Note
>
> Optimally, Guidelines for Success are developed and used on a schoolwide basis. That is, the entire staff creates and agrees to post and use a common list of positive traits. Sprick, Howard, Wise, Marcum, and Haykin (1998) provide suggestions on how to involve staff, students, and parents in developing schoolwide guidelines for success. If your school does not have schoolwide guidelines, plan on developing them for your own class. If your school has already developed and adopted schoolwide guidelines, plan to use them. The advantage of having these guidelines schoolwide is that students are given consistent messages from all school staff about what is required of them to be successful within the school.

Figure 1.2
Sample Guideline for Success

Guidelines for Success

1. Be responsible.
2. Always try.
3. Do your best.
4. Cooperate with others.
5. Treat everyone with respect (including yourself).

Source: Sprick, Sprick, & Garrison (2002).

Developing your guidelines is just the first step. If students are truly going to learn to exhibit these attitudes, traits, and behaviors, you need to make them an ever-present part of your classroom.

Post your guidelines in a prominent place where everyone can see them. Teach them to students at the beginning of the year. As with your long-range goals, let students' families know what your guidelines are. Using the vocabulary from the guidelines consistently and regularly will help to keep them familiar. For example, you can use them to prompt motivation and get your students excited about striving for excellence. You should also use the guidelines as a basis for providing both positive and corrective feedback to students regarding their behavior:

"Shelly, you have been doing much better about getting homework completed. Thank you for being so responsible."

"Fionna, you need to work quietly. The guideline about treating everyone with respect means you don't disturb others when they are trying to get their work finished."

Plan to put your Guidelines for Success and a brief explanation of their importance in the syllabus that you will distribute to students on the first day of the semester.

Note
Whether you are starting to work through this book at the beginning of or during the school year, spend some time implementing this task. Guidelines for Success give your students critical information about how they can accomplish what you expect from them—and this is valuable at any point in the year.

Remember that when students do not receive information about these kinds of attitudes, traits, and behaviors at home, the emphasis that school personnel place on their guidelines may provide critical life lessons. If you find that some of your students have had less of a personal context for understanding and operating from your guidelines, plan to provide more instruction on how students can implement them and be prepared to give those students more encouragement.

Task 6: Adjust the Structure of Your Management Plan Based on the Needs of Your Students

The level of structure in your classroom management plan refers to the degree that you will need to be hands on during class activities to ensure the success of your students. To determine the level of structure necessary, evaluate the students you will be teaching using the worksheet at the end of this section (Exhibit 1.2). The level of structure required for successful classroom management is determined largely by the risk factors of your student body. If you have large numbers of immature students, the risk factors are likely high and you will need a more structured class environment. If your classes have predominantly mature and independent students, then you will be able to follow a more loosely structured plan.

If the risk factors of your class are high and your management plan is not sufficiently structured, student behavior will become problematic. For example, although it is always a good idea to begin instruction quickly at the start of class, in a class with higher risk factors, student behavior can deteriorate quickly if the beginning of class is not particularly structured. If your students have nothing to do for the first five minutes because you are taking attendance or catching up on class housekeeping, they are likely to be talking and wandering out of their seats, and this will make it much more difficult to get them back under control when you are finished with your attendance. For a high-structure class, it is much more advisable to begin instruction immediately after the bell rings and take attendance after you have given out a work assignment.

As you progress through this book, you will find references to how tasks can be implemented differently depending on your students' need for structure in your class. Some groups of students are largely mature, responsible, and independent. This is a *low-structure class*, meaning your classroom management plan can be relatively less rigid, and your students will probably be successful. When groups of students are collectively immature and irresponsible and have difficulty staying focused independently, this is a *high-structure class*, meaning you will need to be more systematic in designing and implementing your classroom management plan. If you have a class needing high structure, you should implement all of the tasks in this book. If you have a low-structure class, you can implement only the tasks you believe will be needed to motivate your class and you can ignore any procedures that you feel will be unnecessary to ensure effective use of instructional time. In a medium-structure class, you should implement most of the tasks in the program, except for those that your students clearly do not need, but you can implement them in a less-structured fashion than may be needed with a high-structure class. The greater the risk factors of your students are, the more they will respond to strong implementation of all the tasks.

The worksheet in Exhibit 1.2 will assist you in determining the risk factors of your class before you begin your classroom management plan and then help you determine which level of structure is most appropriate for your classroom management plan. Plan on reevaluating your class at several times throughout the year. It is highly recommended that you evaluate your class's response to structure after a month has gone by and again after the first long vacation of the year. If a significant number of students are not meeting expectations, adjust the structure of your class accordingly. Suggestions for collecting information and revising your management plan, if necessary, are provided in Chapter Eight.

In Conclusion

To properly integrate the system in this book and to create and maintain an effective classroom management plan, it is essential to understand the core concepts presented in the previous sections. If you are reading this book in the summer, I recommend you return to this chapter for a review before classes begin. This program is highly customizable, allowing you to adapt its concepts and principles to your specific needs, and the more familiar you are with the concepts behind it, the easier it will be for you to make judgment calls on what to retain and what you might be able to do without.

Whenever you have something that works for you, do not feel that it should be immediately discarded simply on the recommendations of this book. If there are aspects of your teaching you wish to retain, you will be the most effective teacher you can be if you add these concepts to strategies that already work for you.

Exhibit 1.2

Management and Discipline Planning: Reproducible Form

1. For each question, circle the number under the statement that best answers the question. When you are unsure about the answer to a question, circle the middle number.
2. Total the scores for all items. You should have a number between 0 and 120.
3. Use the scale at the end of the form to determine the most appropriate structure level for your classroom management plan.

Questions 1–6 relate to the population of the entire school.

1. How would you describe the overall behavior of students in your school?	Generally quite irresponsible. I frequently have to nag and/or assign consequences. 10	Most students behave responsibly, but about 10 percent put me in the position where I have to nag and/or assign consequences. 5	Generally responsible. I rarely find it necessary to nag and/or assign consequences. 0
2. What percentage of students in your school qualify for free or reduced lunch?	60 percent or more 10	10 to 60 percent 5	Less than 10 percent 0
3. What percentage of students in your school typically move in and/or out of the school during the course of the school year?	50 percent or more 10	10 to 50 percent 5	Less than 10 percent 0
4. How would you describe the overall attitude of students toward school?	A large percent hate school and ridicule the students who are motivated. 10	It's a mix, but most students feel okay about school. 5	The vast majority of students like school and are highly motivated. 0
5. How would you describe the overall nature of the interactions between students and adults in your school?	There are frequent confrontations, which include sarcasm and/or disrespect. 10	There is a mix, but most interactions are respectful and positive. 5	The vast majority of interactions are respectful and positive. 0
6. How would you describe the level of interest and support provided by the parents of students in your school?	Many parents are openly antagonistic, and many show no interest in school. 10	Most parents are at least somewhat supportive of school. 5	The majority are interested, involved, and supportive of what goes on in the school. 0

Questions 7–11 relate to students in your class this year. Use your most difficult class, or if you are doing this before the school year begins, simply give your best guess.

7. What grade level do you teach?	Ninth grade 20	Tenth grade 5	Eleventh or twelfth grade 0
8. How many students do you have in your class?	30 or more 10	23 to 30 5	22 or fewer 0
9. What is the reputation of this group of students from previous years? For example, if you teach tenth grade, what was the reputation of these students as ninth graders?	This class is going to be awful. 10	It's a mix, but most students work hard and cooperate. 5	This group is very hard working and cooperative. 0
10. How many students in your class have been identified as severely emotionally disturbed (SED)? Note: This label varies from state to state.	Two or more 10	One 5	Zero 0
11. Not including students identified as SED, how many students have a reputation for chronic discipline problems?	Three or more 10	One or two 5	Zero 0

Total _____

If your total is:	Your risk factors are:
0 to 30	**Low,** which means your students can probably be successful with a classroom management plan that involves **low, medium, or high structure.** The level of structure can be defined by your teaching style.
31 to 60	**Medium,** which means that for your students to be successful, your classroom management plan should involve **medium or high structure.**
61 to 120	**High,** which means that for your students to be successful, your classroom management plan should involve **high structure.** Regardless of your personal preference or style, your students will probably benefit from a detailed, systematic, and organized classroom management plan.

Vision Self-Assessment Checklist

Use this worksheet to identify which parts of the tasks described in this chapter you have completed. For any item that has not been completed, note what needs to be done to complete it. Then transfer your notes to your planning calendar in the form of specific actions you need to take (for example, "August 17, finish Guidelines for Success, write orientation letter for parents").

✓	Task	Notes and Implementation Ideas
☐	*Understand the basic principles of behavior modification and your role in that process.* I have sufficient knowledge of fundamental behavior management principles so I can effectively help my students learn to behave more responsibly. Specifically: 1. I know why and how to promote responsible behavior by: • Recognizing what is prompting behavior; • Recognizing what is encouraging or sustaining a behavior; and • Recognizing what might discourage a certain behavior in the future and then changing conditions to promote desired behaviors. 2. I know why and how to deal with misbehavior by: • Recognizing that any behavior that occurs repeatedly is serving some function for the individual exhibiting the behavior and taking that into account when designing an intervention; • Identifying and then modifying any conditions that may be perpetuating the misbehavior; and • Identifying and then eliminating any positive outcomes that may be resulting from the misbehavior.	
☐	*Understand motivation and the variables that can be manipulated to increase it.* I understand that behavior that is repeated is motivated and that motivation is affected by a mix of intrinsic and extrinsic factors. I also understand that intrinsic motivation is related to a student's proficiency at a task. Therefore, I have: 1. Identified the motivating factors for certain behaviors; and • Modified conditions to increase students' motivation to engage in desired behaviors,	

Vision Self-Assessment Checklist (*continued*)

• Modified conditions to decrease students' motivation to engage in undesired behaviors. 2. Enhanced student motivation using both intrinsic and extrinsic factors; and 3. Identified whether students' lack of motivation is related to a lack of value, lack of expectancy, or both. • For students who are not motivated because of lack of capability, I have modified tasks so that they can succeed.	
Understand the importance of maintaining high expectations for students' academic and behavioral performance. I understand the importance of having high expectations for, and communicating high expectations to, all my students. I will make a conscious effort not to say anything (to students, their families, or others) that would suggest that I have low expectations for any student. I have identified specific ways I can and will convey my high expectations to students, their families, and others. I understand the importance of maintaining a positive attitude toward my students. Therefore, I will: • Develop a wellness program for myself that includes exercise, proper nutrition, and sufficient sleep; • Maintain a positive and realistic vision of student success; • Conduct periodic evaluations of my methods to see what is and isn't working; • Be objective when dealing with student misbehavior; • Make an overt effort to value and to interact positively with every student; and • Consult with colleagues to discuss concerns.	

Vision Self-Assessment Checklist (*continued*)

☐	*Understand the importance of building personal relationships with students.* I understand that I will dramatically increase the probability of having cooperative and motivated students if they perceive that I both like and respect them. Therefore, I will take a personal interest in my students and their success. I will value my students. I will make a concerted effort to maintain a personal connection with my students, and to maintain a positive attitude toward them.
☐	*Develop and implement Guidelines for Success.* I have identified three to six basic attitudes, traits, and/or behaviors that are important for my students to succeed in my classroom and in their lives. From them, I have created a set of Guidelines for Success (or "Guiding Principles," "Goals," etc.). I have posted the Guidelines for Success in my classroom, communicated them to students' families, and included them in my syllabus.
☐	*Adjust the structure of your management plan based on the needs of your students.* I have filled out the "Management and Discipline Planning" worksheet and carefully considered all factors, especially the needs of my students, to determine whether my classroom management plan needs to involve high, medium, or low structure. I have noted in my planning calendar times throughout the year to reevaluate the level of structure my classroom needs. Specifically: • During the fourth or fifth week of school, I will conduct CHAMPs or ACHIEVE Assessments (Chapter Eight). • Shortly after winter vacation, I will conduct the CHAMPs or ACHIEVE Assessments (Chapter Eight).

Vision Peer Study Worksheet

Schedule one to two hours with one to five colleagues. Each participant should have read Chapter One and worked through the self-assessment activities in advance of this discussion time. By discussing each participant's policies, procedures, and questions regarding the tasks in Chapter One, each participant will gain a deeper understanding of the chapter and learn tips and techniques from colleagues.

Begin the discussion by prioritizing the seven tasks, that is, which task interests participants most (for which task do you want to hear the procedures and policies of colleagues?). Which task is the next highest priority? In this way, if there is not adequate time to discuss all seven tasks within the hour, discussion will focus on the tasks of greatest interest to you and the other participants. Work through the prioritized tasks by discussing the questions or topics within that task. Then go on to the next highest priority. Continue this process and complete as many of the tasks as possible within the scheduled time.

Task 1: Understand Basic Principles of Behavior Modification and Your Role

    A. Have group members share whether this summary of behavior modification matches their prior training and whether the concepts provide a useful framework for examining classroom management plans.

Task 2: Understand Motivation and the Variables That Can Be Manipulated to Increase It

    A. Identify the three categories of procedures for promoting responsible behavior.

    B. Identify the three categories of procedures to take into account once you have identified the reason a chronic misbehavior may be occurring (for example, the student loves getting attention from other students by making rude comments in class).

    C. Have group members discuss whether this organization for categorizing behavior management strategies is useful. Ask them to share specific examples.

Task 3: Understand the Importance of Maintaining High Expectations for Students' Academic and Behavioral Performance

    A. Have group members share what they do to avoid developing low expectations for a student who is chronically behaviorally challenging.

    B. Objectively consider whether the atmosphere at your school is one of positive expectations for students (for example, evaluate the kinds of comments about students that are made in the faculty room). If it is not, identify how those of you who are in the group might help your whole staff develop more positive expectations.

Vision Peer Study Worksheet *(continued)*

Task 4: Understand the Importance of Building Personal Relationships with Students

   A. Have the group discuss the fine line between building personal relationships with students as compared with trying to be "friends" with students. Discuss whether there are risks in building a relationship with the student, in that there may be a reduction in the degree to which the students respect the authority of the teacher's role. If so, what can be done to diminish this?

Task 5: Develop and Implement Guidelines for Success

   A. If your school does not have schoolwide Guidelines for Success, have each group member share his or her guidelines with the other group members.

   B. Brainstorm at least six different strategies, other than those identified in the text, for using Guidelines for Success in the classroom to help students understand and internalize them.

   C. If your school does not have schoolwide Guidelines for Success, discuss (1) whether it would be worth trying to develop schoolwide agreement so that all staff emphasize the same set of attitudes, characteristics, or traits, and (2) what actions would be necessary to get a schoolwide development process started.

Task 6: Adjust the Structure of Your Management Plan Based on the Needs of Your Students

   A. Have each group member share his or her completed "Management and Discipline Planning" worksheet (Exhibit 1.2).

   B. Have group members discuss how the level of structure they have identified will affect their classroom management plan.

Briefly discuss why you should periodically reevaluate the level of structure required for your class, and have each group member identify when he or she will reevaluate the level of structure necessary for his or her class.

Chapter Two

Grading

Design instruction and evaluation systems

Mrs. Allen teaches high school biology. She has always enjoyed teaching but finds working with unmotivated students frustrating. Mrs. Allen knows that many staff members feel the same way. She has heard them complain, "Every year it seems as if I get more and more students who don't care about their grades. They don't even try to pass my courses, and it really doesn't matter to them when they fail. Their parents must not care either."

Motivating students to achieve academic success can be a difficult job. Teachers often work with students who have been neglected or abused and may face a lack of parental support. Drug problems, absenteeism, and general apathy can make it seem as if student motivation is beyond a teacher's reach.

Certainly many factors affecting student motivation are outside your control. You cannot control a student's home life or eliminate drug use. You cannot make each minute of instruction fascinating for every student in your class. Part of every course is going to be hard work. However, the way you organize instructional content and evaluate student mastery of that content can play a major role in whether students' expectancy of success is high or low (Harniss, Stein, & Carnine, 2002; Paine, Radicchi, Rosellini, Deutchman, & Darch, 1983). In addition, a well-designed grading system can increase students' motivation to behave in ways that will help them engage with the instructional content you design. When an effective grading system is paired with effective instruction, even low-performing students are more likely to succeed.

The most unmotivated students tend to consistently get poor grades. These students may view grades the same way many people view the lottery: it would certainly be nice to win, but the odds are stacked heavily against it, so why try? Most students would love to get an A or a B, but many know from experience that their efforts will do little to change the odds. When teachers hand back tests or papers, it is rare to see a student who does not care enough to quickly check his grade. While students may give up trying, they do not usually give up hoping. An effective grading system can teach students that they do have some control over their grades. This chapter will help you design instructional units and grading procedures that will increase your students' expectancy of success, thus increasing their motivation.

This chapter has four tasks that will help you demonstrate to your students that hard work and appropriate behavior can lead to passing your course and earning the grade they desire:

Task 1: Develop clear goals for each class you teach.

Task 2: Design instruction and evaluation procedures that create a clear relationship between student effort and success.

Task 3: Establish a system to provide students feedback on behavior and effort. Incorporate this into your grading system.

Task 4: Design procedures for students to receive feedback on each aspect of their behavioral and academic performance and to know their current grades.

Tasks 1 and 2 provide basic suggestions on effective instructional practices. For more information on effective instructional practices with secondary students, explore the Strategic Instruction Model (see Exhibit 1.1) developed by Deshler, Schumaker, Lenz, and their colleagues at the University of Kansas Center for Research on Learning. You can also visit the University of Kansas Web site at www.ku-crl.org, or read the following:

Schumaker, J. B., Deshler, D. D., & McKnight, P. (2002). In M. A. Shinn, H. M. Walker, & G. Stoner (Eds.), *Interventions for academic and behavior problems II: Preventive and remedial approaches* (pp. 791–823). Bethesda, MD: National Association of School Psychologists. This chapter summarizes key components of an innovative model for providing services to students in general education classes. It includes descriptions of learning strategies and content enhancement routines.

Deshler, D. D., Schumaker, J. B., Lenz, B. K., Bulgren, J. A., Hock, M. F., Knight, J., & Ehren, B. J. (2001). Ensuring content-area learning by secondary students with learning disabilities. *Learning Disabilities Research and Practice, 16*(2), 96–108. This article describes the broad array of services that must be available to students with learning disabilities so they can succeed in learning subject-area content. It includes a summary of how SIM components relate to these requirements. The Self-Assessment Checklist at the end of this chapter will help you determine which tasks you will need to work on as you build or revise your management plan. The Peer Study Worksheet that follows the checklist has a series of discussion questions you can use with one or more of your fellow teachers to share information on how they have improved their own teaching practices. The worksheet also presents a series of activities that can be used by two or more teachers who want to share information and peer support as they work to improve together.

Task 1: Develop Clear Goals for Each Class You Teach

Before school begins, determine what you hope to accomplish with your students by the end of the school year (Colvin & Sugai, 1988; Sprick, Garrison, & Howard, 1998). Determine four to seven major goals that summarize why your class will be a worthwhile experience for your students. Specifically, you need to identify what skill or knowledge they will develop that they did not have on the first day of school (National Research Council, 2000).

Long-range goals can be a mix of academic and behavioral goals. Academic goals focus on what your students will be able to do differently relative to the content you teach. Behavioral goals focus on the attitudes or traits you hope to instill in your students. Whether your goals are predominantly behavioral or predominantly academic is entirely up to you and what you think your class needs.

Having these long-range goals will help you plan and make decisions on a daily basis throughout the year. For example, if one goal is for your students to be able to plan long-range projects and bring them to completion, plan on devoting time to several long-range projects over the course of the year. If this is not a goal of yours, plan for students to engage in more short daily activities and spend less time and energy on long-range projects.

Sharing your goals with your students and their families at the beginning of the year will let them know what you feel is important and where you hope to guide your students. One effective way to do this is to list your goals prominently within your course syllabus. Detailed information about how to share goals with students initially and throughout the year is covered in detail in Chapters Seven and Eight. Keeping your long-range goals in mind can be particularly important as you move on into the school year. Teachers can easily get so busy and immersed in daily details that they lose sight of what they are trying to do and what they hope to accomplish. With long-range goals in mind, you can stay focused on your goal and periodically ask yourself if what you are doing on a daily basis is aiding (or hindering) your efforts to help students reach these goals.

The following are examples of long-range goals for different grade levels and subject areas.

Ninth-Grade Band: All students will:

- Practice independently for a minimum of four hours a week.
- Perform in the band recital at the halfway point of the semester.
- Prepare an individual recital piece to be performed at the end of the semester.
- Be able to demonstrate a marked improvement between the beginning of the semester and the end.
- Demonstrate capability to complete independent work and practice.

AP Literature: All students will:

- Write an in-class essay on the literary school of your choice at the end of the third week.
- Make a team presentation on an assigned author at the end of the sixth week.
- Take a comprehensive, closed-book midterm essay and short-answer exam.
- Write a position paper, and make a solo presentation on an author or work of your choice.
- Read the work of four different transcendentalists and present a compare and contrast paper on them at the end of the semester.
- Demonstrate the ability to analyze and write clearly about an assigned topic.

Ninth-Grade Math: All students will:

- Demonstrate mastery of the quadratic equation by the end of the second week.
- Perform an equation of the teacher's choice before the class at the end of the fourth week.
- Demonstrate comprehensive mastery of all concepts on the midterm.
- Write a paper on the real-world application of one math technique learned in this class.

- Complete a comprehensive final.
- Demonstrate independent study skills and the ability to analyze problems on your own.

Tenth-Grade U.S. History: All students will:
- Memorize twenty key events in U.S. history including the year the Constitution was ratified, the beginning and ending years of the Civil War, and the year the United States entered World War II, and be able to place those events on a time line.
- Be able to describe and apply five essential concepts of the U.S. Constitution, including the three branches of government and the First Amendment right of free speech.
- Be able to learn new facts and issues from U.S. history and analyze them using the time line events and constitutional concepts noted above.
- Learn to take notes from lectures, films, and readings, and use them to analyze and synthesize information on tests and projects.
- Learn to study independently and stay on task both in class and with homework.

To develop your long-range goals, consider the following suggestions before determining your own goals:

- Ask yourself what you want students to be able to know and do at the end of the year that they may not be able to do now. What knowledge, processes, attitudes, behaviors, or traits do you want your students to have? What do you want students to take with them after a year with you?

- Find out what the school, district, and state standards are for your students in the grade level or subject you teach. Your goals should incorporate this.
- Talk to other teachers within your department about the goals they have for their students. Ask your colleagues at the next grade level what they believe students coming into their class will need to be successful.
- If there will be accountability testing, such as AP or statewide tests, in your subject, be sure that your goals are connected to this testing so that students can see that striving toward the goals you have identified will help ensure they do well on it.

> **Note**
> These samples of long-range goals are included to prompt your thinking. They are not meant to suggest *your* long-range goals.

> **Note**
> If you are starting to work through this book during the school year, implementing this task should be a lower priority. Before the next semester begins, however, you should give careful thought to what your long-range goals will be.

Include this information in your syllabus, and clarify that everything in the syllabus is designed to help students achieve success in your class. Clarify that meeting the goals in the syllabus and completing the assigned work ensures a passing or better grade in the class. Chapter Seven includes an example of a teacher's course syllabus for a high-structure class.

Task 2: Design Instruction and Evaluation Procedures That Create a Clear Relationship Between Student Effort and Success

This task provides suggestions on how to adapt your goals into small units of instruction. You will also determine the evaluation methods and process you will use to verify that students are learning what you teach them. The goal of this process is to clearly show students the link between learning, doing work and participating, and receiving a passing grade (Brophy, 1998). This should also illustrate that above-average work will result in above-average grades, etc. First, however, consider what not to do.

Two common pitfalls with instruction and evaluation. Some teachers view all information and concepts they teach as equally important. If this is the case, then evaluation can often consist of a random sampling of that information to determine student mastery. Consider an extreme (but true) example of what can happen if a teacher designs instruction evaluation based on this sampling form. In an undergraduate history course, a college instructor assigns twelve hundred pages of reading. Every three weeks, students are to be tested on a four-hundred-page section of the reading and on three weeks of lecture. The final grade will be based entirely on the three tests. Prior to the first test, students are not provided any information that will help them prepare for the test. When they ask what information from the text will be important, the teacher tells them, "Everything will be important."

The first test is a single essay question covering a topic that has not been mentioned in class and was discussed on only three pages of the text. Out of fifty students, one receives an A, three receive B's, fourteen receive F's, and thirty-two receive C's and D's. Students complain that the test was unfair: "How could we know which three pages were important? There is no way to memorize four hundred pages of text!"

The instructor replies, "I tested you on those three pages not because they were the most important but because anyone who knew those three pages would also have learned the material on the other 397 pages." On hearing this reply, half the students drop the class before the second test. Think about the probable attitude and motivation of the students who remain. Keep in mind the Expectancy × Value theory of motivation from Chapter One.

This example demonstrates how a course can seem impossible when important objectives are not made clear to the students. Even sophisticated college students may choose not to try when there are overwhelming odds against knowing what to study. The instructor made an error in assuming that it was the responsibility of the students to identify what content was important. He felt that his job was only to *give* information. This misconception not only made it impossible for students to know what to study, but it also resulted in many students' having a decreased expectancy of success and reduced their motivation.

One skill many academically successful students have is the ability to determine critical objectives. If testing is on random information, they still have a chance to succeed because they start with more background knowledge, are more likely to be adept at remembering information, and are probably skilled at guessing what the teacher will choose to include on the test. Less capable students will have difficulty sorting out critical objectives and less chance of remembering unconnected bits of information. In order to increase motivation for all your students, you need to clarify your instructional objectives and then evaluate students only on the basis of those objectives (Kame'enui & Simmons, 1990).

The other major pitfall of instruction and evaluation is grading on a curve. A major percentage of the final grade should reflect each student's mastery of the course objectives. A failing grade should indicate that a student has not mastered the objectives. Students who master the objectives should receive a C, and students who exceed the objectives should receive an A or a B. Grading on the basis of student mastery of objectives instead of on the curve means that every student has the opportunity to pass. This means that you should avoid grading on the standard curve, which distributes the class's grades according to predetermined percentages. In a standard curve, those percentages are:

  2 percent of the students receive an A

14 percent of the students receive a B

68 percent of the students receive a C

14 percent of the students receive a D

  2 percent of the students receive an F

Grading on a curve takes all incentive away from lower-performing students. They soon realize that their grades have little to do with how well they master course content. They realize that they have to beat higher-performing students to succeed. No matter how hard they work, their performance will always be evaluated relative to that of another student. However, if students know they can pass a course because they have mastered the course objectives, they will soon learn that they can succeed regardless of their relative position to other students. Your goal should be to provide instruction that gives all students what they need to get a C or better. You would not give away passing grades, but rather give them to students who have earned them.

One of the benefits of organizing a grading system around specific objectives is that students will not have to second-guess what they are supposed to learn (Woodward, 2001). Many students do not know enough about a given subject to identify the most important material to learn, and trying to second-guess their teacher would be impossible. When students understand a class's objectives, they will know what they are supposed to study. This will increase the likelihood that they will make the effort and make it easier for you to evaluate their performance. The remainder of this task suggests steps that can allow you to turn your established class goals into meaningful units of instruction and evaluation.

Break down the semester's content into one- or two-week units of instruction. If you think of the goals you established within Chapter One as the final destination of a journey, then your units of instruction will be the steps that you will take to reach that destination. Decide if you will use the midsemester point for a formal midterm evaluation. If you will not have formal midterm exams, simply divide the content you intend to teach over the entire semester into logical units. Depending on how you build your class, this may be defined for you by curriculum guides or the structure of a textbook you are using. If you plan on giving formal midterms, divide the semester in half, and then divide each half into units.

For students to join you on this journey they need a vision of the final destination. Remember, though, that this vision can be daunting to some students, particularly those who have experienced past failure. Let your students know that their success will come one step at a time, one unit at a time, not all at once.

Determine the percentage of mastery that will be used to determine student grades. Most teachers use something like the following:

90 percent or better equals an A

80 to 89.9 percent equals a B

70 to 79.9 percent equals a C

60 to 69.9 percent equals a D

59.9 or less equals an F

Check with your school administration to determine if these breakdowns are already specified by policy or if you can make the choice yourself. Whether you use the percentages above or something different, the important thing is to realize that the grade distribution is based on each student's performance, not by the curve. Include this information in your syllabus.

> **Note**
> For simplicity and clarity throughout the rest of this book, it will be assumed you are using the "90 percent for an A" breakdown specified above.

Prior to designing instruction, identify the essential objectives for each unit that you want your students to master and retain for the rest of the semester. What are you going to hold students accountable for knowing, not just for this unit but for the remainder of the semester and on the final if you plan to give one? These essentials may be facts, higher-order processes, operations, or some combination of them.

One way to identify these essential objectives is to begin the process of designing your units of instruction. To do this, determine your method of student performance evaluation. In most cases, this will be a test. However, in some cases, the essential objectives may be evaluation of a product, in which case your first step is to determine the criteria by which you will evaluate the end product. By settling on your final evaluation tool (test or evaluation criteria) first, you can then identify exactly what you want students to know or be able to do and then determine the essential content you will need to teach. If you are using predesigned tests from your district curriculum guide or the textbook publisher, this step involves examining what is on that test and editing it as needed.

Break these essential objectives into a manageable number of concepts that are essential for a person to be literate in this subject. If you are basing instruction on a textbook, you may find that many texts have only a few essential concepts and lots of embellishment with interesting but nonessential information. Do not worry if your essentials comprise only a small percentage of the content of a given chapter of the book. Plan to teach these essential objectives directly, and provide multiple practice opportunities in the form of daily assignments and homework to help students reach mastery of this content.

These essential competencies will comprise 80 percent of the point value of unit tests and 80 percent of the point value of major assignments and projects. This organizational structure allows you to communicate to students that you will directly teach everything they need in order to get a passing grade for the class. For students who have experienced academic failure in the past, you can use this concept to let them know that you will do everything possible to help all students pass—not by giving away grades but by being direct in telling them the essential objectives and creating lots of practice and feedback opportunities to help them get there. One common concern that some teachers express is, "But I don't want to tell them what will be on the test." However, remember that the essential competencies comprise only 80 percent of the point value on the test. Thus, you are letting students know everything they need to know to get a high C or the very lowest possible B.

Another advantage of directly teaching the essential competencies is that it allows you to create a challenge for students who want to earn an above-average grade. The remaining 20 percent of point value on tests and major assignments will not be directly taught. To gain this content, students will need to read the textbook carefully and generally demonstrate an above-average mastery of the subject. You can inform students that while you directly teach what is needed to get a high C or low B, if they want to earn an A or a high B, they will have to demonstrate performance above and beyond that. Thus, 20 percent of the point value of tests and major assignments can be based on advanced objectives. The advanced objectives could be any content from the textbook, lectures, videos, and other material that students were exposed to but that was not emphasized or directly taught.

This 80/20 analysis prevents the problem in which a teacher views his or her job as covering 100 percent of the content and testing to see what students have learned. That does not take into account that in most subjects, much of the content is not absolutely essential to literacy in the subject. Read any chapter from any science, health, or social science book and notice that much of the material in that chapter is not essential to understanding the really important concepts, or "big ideas," and is probably not essential to understanding later chapters of the book.

Some teachers label each test item as being an essential or an advanced objective to demonstrate to students a direct connection to what you do in class and being able to pass the class.

Build cumulative review of essential objectives into subsequent units of instruction. After the first unit test, provide a one- or two-page summary of the essential objectives covered for that unit of instruction. Let students know that the second unit test will have a review section on the essential objectives from unit 1. Here is one way to do this:

Unit 1
80 percent of the point value covers essential objectives from unit 1

20 percent of the point value covers advanced objectives from unit 1

Unit 2
60 percent of the point value covers essential objectives from unit 2

20 percent of the point value covers advanced objectives from unit 2

20 percent of the point value covers the essential objectives from unit 1

Unit 3
60 percent of the point value covers essential objectives from unit 3

20 percent of the point value covers advanced objectives from unit 3

20 percent of the point value covers the essential objectives from units 1 and 2

Unit 9
60 percent of the point value covers essential objectives from unit 9

20 percent of the point value covers advanced objectives from unit 9

20 percent of the point value covers the essential objectives from units 1 through 8

By following this structure, students can be taught to study the review sheets you give out at the completion of each unit. Studying these review sheets will prepare them for 20 percent of the point value of each test. To get a passing grade, if they are correct on most of the essential objectives for the current unit and the essential objectives for past units, they will get a high C. If they want an A or B, they will have to demonstrate above-average mastery of advanced objectives from the current unit. Do not include review items that cover advanced objectives from previous units. You want to demonstrate that you hold them responsible only for keeping track of the essential objectives.

One huge advantage of this cumulative review strategy is that students will perform better on finals and statewide tests. Since they have been reviewing the essential objectives again with each new unit, this information stays fresher in their minds. Most adults do not remember their locker combination from when they were sophomores in high school. You knew this information very well at one time and throughout the year successfully opened that lock hundreds of times. Why don't you remember it now (assuming you are not one of those rare individuals who can remember)? Because it has been years since you have needed to use that information, and through lack of use that information has faded from your memory. Do not let that happen to your essential objectives. Keeping that information fresh in students' minds throughout the semester or the entire year will allow your students to retain the information much better, and for much longer.

Task 3: Establish a System to Provide Students Feedback on Behavior and Effort. Incorporate This into Your Grading System

Among the several sections of math that Mr. Nakamura teaches is a sophomore geometry course. He has designed his course to include lectures, class discussions, and assignments Monday through Thursday. Each Friday, students are given a quiz on the material they covered during the week. Class discussions and lectures typically focus on the previous day's homework. Mr. Nakamura has designed his schedule to allow students to work on problems independently and then to resolve any difficulties as a group.

During class activities, not all of the students work diligently. Some do not seem to care whether they learn to solve the problems. The students who goof off during class work times are not learning what they need to. Although they may not get out of hand, they are not learning content they are expected to master.

Highly motivated and academically successful students have learned that their daily performance has a cumulative effect on their grade. They understand that each day's work will affect how much they learn, which will in turn affect their test performances and their final grade. Academically motivated students can take the long view that their daily efforts will affect their future schooling options and even job opportunities, whereas less mature and lower-performing students do not understand these relationships. These students may not realize that the reason they are not passing is that they do not work or listen during class.

Most grading systems in secondary school are structured similarly to those in college. Attendance and behavior do not in themselves affect the grade. The grade is usually based solely on assignments, tests, and quizzes. In this type of system, there is no immediate accountability for goofing off. By the time a student fails a test, it is too late to make improvements. The delayed consequence is too weak to be effective with immature students, who may need more frequent reinforcement to stay on task.

An effective grading system at the secondary level must teach less sophisticated students the skills that more sophisticated students learn on their own. The grading system must demonstrate to the students that daily work and attention have a cumulative effect on their grades. Less motivated students in the typical secondary classroom must be taught to evaluate the long-term consequences of their daily actions. This can be accomplished by basing a percentage of their

[handwritten margin note: College prepatory school, but can we expect students to arrive at that level immediately?]

final grade on behavior and effort. Students will learn appropriate classroom behavior and that what they do in class each day is an important part of earning their final grade (Lam, 1995).

Some districts have a policy that prohibits teachers from using behavior in class as criteria for grading. If that is the case, look closely at the policy to find out if the intent of the policy is to restrict you from lowering a student's grade because of misbehavior. If so, you may still be able to use a system that partly bases a grade on behavior by saying that your class objectives involve teaching students the overall behaviors they need to be successful in any educational setting. For example, in a chemistry class, the abilities to stay on task, follow directions, and follow safety rules are critical factors for success. This same argument can be used to justify grading on behavior and effort in more traditional academic classes like English or history. By including behavior and effort as part of grading, you will be demonstrating to students that learning independent study skills, knowing how to listen, and taking responsibility for assignments and materials have a direct relationship to success and good grades. These behaviors are necessary for all future educational and professional endeavors and are therefore important objectives. Your district may agree that since these behaviors represent sound educational objectives, it is reasonable to base a percentage of each student's grade on these behaviors.

If district policy prevents you from incorporating behavior and effort into your grading system, find out if you can run a parallel system of providing a weekly behavior and effort score that affects the academic grade only if a student is just below the cutoff for receiving a higher grade. If this is acceptable, you can modify the system described in the remainder of this task so that it comes into play only if a student is not more than 2 percent below the cutoff for the next higher grades. Then you can establish criteria like the following:

- If you are 1 percent or less away from the next highest grade but have 80 percent or more of the behavior and effort points, you move up to the next grade.

- If you are 2 percent or less away from the next highest grade but have 90 percent or more of the behavior and effort points, you move up to the next grade.

> ## Note
>
> Some high school teachers and college professors track verbal participation in class. For example, each time a student speaks up in class by participating in a discussion or verbally answering a question each day, the student gets a point added to his or her academic grade. This type of system can be unfair to shy, quiet students. In addition, it can result in each student's saying something each day just to get checked off for speaking in class. The system described in this chapter for evaluating behavior and effort is different: students are given points on both the degree to which they follow the rules and to which they demonstrate significant effort. These effort points could be for verbal participation, but could also be given for cooperation, demonstrating respect, actively participating in activities, and so on.

If even this moderate influence of behavior and effort on the course grades is unacceptable in your district, you should still implement systematic feedback on behavior and effort like the system described in the remainder of this task. Instead of affecting their grades, however, behavior and effort points will have to count toward something else. To reinforce these ideas, there must be a positive motivator and a negative motivator—for example, evenings without homework, free time for

[handwritten margin note: To master criteria, you must master these skills which are crucial to learning...]

the positives and extra homework, or loss of a privilege for the negatives. The planning steps that follow assume you will base a percentage of the academic grade on behavior and effort. Adapt these procedures as necessary to ensure that you are within the policy guidelines of your district.

Planning Step 1: Establish a Grade Percentage for Classroom Behavior/Effort

To teach students that daily effort affects their final grade, establish a set percentage of the final grade for classroom performance. The exact percentage should vary from class to class according to several factors.

Subject. Some subjects must have grades that are based heavily on competency. For example, students in a ninth-grade writing class must demonstrate competency in basic writing skills to pass the course. If too high a percentage of the grade is based on behavior and effort, a student could potentially pass the class without demonstrating mastery of the basic course objectives. For this type of class, do not allocate more than 10 percent of the total possible points for behavior and effort. In a chorus class, it might be appropriate to have as much as 50 percent of the grade based on behavior and effort. This would give credit to students who work hard, even if they are not exceptionally talented.

Maturity and self-motivation. If you are working with students who are not yet sophisticated with grading systems, base a larger percentage of the grade on class performance. The higher the structure of your class, the more the grade percentage should depend on behavior. In general, this means that ninth-grade classes should have a higher percentage of the grade affected by behavior than a twelfth-grade class.

Course level. The level of student experience in a given subject should affect how much of their grade is based on behavior and effort. Students beginning a new skill should have a higher percentage of the grade based on classroom performance than those with experience. When students acquire a new skill, effort will determine whether students move beyond the beginning stages. It is during this time that students need the most encouragement. As they gain proficiency in any skill area, that skill becomes more intrinsically reinforcing. For example, beginning string students need encouragement as they learn to read and play notes. Advanced string students are able to enjoy their own ability to play complex pieces and interpret music.

Table 2.1 provides several examples of different types of classes and the kinds of percentages that might be reasonable to assign for behavior and effort.

Determine in advance what percentage of the final grade your students can earn for daily behavior and effort in class. Throughout the term, you will need to monitor and record student behavior. Be sure to inform students at the start of the semester, so that students know what to expect, rather than after problems occur. If this procedure is implemented without students' being aware that their class behavior has an impact on their academic grade, it becomes an unfair and arbitrary system.

Planning Step 2: Determine the Approximate Number of Total Points Students May Earn During the Term

Count the units of study you hope to cover during the term, working from the district text or a district curriculum guide. Next, using the number of units you hope to cover, estimate the

Table 2.1.
Differing Percentages for Behavior and Effort

Type of Class	Estimated Level of Student Maturity	Behavior and Effort Percent
Introductory Drafting	Mixed	40 percent
Advanced Composition	Highly motivated, excellent skills	5 percent
Remedial English	Poorly motivated, low performing	20 percent
Biology	Mixed	20 percent
Intermediate Band	Some mix, primarily motivated	30 percent
Advanced Art	Highly motivated	20 percent
Twelfth-Grade History	Mixed	10 percent

number of tests, assignments, and projects students will be taking during the term. Although you are projecting what you hope to accomplish during the term, these preplanning steps should not lock you into a system. By estimating the number of tests, assignments, and projects students will be graded on, you can prepare the students for how you plan to evaluate them. You do not have to plan the assignments or write out your tests in advance. You can adjust the number of assignments and tests as you work to meet the needs of your students.

Assign point values to the tests, assignments, and class projects. The point value of each type of work will vary according to the organization of your course and how you want to balance the points for different tasks. Once you have assigned approximate point values, add them together. This will give you an approximate number of work points that students may earn during the term.

Planning for a history class might look something like this:

Nine Units Covered in the Nine-Week Term

8 unit tests, 100 points each	800 points
8 quizzes, 25 points each	200 points
16 homework assignments, 20 points each	320 points
Final exam	200 points
1 term paper	200 points
Total work points	**1,720 points**

Planning Step 3: Determine the Approximate Number of Total Points Based on Behavior and Effort

Using the total work points from step 2 and the percentage of the grade that will be based on behavior and effort from step 1, determine the approximate number of points possible based on behavior. Using the history example, there are 1,720 work points. If this teacher wanted the behavior portion of the grade to have about a 10 percent influence on the grade, she would take 10 percent of 1,720 and say that there would be approximately 172 points possible for behavior and effort. She could then divide this number by the number of weeks in the term to determine how many behavior points were possible for each week—in this case, 19.11. However, since she does not want to bother with fractions of points, she will round up or down. For the sake of ease, this teacher will inform students that they can earn up to 20 points each week. This information should be included in your syllabus. See the example in Exhibit 2.1.

> ## Note
> You may note that in Exhibit 2.1, the teacher wanted behavior and effort to be about 10 percent of the grade, but she ended up with 1,900 possible and only 180 for behavior and effort, which is less than 10 percent. There are formulas for doing this more accurately that you can figure out on your own, but in most cases it is perfectly acceptable for the point values for behavior and effort to be slightly less than the original percentage you had estimated for this category.

Exhibit 2.1
Grading Information

Nine units covered in the nine-week term

8 unit tests, 100 points each	800 points
8 quizzes, 25 points each	200 points
16 homework assignments, 20 points each	320 points
Weekly behavior/effort, 20 points each	180 points
Final exam	200 points
Term paper	200 points
Total points possible	**1,900 points**

Planning Step 4: Design an Efficient System for Monitoring and Recording Daily Classroom Behavior Points

To demonstrate how daily performance affects the final grade, students need to see that their daily behavior is being monitored and recorded. Exhibits 2.2 and 2.3 show examples of a sheet that can be used to quickly note any information related to a student's classroom performance.

The behavior record form provides space to record each student's behavior during the week. It can be used to note attendance, assignments, behavior, classroom performance, and weekly point totals. At the bottom of the form is a place for a code. First, identify three or four positive traits or behaviors you wish to encourage at a classwide level. These will likely have several points in common with your Guidelines for Success. Then identify the three or four particular misbehaviors that represent rule violations you wish to address and reduce at a classwide level. For each positive and each negative behavior, assign a code that you will use

Exhibit 2.2

Behavior Record Form

Date _____   Reminders _____

Name	Fri.	Mon.	Tues.	Wed.	Thurs.	Total

Codes:

Exhibit 2.3
Behavior Record Form

Date _____   Reminders _____

Name	Fri.	Mon.	Tues.	Wed.	Thurs.	Total

Codes:

to record occurrences of that behavior on your record sheet. Table 2.2 shows a sample of such codes. When you have the codes completed, fill out an alphabetical listing of student names for each class that you teach. Thus, if you teach five classes, you will have a different sheet for each class.

Notice that the form begins with Friday of one week through Thursday of the following week. That way, you can calculate and post the grades on Friday to show how your students did on the previous five days. Posting these grades on Monday may be too much of a delay and can reduce the interest in the behavior and effort score of some of the less mature students.

Keep the behavior record form readily accessible at all times, especially when you are circulating throughout the classroom monitoring student behavior during independent work and cooperative group activities. Some teachers keep forms for each class on a clipboard, while others use a notebook. Throughout the period, students should see you using the record form. If a student comes in late, you can quickly mark a t for tardy. If a student needs to be reminded to get to work, simply note an o for "off-task" next to the student's name. Immediate notation of these negative behaviors will teach students that they are immediately accountable for their actions every day. (See Exhibit 2.4 for a partially filled-in sheet.) When students excel, you can record an A for effort or a C for cooperation on the form. You will have to determine when you start using this system how publicly you wish to acknowledge student behavior. When a student receives an A, will you announce it in front of the class, or will you tell the student later on, privately? (For additional information on giving students positive feedback without embarrassment, see Chapter Six.) Consistently using the behavior record form during class will allow you to record behavior grades as they happen without cutting into your class time.

> **Note**
>
> If you are working with low-performing students in a remedial setting of any kind, consider giving behavior and effort points daily instead of weekly. This increased immediacy in feedback will help motivate students who may have given up. The major disadvantage to this is the amount of time required. Therefore, use daily grades only with smaller classes. With a smaller class, assigning and recording daily performance grades should take only two or three minutes at the end of each period. A system of this type can also be incorporated into any behavior plan a student may have, such as a behavior card.

[handwritten margin note: Post Friday instead of Monday to show how grade is effected by participation. IMMEDIATELY.]

Table 2.2
Sample of Codes for Behavioral Grading

Misbehavior	Code	Positive Trait	Code
Off-task	o	Doing your best (effort)	A
Talking (at the wrong time)	t	Be responsible	B
Disruptive	d	Respect/cooperation	C

Exhibit 2.4
Partially Filled-In Behavior Record Form

Name	Fri.	Mon.	Tues.	Wed.	Thurs.	Total
Andersen, Gina	dd	cc	dA	d		14
Bendix, Frank	c	c	AA	B	B	20
Bigornia, Brad	o		A		A	16
Collias, Zona	t	B tt	t t t		C B	12

Each time you record a positive behavior add 1 point to that student's current total for the week. Each time you record misbehavior subtract 1 point from that student's current total. Since you are unlikely to be able to give every student enough positive marks to get them all to the A or B range, determine a number of points that each student should start with at the beginning of each five-day period. This should be approximately mid-C level—in this case, 15 points. In this way, you can inform students that every week, they start with 15 points and will move up or down from there based on the marks they receive. In Exhibit 2.4, if you start with 15 and subtract a point for each lowercase letter and add a point for each uppercase letter, you come out with the total in the far-right column. The one exception in the sample is Frank Bendix. He has six positives but receives only 20 points—not 21. Inform your students that no matter how many positive marks, they will not get more than the total possible, in the same way that if an essay is worth 100 points, they are not going to get a score of 110 no matter how many positive comments are written in the margins.

Planning Step 5: Determine the Impact of Excused and Unexcused Absences on Your Grading of Behavior and Effort

Determine how you will deal with students who are not in class. Obviously, a student who is not in class cannot be evaluated on behavior and effort. However, you do not want to have a system that penalizes students who have legitimate absences. Below are some recommendations for you to consider:

• *Unexcused absences.* An unexcused absence removes the student from the learning environment, makes her fall behind, and can distract other students. There must be a negative consequence equal to all the points that could have been earned with the student's presence. Thus, if there are 20 points possible for the week, students would be penalized 4 points for each day they have an unexcused absence.

• *Excused absences.* Students who have an excused absence will be allowed to earn back the credit they have missed. Note that they will not automatically earn performance points on the days they are gone. Instead, they will have an opportunity to do extra credit to make up the lost class time. This procedure is not designed to penalize students who are ill; rather, it is designed to demonstrate how valuable class time is. When students miss class time, they also miss learning. Thus, a small extra-credit assignment must be completed to compensate for the lost time. Students will learn that they are accountable for making up missed time. This procedure also applies to students who miss class due to involvement in sports, student government, and other extracurricular activities. You are not discouraging students from participating in other activities; you are holding them accountable for class time. A student who is pulled out regularly for special services of some type, such as English Language Learning or speech therapy, should not be required to make up the participation points that he or she missed.

• *Sent out of class.* A student who is sent out of class has lost the opportunity to earn performance points for the class period and will lose points based on the remaining amount of class time missed. A student who misses half the class will lose half the behavior points for that day, in addition to any other behavior coding recorded before the removal.

Exceptions can be made for students who are out of school with a serious or long-term illness. If a student is out of class for an extended period of time, award performance points as regular work is made up.

Not all administrations will allow you to require makeup work for behavior and effort points in the event of an absence. If this is the case, make sure your grading policies and behavior and effort points reflect this. You should make the other requirements balance without using excused absences as a criterion for points.

Planning Step 6: Assign Weekly Performance Points and Provide Feedback to Students

Every Thursday, your behavior record form will have all the information you need to determine the student's weekly performance points. Simply follow these steps:

1. Begin with the number of points students can earn for average performance.
2. Add the appropriate number of points for each notation of excellence.
3. Subtract the appropriate number of points for each notation of inappropriate behavior.
4. Record the total number of points earned on the behavior record form.

The first few weeks will be a period of adjustment as you get used to regularly noting performance, but as you continue, the task will become automatic. After some practice, you will be able to scan the performance sheet and quickly take in totals. Noting behavior in class should not take extra time once you get used to it, and totaling and awarding the points each week should take no more than five minutes.

When students enter class on Friday, they should be given their weekly performance points for the previous five-day period and informed that the new five-day period has just begun. If they do not receive the point totals before they go home for the weekend, the mental connection between their performance and their grades will weaken. Students need frequent and consistent feedback, especially with the implementation of a system to encourage them to follow the rules and give their best effort. There are several ways to give each student information on their points while maintaining an element of confidentiality:

• If you are using a computerized grading program, print out each student's current grade status, using student numbers for confidentiality.

• Post the sheet on which you have totaled the previous week's points, using a coded number to cover the student names on the far left. This may take a few more days to implement, and it would be best to use something only the student knows (like the last four numbers of his or her social security number). Once you have created a form with codes instead of names, the procedure should not take any longer than any other method. Some students may share their numbers with each other and defeat the coding method, but if this is their choice, it does not negate your effort to respect students' confidentiality.

• If you have a high-structure class or a small-size class, the best way to give feedback is a personal form for each student that breaks down the totals of the weekly performance points. This provides the students with the most immediate and direct information. It also keeps the process private for each student. The drawback of this method is that it will take longer than five minutes to prepare these for every student in your class.

When you have logged the performance score in your grade book, file the behavior record form. Keeping these records can be useful for several reasons, the most important being to provide answers to any questions about a student's grade. The record sheets provide detailed information about a student's behavior and motivation. This information is useful in conferences with students, parents, and administrators. It can also be useful for determining a special education placement or for any formal hearings or meetings about a particular student.

Keeping the behavior record forms on file can also provide useful information to you about revising your teaching methods with a particular group. For example, if you are concerned about off-task behavior in your seventh-period class, you can look at the record forms for the past four weeks and track the problem. If there are many o's (for "off task") marked on the sheet, then you should be concerned and make a plan of action. You may want to consider giving your class more structure. If there are steps you have not taken from this book, explore them. Talk with colleagues who may have a similar group of students, and find out what steps they have taken. You should be able to use the record sheet to get a sense of how your class is doing as a whole, not just to evaluate students on their own.

Summary of Behavior Feedback Within Grading Systems

By including a behavior and effort grade, your grading system will become more than a simple evaluation tool. It will become a systematic monitoring device that demonstrates to students that they are accountable for their efforts each day, and that such an effort will result in a better grade at the end of the term ("Teachers favor standards," 1996).

The Academy of Irving

One exciting variation of behavior and effort grading comes from the Academy of Irving, Independent School District in Irving, Texas. The academy is a high school in which students are graded on employability skills (ES). (The following information was provided by Patrick Martin, lead special education teacher, and Robin Wall, principal.)

The academy is a school of choice where entrance selection is made based on a lottery system; a failure by the student to maintain the required grade could potentially result in being returned to his or her home campus. The ES grade is based on a rubric developed in conjunction with business leaders. The skills measured are:

- Keeps appointments on time
- Completes assignments on time
- Exhibits professionalism in the areas of courtesy, appropriate language, and dress
- Works toward achieving individual and group goals
- Adheres to the ethical use of technology in regard to property, privacy, and appropriateness

The grading scale for these five areas runs from 1 ("rarely does any of these") to 5 ("always does these"). Each of the five areas is graded individually. Let's say that a student receives a 3 in each of the five areas. At this point, the total score is 15. That number is then multiplied by 3, to arrive at 45, and then added to 25 for a graded score of 70. Each grade level has a passing score that must be achieved in order for the student to be invited back the following academic year. The score is 70 for freshmen, 80 for sophomores, and 85 for juniors and seniors.

At the beginning of the school year, each parent and student receives a briefing regarding the expectations and performance criteria established by the academy. What we have noted is that the grades in academic subjects closely parallel the ES grade. It is unusual for a student to have a high ES grade and be low academically. The underlying philosophy for the program is that the skills needed to succeed at the academy in academics are the same skills employers want and employees need for success in the adult working world.

Task 4: Design Procedures for Students to Receive Feedback on Each Aspect of Their Behavioral and Academic Performance and to Know Their Current Grades

The first part of this task is obvious but difficult: get graded work back to students as quickly as you can. The longer a student goes between completing a task and getting feedback on it, the less the student will apply the feedback academically. The longer the delay is, the less impact a grade will have, good or bad.

In addition, you want students to know their current status in your class at all times. It is imperative that students be able to track their own grades, so they can measure the effect their effort has against their grade performance. If you are using a computerized grade program, printing out current grades and assignment status can be done easily on a weekly basis.

If you are not using a computerized system, you can teach students to keep a grade sheet. In Task 3 you identified the approximate number of tests, assignments, and class projects students would complete during the term and the number of points each would be worth. List this information on a student grading sheet with spaces for students to record work points, weekly performance points, and point totals. A sample is shown in Exhibit 2.5.

The maturity and level of sophistication of your students will serve as a guide for determining how much prompting you must give students to record their grades. A typical ninth-grade class may have many students who will need to be taught how to keep this sheet in an easy-to-find place in their notebook and how to track their grades. Each time they receive a grade, they record it. It may be necessary to inform students that you will conduct periodic spot checks to be sure they have kept their grading sheets up to date. Students in a very high-structure class may need to have recording their grades reinforced with the awarding of bonus points for keeping this sheet up to date.

If your students are fairly sophisticated (low-structure), the grading sheet may simply be a useful tool for them. Hand out the sheet at the beginning of the term and let students know that you will occasionally check to see if they are properly recording their grades. A grading sheet will be a useful tool for all your students, especially as you can use it to illustrate your grading plan. You may need to make some minor adjustments if you decide to add or remove assignments as the term progresses, but the students will have a clear outline of their activities and the relative grade values for different assignments.

In Conclusion

An effective grading system is more than an evaluation tool; it is an instructional and motivational tool as well. If properly designed and implemented, a grading system can encourage students to try their best every day (Detrich, 1999). An increase in daily motivation increases the chance that students will keep up with course work and learn to demonstrate mastery of course objectives. When students discover they can be successful in your class, they will remember their success. This will increase the likelihood that they will try to succeed in the future.

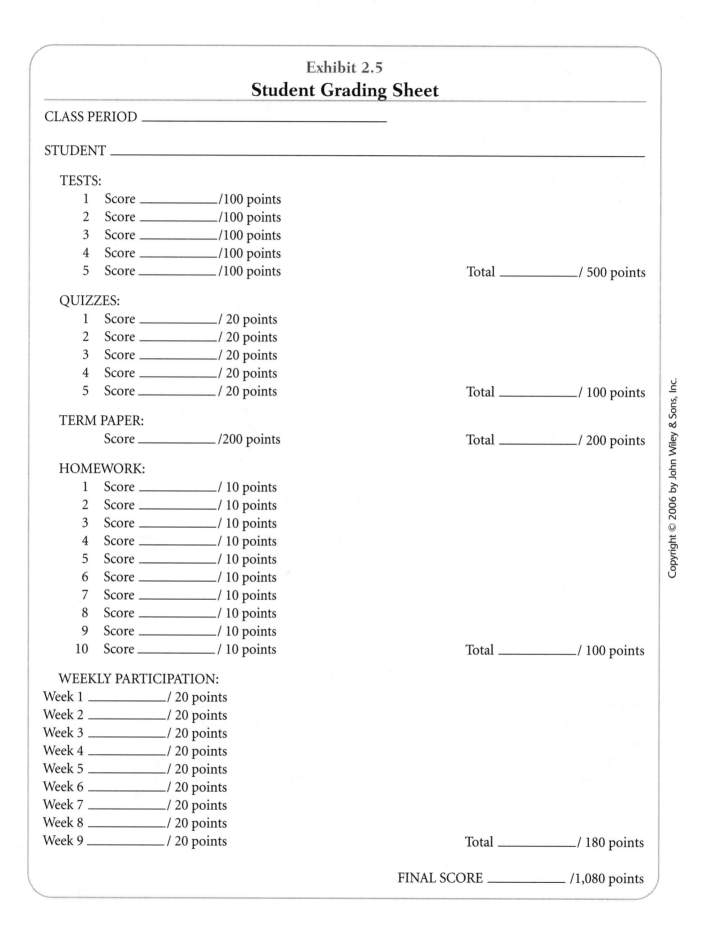

Exhibit 2.5
Student Grading Sheet

CLASS PERIOD _____

STUDENT _____

TESTS:
    1 Score _____/100 points
    2 Score _____/100 points
    3 Score _____/100 points
    4 Score _____/100 points
    5 Score _____/100 points   Total _____ / 500 points

QUIZZES:
    1 Score _____/ 20 points
    2 Score _____/ 20 points
    3 Score _____/ 20 points
    4 Score _____/ 20 points
    5 Score _____/ 20 points   Total _____ / 100 points

TERM PAPER:
      Score _____ /200 points   Total _____ / 200 points

HOMEWORK:
    1 Score _____/ 10 points
    2 Score _____/ 10 points
    3 Score _____/ 10 points
    4 Score _____/ 10 points
    5 Score _____/ 10 points
    6 Score _____/ 10 points
    7 Score _____/ 10 points
    8 Score _____/ 10 points
    9 Score _____/ 10 points
   10 Score _____/ 10 points   Total _____ / 100 points

WEEKLY PARTICIPATION:
Week 1 _____ / 20 points
Week 2 _____ / 20 points
Week 3 _____ / 20 points
Week 4 _____ / 20 points
Week 5 _____ / 20 points
Week 6 _____ / 20 points
Week 7 _____ / 20 points
Week 8 _____ / 20 points
Week 9 _____ / 20 points   Total _____ / 180 points

            FINAL SCORE _____ /1,080 points

Grading Self-Assessment Checklist

Use this worksheet to identify which parts of the tasks described in this chapter you have completed. For any item that has not been completed, note what needs to be done to complete it. Then transfer your notes to your planning calendar in the form of specific actions you need to take (for example, "October 10, finish determining the percentage of mastery used to determine student grades").

✔	Task	Notes and Implementation Ideas
☐	*Develop clear goals for each class you teach.*	
	I have developed and written down four to seven major goals (instructional and/or behavioral) that I want to accomplish with all my students by the end of the school year.	
	I have identified specific ways in which I will use these goals to guide lesson planning and decision-making throughout the year.	
☐	*Design instruction and evaluation procedures that create a clear relationship between student effort and success.*	
	I have determined the evaluation methods and processes I will use to verify that students are learning what I am teaching so they can clearly see the link between learning, doing work and participating, and receiving a passing grade.	
	In order to increase motivation for all my students, I have clarified my instructional objectives and will evaluate students only on the basis of those objectives.	
	I have made sure my students understand my class objectives, so they will know what they are supposed to study to increase the likelihood they will make the effort. Moreover, I have organized my grading system such that if a student meets specific objectives, he or she will pass. It is not based on a curve. I have done the following to help me establish my goals into units of instruction and evaluation: • Broken down the semester's content into one- or two-week units of instruction; • Determined the percentage of mastery that will be used to determine student grades; • Identified the essential objectives for each unit that I want my students to master and retain; and • Built cumulative review of essential objectives into subsequent units of instruction.	

Grading Self-Assessment Checklist (continued)

Establish a system to provide students feedback on behavior and effort. Incorporate this into your grading system.

I understand that my grading system must demonstrate that daily work and attention have a cumulative effect on grades. I need to teach less motivated students that learning independent study skills, knowing how to listen, and taking responsibility for assignments and materials have a direct relationship to success and good grades. I will accomplish this by basing a percentage of their final grade on behavior and effort.

I have done the following to assist me in accomplishing this:

- Established what percentage of the final grade will be for classroom behavior and effort, taking into account the subject, maturity and self-motivation of students, and course level

- Determined the approximate number of total points students may earn for tests, assignments, and class projects during the term

- Determined the approximate number of total points students may earn for behavior and effort

- Designed an efficient system for monitoring and recording daily classroom behavior points (using the behavior record form)

- Determined the impact on grading that students not being in class will have, making sure not to penalize excused absences

- Planned to total points on the behavior record form weekly, and give them to students

Design procedures for students to receive feedback on each aspect of their behavioral and academic performance and to know their current grades.

I understand the importance of getting students their grades back quickly and the importance of them knowing their current status in class at all times so they can measure the effects their effort has against their grade performance. Therefore, if I am using a computerized grade program, I will print out current grades and assignment status on a weekly basis. Otherwise, I will use a student grading sheet to prompt students to record their grades.

Grading Peer Study Worksheet

With one or more of your colleagues, work through the following discussion topics and activities related to the tasks in Chapter Two. If necessary, refer back to the text to get additional ideas or for clarification. (See the Vision Peer Study Worksheet in Chapter One for suggestions on structuring effective discussion sessions.)

Task 1: Develop Clear Goals for Each Class You Teach

    A. Have all group members share their goals and explain why they chose those goals.

    B. As a group, examine each member's goals individually, giving positive and constructive feedback on their content and language.

    C. Have all group members share how they plan to communicate their long-range goals to students and students' families.

Task 2: Design Instruction and Evaluation Procedures That Create a Clear Relationship between Student Effort and Success

    A. Have all group members discuss how they create a direct link between state and district standards, daily instruction, and assessment tools (such as unit tests).

    B. Have all group members share any ideas on how to directly teach students to understand that effort and hard work will have a direct relationship to quality of performance on assignments and tests and, consequently, their grades.

    C. Discuss whether group members plan to structure lesson and test design with the essential objectives/advanced objectives organizational pattern.

Task 3: Establish a System to Provide Students Feedback on Behavior and Effort. Incorporate This into Your Grading System

    A. Have group members discuss their understanding of school and district policies relative to grades being based partially on behavior and effort.

    B. If any group members are using this sort of grading procedure, have them share details on what they have done and the results achieved. In particular, address what percentage of the total grade is influenced by behavior and effort, how these grades are determined, and how excused and unexcused absences are dealt with.

Task 4: Design Procedures for Students to Receive Feedback on Each Aspect of Their Behavioral and Academic Performance and to Know Their Current Grades

    A. Discuss what type, if any, of computerized grade book group members use. What are the pros and cons of any in use? What are the procedures for providing students with regular feedback on current status of grades; for example, is there a "Weekly Report" feature or something similar? If computer grade books are not in use, how are group members providing students with regular feedback on grade status?

What do different group members do to maintain student confidentiality when posting grades and handing out grade-status reports?

Chapter Three

Organization

Prepare routines and procedures

Picture two different college classes: one has an organized professor who starts class on time, uses class time efficiently, and clearly states the requirements of assignments and their due dates. The other class has a disorganized professor who never starts on time. He is often sorting his notes or overheads until ten minutes into class. Then he takes up class time to talk about things that interest him, not the class topics. His students are never clear on what their assignments are or when they're due. In which of these classes would you do better? Never doubt that a teacher's organization affects his students. If he is clear and motivated, his students are likely to be as well (Moran, Stobbe, Baron, Miller, & Moir, 2000; Simola, 1996).

The five tasks presented in this chapter will help you organize your classroom in a manner both efficient and likely to prompt responsible behavior from your students. Whenever possible, you should complete the tasks before the school year begins so that you have a solid organizational structure in place from the start (Bell, 1998; Schell & Burden, 1985). In addition, once you have finished the tasks, the essential information should be included in your course syllabus. (See Chapter Seven.)

If you are starting this chapter during the school year, address the tasks one at a time and implement them gradually so as not to make too many changes to your classroom routine at once.

Five tasks are presented and explained in this chapter:

Task 1: Arrange the schedule of activities for each class period so it maximizes instructional time and responsible behavior.

Task 2: Arrange the physical space in your classroom so that it promotes positive student-teacher interactions and reduces disruptions.

Task 3: Decide on a signal you can use to immediately quiet your students and gain their full attention.

Task 4: Design efficient, effective procedures for beginning and ending the class period.

Task 5: Design efficient, effective procedures for assigning, monitoring, and collecting student work.

At the end of this chapter are two worksheets for you to complete. The Self-Assessment Checklist will help you determine which tasks, or parts of tasks, your classroom management plan will need. The Peer Study Worksheet presents a series of discussion questions that you can use with one or more teachers to share information on how they have improved their own classroom management practices.

Task 1: Arrange the Schedule of Activities for Each Class Period So It Maximizes Instructional Time and Responsible Behavior

How you schedule activities within a class period and through the week can have a tremendous influence on student behavior (Kame'enui & Simmons, 1990; Tanner, Bottoms, Caro, & Bearman, 2003). For example, the teacher who schedules independent work for the last half of the last period of the day may find that students engage in high rates of off-task behavior because they are fatigued and restless. During the last half-hour of the school day, you will keep students more engaged if you schedule only brief independent work tasks and implement more interactive and teacher-directed tasks. This may even mean that if you have two classes of freshman English, one first period and one seventh period, you will teach the same content in both classes, but the schedule and type of activities you use may be different in the two periods. An effective schedule provides enough variety that students will be able to stay focused on any task. An effective schedule also takes into consideration your skill at keeping students on task and the maturity of your students.

> ## Note
> The level of structure your class requires has a direct impact on how you approach scheduling. If you have determined that your students are likely to be successful with a low-structure management plan, you may not need to closely attend to daily schedule issues. Low-structure students are more likely to be able to stay on task for extended periods and should be able to begin class with an independent or cooperative (as opposed to teacher-directed) activity. If your class requires a medium- or high-structure plan, carefully consider the information in this task and use it to get the most out of your daily schedule.

The information in this task is designed to help you evaluate and change your schedule to ensure that it promotes effective student behavior. Along with specific scheduling suggestions, this task will also identify specific times of the day during which students are more prone to irresponsible behavior and what you can do to increase productive behavior at those times.

To begin evaluating your schedule, list the subjects you teach and the length of your class periods. Then list the activities that typically occur during each class and the amount of time each activity takes. Finally, list whether the activities are independent or directed by you. The end result should be a schedule that lays out each period like this:

2 minutes	Independent warm-up exercise and attendance
5 minutes	Teacher-directed review of previous concepts
10 minutes	Teacher-directed introduction of new concepts
8 minutes	Teacher-directed guided practice, working on assignment
20 minutes	Independent work or cooperative tasks (depending on task)
5 minutes	Teacher-directed corrections and guided practice to help students identify errors or misunderstandings

Create a balance of teacher-directed, independent, and group tasks. Your goal is to balance the kinds of activities you have your students doing. Especially watch for a tendency to schedule too much of a good thing. For example, if you like having students work in cooperative groups and feel strongly that students learn the most by working cooperatively, you may inadvertently schedule too much of your class period for group activities. Similarly, if you prefer teacher-directed activities (that is, lectures, discussions, demonstrations), you may have a tendency not to schedule enough time for independent work and group tasks.

Look at your daily schedule, and estimate the approximate percentage of class time your students spend on various activities. You may find your schedule looks something like the following:

40 percent teacher directed

35 percent independent work periods

25 percent cooperative groups

There are no absolute rules on balance in the classroom. A technology class would have far more independent work, while a history class would have more teacher instruction. Look closely at what type of task takes up the highest percentage of your class time, and honestly ask yourself if that task is appropriate for the class or if it represents "too much of a good thing."

Whenever students engage in one particular type of task for too long, behavior problems can result. When teacher-directed instruction goes on too long, students tend to become inattentive. When students have to sit and do independent work for an extended period, they may get bored and stop working.

There are no absolute rules about how long is too long or how much is too much, but a good rule of thumb is keeping all activities under thirty minutes. The amount of time can depend in part on your skills and talents as a teacher. A teacher who designs clear, interesting, and fun independent assignments can successfully engage students for longer periods. A teacher whose presentation style is dynamic, organized, and humorous can sustain student attention for longer periods of teacher-directed instruction. If you have found in the past that student behavior deteriorates as a particular activity progresses (for example, students do well at the start of independent work but get increasingly off-task after about fifteen minutes), schedule shorter time periods for that particular type of activity.

If you teach in ninety-minute blocks, pay particular attention to keeping each activity to a reasonable length of time. You should schedule more activities within the period, instead of longer activities—for example:

2 minutes	Independent warm-up exercise and attendance
6 minutes	Teacher-directed review of previous concepts
10 minutes	Teacher-directed introduction of new concepts
10 minutes	Teacher-directed guided practice, working on assignments
15 minutes	Independent work
5 minutes	Teacher-directed correcting and clarifying
5 minutes	Introduction to cooperative exercise
15 minutes	Cooperative group task
5 minutes	Teacher-directed clarification
10 minutes	Independent work
5 minutes	Teacher-directed introduction to homework

Schedule independent work and cooperative group tasks so that they immediately follow teacher-directed tasks. Teacher-directed instruction is an excellent way to generate classroom momentum, while starting class with independent projects can result in lower rates of on-task behavior. Starting the period by reviewing previous concepts, introducing some new concepts or skills, and then moving students into independent work or cooperative tasks allows you to clarify what students should be working on, creates cohesive and clear expectations for on-task behavior, and maintains the momentum that you create at the beginning of class (Kame'enui & Simmons, 1990).

There are exceptions to this rule. For example, many teachers have their students work on review exercises or a challenge problem as soon as they enter the room while the teacher takes attendance and deals with other housekeeping tasks. This strategy usually involves brief (two to five minutes) independent or cooperative activities and is a structured part of the daily routine. This can be a highly effective practice. Another exception may be a class in which students work mainly on extremely clear and highly motivating independent tasks—a computer lab, for example.

As you develop your daily schedule, remember that in general, teacher-directed instruction is the best way to begin class; therefore, avoid beginning class with a long period of independent work time. Also keep in mind that for a class needing high structure, brief periods of independent work are more likely to result in high rates of on-task behavior than an independent work time that lasts more than twenty minutes.

Implementing these suggestions as you schedule daily activities is an excellent way to reduce the likelihood of irresponsible student behavior. Another way is to identify and address those specific activities and times of day during which students typically exhibit the most distraction or misbehavior. For problem activities or times, make a point of diligently teaching students what your expectations are and how to meet them. What follows are times that are particularly troublesome for many teachers, along with some suggestions on how to address the increasing irresponsible behavior during those times.

The last hour of the day. Students (and teachers!) tend to be tired by the end of their day. Students are more likely to be distracted at this time, so you should avoid scheduling too much independent work then. This can be an effective strategy even if you teach several units of the same class at different times. If you teach two classes of tenth-grade English—one first period and one seventh period—it would be reasonable to have the first class begin with teacher-directed instruction and then assign students to work on a long-range project for thirty minutes. Students in the last class would find it more difficult to stay on task for such an extended independent work period. You would be better off giving teacher-directed instruction, then fifteen minutes of project work, and then more teacher-directed instruction before guided practice to end the class. You would be covering the same amount of information as you did in the first period, but split into two units.

The last five minutes of a class period. Try to end each class period with a few minutes of teacher-directed instruction. If you schedule independent work time during the last part of the class, students will begin to take advantage and let their work slide as the clock winds down. The more they get away with this behavior, the more time they will waste, and utimately the last fifteen minutes of your class may be wasted altogether. By scheduling the last class activity as a teacher-directed task, you set a precedent that class time is used only for class work. This should not be complicated. If you have students working in groups during the second half of class, you can monitor their progress and make corrections. As the period draws to a close, you can get everyone's attention and discuss any common mistakes: "Class, for the last fifteen minutes of class, we'll be working on this problem. We'll finish class by looking at the problem together. Before you leave, I'll give you the homework assignment for tonight. While you're working, keep in mind . . ."

In addition to giving students feedback or information about the current task, you can use those final minutes to review homework expectations or remind your students about long-range projects: "Class, do not forget that you should be done with your outline for the projects by Wednesday, and tomorrow is the last day to get your permission slips in for the field trip."

If you do not end the class with teacher-directed instruction, your students may begin to act as if independent work time is free time. One example of how to accomplish this is to use the last three to five minutes to draw names and have the students answer pop questions for bonus points. This can be an enjoyable and fast-paced way to keep students focused on the academic subject right up to the end of the period.

A well-designed schedule ensures that students experience a varied and balanced range of activities within class. If students are kept engaged with activities that are scheduled for reasonable lengths of time, responsible behavior will result. If students are required to engage in the same type of activity too often or for extended periods, they may become bored, distracted, and even disruptive.

Task 2: Arrange the Physical Space in Your Classroom So That It Promotes Positive Student-Teacher Interactions and Reduces Disruption

The physical organization of the classroom has a significant influence on student behavior. If student desks are arranged in a manner that makes it difficult for the teacher to circulate

> **Note**
>
> Teachers may not always have control over the physical layout of their classroom environment. If you teach in a classroom that isn't yours, have inherited affixed student desks or other permanent fixtures, or have a large class in a small space, adapt the principles in this task as well as you can.

through the room, student behavior is likely to be less responsible than if the room is arranged so that the teacher can easily be among the students. This task covers the four aspects of a classroom's physical arrangement that you can address to increase responsible student behavior. If you have a high-structure classroom management plan, carefully consider how you can implement all four aspects of physical space presented in this task. Well-designed physical space can prevent a wide array of potential behavioral problems.

The basic rule regarding physical arrangements is this: change what you can and make the best of what you can't. If you must teach English in a science lab, you will have to put more energy into teaching your students to stay on task than you would if they could work at individual desks. Manage the aspects of the physical space over which you have no control by manipulating other variables, such as teaching more expected behavior and monitoring student behavior more closely.

To whatever extent you can control the physical space in which you teach, consider the following suggestions:

• *Make sure you have easy access to all parts of the room.* One of the most effective behavior management strategies a teacher can implement is to circulate through the class as often as possible. To this end, however you organize the desks and chairs in the class, make sure you're able to move around them freely.

When students are working independently or in groups, your proximity will have a moderating effect on their behavior. As you circulate, you will be able to provide corrective feedback to students who are off-task, give positive feedback to students using their work time well, and answer the questions of students who need assistance. While assisting a student, if you notice another student who is off-task, you should be able to go directly to that student. This will keep the students aware of your proximity, which will keep their behavior in check.

• *Arrange student desks to optimize the instructional tasks that students are most likely to engage in.* Following are descriptions of common arrangements for desks with information about their relative pros and cons:

Desks in Rows, Front to Back (Figure 3.1)
- Excellent if you frequently schedule whole-class instruction or have students do tasks at the board
- For occasional cooperative learning activities, students can be trained to move quickly into and out of groups of four
- Allows students to interact, but the spaces between desks will help to keep off-task conversation down
- Directs student attention to the front of the room
- Allows easy circulation among students
- Effective for medium- to high-structure classes

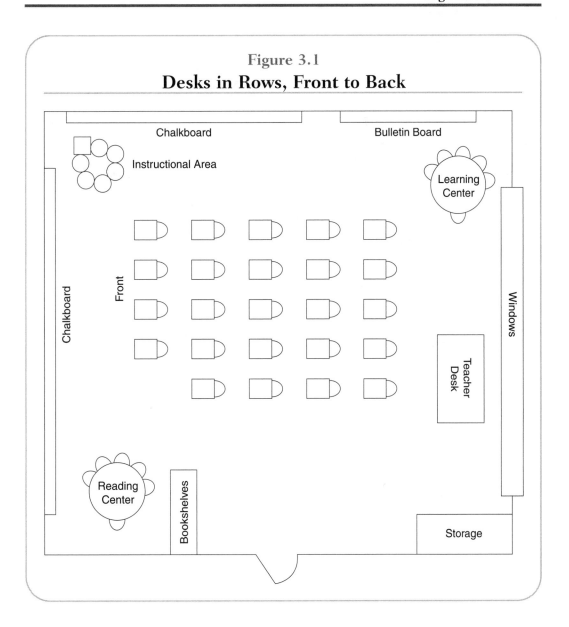

Figure 3.1
Desks in Rows, Front to Back

Desks Side to Side (Figure 3.2)

- Excellent if you use frequent whole-class instruction where you have students do tasks for which they must see the board
- For occasional cooperative learning activities, students can be trained to move quickly from the rows into groups of four and back to the rows when the cooperative activity is completed
- Allows more student interaction, which is helpful for group study but can result in off-topic conversation
- Directs student attention to the front of the room
- Best for a low- to medium-structure classroom

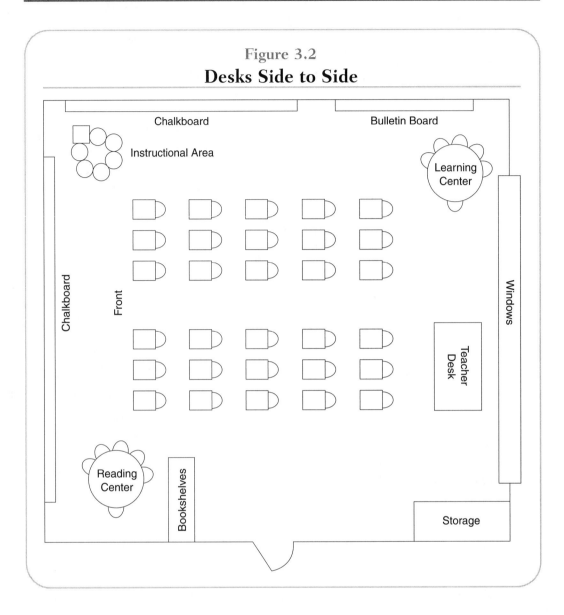

Figure 3.2
Desks Side to Side

- May be necessary for larger classes
- Grouping desks in rows of three creates aisles for easy access

Desks in Clusters (Figure 3.3)
- Allows easy circulation and access to all students at any time
- Excellent if you schedule frequent cooperative learning tasks
- If students are easily distracted, the small groupings may draw attention away from activities
- Requires some students to turn in their seats to see the board for teacher-directed instruction
- May lead to off-topic conversation due to student proximity
- Best for low-structure classes; cluster may prompt inappropriate student interaction in a class needing high structure

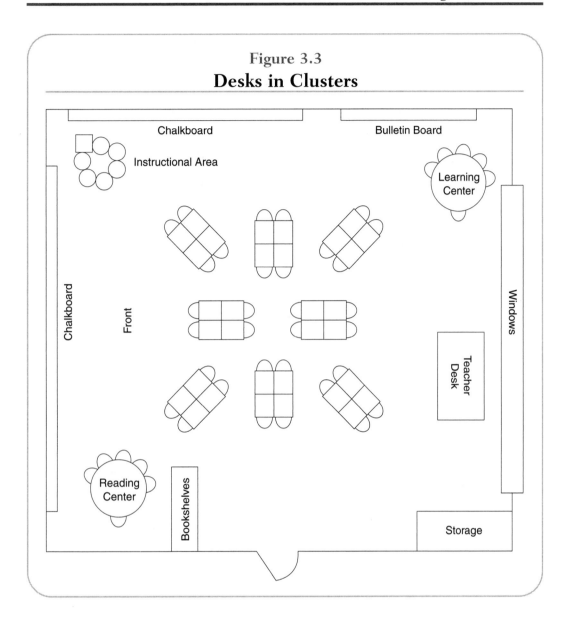

Figure 3.3
Desks in Clusters

Desks in U-Shape (Figure 3.4)

- Excellent for class discussion and teacher-directed instruction with student participation
- Excellent for teacher proximity and circulation
- Does not lend itself to group activities
- Inefficient use of space; may not be useful for labs and small group instruction, for example
- Cannot be used with a large class
- U shape may require breaks to allow easier student circulation—for example, to the teacher's desk or the exit
- Best for classes that need low to medium classroom structure; can be adapted to work for a smaller high-structure class if the teacher is committed to circulating and giving frequent feedback

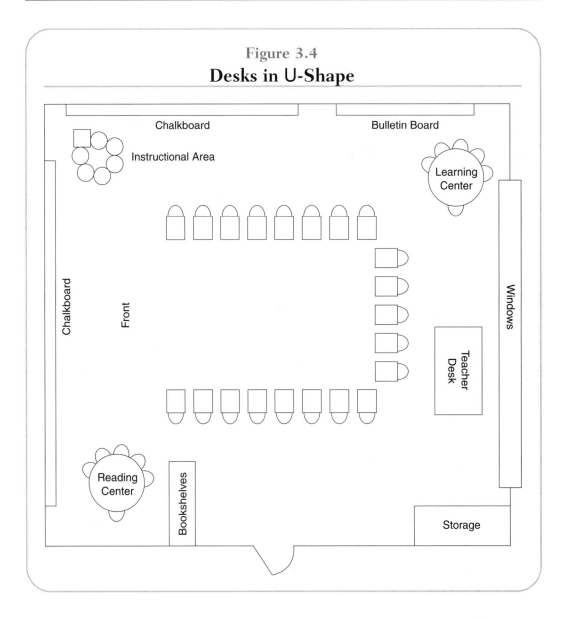

Figure 3.4
Desks in U-Shape

As you consider what arrangement you want for your classroom (one of the four or one of your own), keep in mind the tasks your students will be participating in and the level of classroom structure they will require.

• *Minimize the disruptions caused by high-traffic areas in the class.* There are a number of legitimate reasons that students need to move about the classroom during the day. Any time students are out of their seats, however, there is a greater potential for misbehavior. When setting up your classroom, give thought to high-traffic areas. As much as possible, you should keep desks away from the areas where students will do the following:

• Get supplies
• Sharpen pencils
• Turn in work
• Have small group instruction
• Use lab stations

If you can't avoid having student desks near one or more of these high-traffic areas, you will need to teach students how to be in these areas without distracting other students.

Conclusion. Arrange the physical space in your classroom to prompt responsible behavior from students. One way to accomplish this is to make sure there is easy access from any one part of the room to any other part of the room, so that you can circulate <u>unpredictably</u> among students and so that students can move about without disturbing each other. In addition, desks and traffic patterns should be arranged in a manner that takes into account the major types of instructional activities you use and the level of structure needed in your classroom management plan. Your goal is a physical environment that is comfortable and functional for you and your students.

Circulate unpredictably

Task 3: Decide on a Signal You Can Use to Immediately Quiet Your Students and Gain Their Full Attention

Getting and holding students' undivided attention is an important management tool for any teacher. Just as a conductor uses a baton to gain the attention of the orchestra, so you need a signal to draw your students' attention to you so that you can give directions or provide instruction.

There are many times and situations when an attention signal is useful. Imagine a class of twenty-eight students working in small groups. As the teacher monitors her class, she realizes that her students do not fully understand their assignment. Using a well-practiced signal, she can get her class's attention in less than five seconds. After briefly clarifying the directions and answering any new questions, she can then return them to their small group work. Without a well-practiced signal, it is likely to take the teacher several minutes of yelling over the noise of the class to get their attention. It is even possible that not all of the students will hear and understand the correct assignment if the class never really quiets down.

To implement this task successfully, first identify what you will use as a signal. One effective method is saying in a firm, loud voice (but without shouting), "Class, your attention please," while at the same time swinging your right arm in an arc (from nine o'clock to twelve o'clock on a clock face). Then hold your hand in the twelve o'clock position until all students have also raised their hands. This prompts each student to stop talking, look at you, and raise his or her own hand until all students are quiet and looking at you with their hands raised (see Figure 3.5).

> **Note**
>
> Whether your class requires a low-, medium-, or high-structure classroom management plan, an attention signal is an important behavior management strategy for any class with more than fifteen students. Regardless of what structure level your class needs, you need a way to get students to make the transition from active and potentially noisy group activities into activities that demand the attention of the whole class.

This signal has several advantages. First, it can be given from any location in the room. Second, it can be used outside the classroom, in the hall, or even on a field trip. Third, it has a visual and an auditory component, so students who miss one component may notice the other. A fourth advantage of this signal (and others like it) is its ripple effect: students who

Figure 3.5
Attention Signal

"Class, your attention please."

miss the signal will see the reactions of other students and be aware of the signal, without having to see it themselves.

Some teachers find that high school students may consider having to raise their hand as part of the signal process to be beneath them. If you think this might be the case, you can let students know that they do not have to raise their hands, but it becomes the students' responsibility to make sure that all students around them (for example, the other students in their small group) are aware that the signal has been given. In this way, the teacher will still be able to get the attention of the entire class, even without requiring raised hands. If this adaptation is not effective, go back to requiring raised hands until students can become quiet without participating by raising their hands.

Regardless of the signal you use, you must be able to get the attention of the entire class within five seconds. To this end, you must teach students the signal and how to respond to it from the first day of class. (Information on when and how to teach your attention signal is provided in Chapter Seven.)

Task 4: Design Efficient, Effective Procedures
for Beginning and Ending the Class Period

How you start and end each class period will have a significant influence on the climate of your classroom. Established procedures for beginning and ending class will foster an invitational and supportive atmosphere (Reddy, Rhodes, & Mulhall, 2003). The more efficiently you use the time you have, the more you communicate to your students that time in your class will not be wasted. This will make a difference in student behavior (Burnette, 1999; Harlan, 2002). Consider the following two scenarios.

Teacher A begins the day by warmly greeting students as they enter the classroom. She has previously taught students that when they enter the room, they are to take their seats immediately, get out any required materials, and begin working on the challenge problem written on the board. Students who do not have their materials do not interrupt the teacher while she is greeting students because she taught them specific procedures for dealing with this situation. When the bell rings, the students continue to work on the challenge problem while the teacher takes attendance. Within one minute of the bell ringing, the teacher has taken attendance, secured the attention of the class, and started teaching. In the next ten minutes, two students enter late, but she does not stop teaching. Her students know her tardiness procedures, which are designed to ensure accurate record keeping without disrupting class. Suggestions on how to achieve this kind of efficiency are provided later in this task.

The situation is different in Teacher B's class. As students enter the class, the teacher is seated at his desk trying to finish last-minute preparations for the lesson. Some of the students take their seats, while others socialize in groups. When the bell rings, Teacher B looks up from his work and acknowledges that students are there by saying, "Quit talking and sit down. It's time to begin class." After two minutes of nagging, the students are finally in their seats and reasonably quiet. He instructs students to get out their materials and then spends several minutes assisting students who are not prepared, all the while telling them to be more responsible. Five minutes after the bell rings, the teacher finally begins teaching. In the next five minutes, two more students arrive. Both times the teacher stops teaching to determine if the tardiness is excused or unexcused and to fill out the necessary paperwork. Each incident requires him to stop teaching as he deals with the late individual.

Note that Teacher A spends only one minute on attendance, materials, and tardiness procedures, and even during that minute students are engaged in an instructional task. Teacher B spends over ten minutes on attendance, materials, and tardiness. Students who arrive on time with all of their materials are forced to sit and do nothing while the teacher deals with these procedures. In both scenarios, some students did not have their materials and two arrived late, things that will happen to every teacher. The difference is that Teacher A anticipated these problems and has taught her students procedures for handling them so that all of her class time is used efficiently.

Task 4 addresses how to begin and end class with a positive tone and how to maintain maximum time for instructional activities. There are eight goals related to beginning and ending class, each supplied with suggestions on how you can best implement them.

As always, if your methods are working for you, remember that this book presents you only with an alternative. If your class begins and ends in an organized manner, then there is

> **Note**
>
> If you need a medium- or high-structure classroom management plan, you should address all the issues outlined in this task. In particular, it will be important for you to be in your classroom (or in the hall near your door) when students enter. Plan to keep students occupied from the moment they enter the room. For a low-structure class, you may be able to let students occupy themselves for a minute or two between their arrival and engagement in an instructional task.

no reason to change your methods. If you are struggling, try these suggestions in addition to consulting your colleagues on their own methods.

Entering Class

Goal: Students will feel welcome and will immediately go to their seats and start on a productive task.

Greeting students as they enter your classroom helps them feel welcome and reduces classroom behavior problems. A brief greeting communicates to students that you are aware of and interested in them not just as students but as individuals. Learn student names as soon as possible. Using a student's name as you greet her demonstrates a level of respect and communicates that you are aware of this person as a valuable individual. One high school physics teacher took a digital photograph of each row of students on the first day of class and had students write their names on a seating chart. By the end of the week, he was calling each student by name in each of his six classes: "Charlene, how did things go at the choir concert last night?" In addition, greeting students as they enter provides a subtle but powerful message that you are aware of students and what they are doing from the minute they enter class, not just when the bell rings.

When possible, greet students at the door. Although you can greet students while seated at your desk, the effect is not as powerful as being at or near the door as they enter.

Greeting students at the door also allows you to assist in supervising the hallway. High schools in which most teachers are at their doorways between classes have fewer problems with misbehavior in the halls, and students are, as a result, calmer and ready for instruction when they enter class. If you are supervising the hall outside your room, you can greet your students before they even enter the class.

Have a task that students can work on as they arrive. This gives students something to do while they wait for the bell to ring and while you take care of any attendance or housekeeping tasks in the first minutes of class. Having students work on a daily task like this communicates to them that every minute in class should be used as efficiently as possible.

Keep the task short—one that will require only three to five minutes of work from students. It should be a review task that students can perform independently but also instructionally relevant—not just busywork. For example, math teachers might give a short daily quiz on the previous night's homework assignment, or language arts teachers might have students work in their journals or do a short writing exercise.

When you have finished taking attendance, give the students feedback on the correct responses for their short task and have them trade with a neighbor for corrections. Then collect the papers so that you can later record the grades and note the students' involvement. If students know that this initial task does not count, they will soon stop completing this opening task.

Opening Activities

Goal: Students will be instructionally engaged while you take attendance.

When the bell rings and as students work on the assigned task, use a seating chart rather than calling out names and having students reply to determine who is present and who is not. This eliminates the need for you to read a boring litany of names every day and allows students to continue focusing on the work they are doing.

Goal: You will develop procedures for dealing with tardiness.

This goal will:

- Ensure that students who are tardy do not disrupt class or take your attention away from teaching.
- Allow you to keep accurate records of excused and unexcused tardies.
- Let you assign consistent corrective consequences for unexcused tardiness.

One recommended procedure for dealing with tardy students involves having a three-ring binder with forms like the reproducible Record of Tardies (shown in Exhibit 3.1) on a table or shelf near the door to the classroom.

During the first week of school, train your students that when they are tardy, whether excused or not, they are to quietly enter the classroom without interrupting you or any students in the class, put their name in the box for the appropriate period, indicate excused or unexcused, attach the excuse if they have one, and then quietly take their seat.

Each day before students arrive, make sure that a new page is showing with the correct day and date filled in at the top. Attach paper clips to the page so students with excused tardies can attach the excused paperwork.

> ### Note
> If tardiness is a chronic problem in your school, a schoolwide program should be considered. If possible, mention to the administration that tardiness should be addressed. START on Time! (Sprick, 2004), a DVD-based in-service program, has reduced tardiness in some high schools up to 90 percent.

When a student enters late, do not stop what you are doing. Visually monitor to make sure that the tardy student goes to the notebook and writes something. If the student does not go to the notebook, provide a verbal reminder: "Paul, before you sit down, put your name in the notebook by the door and indicate if you have an excused or unexcused tardy. Now class . . ."

Later in the period, when the class is engaged in independent work or cooperative groups, check the information on the tardy student in the notebook. Record the information in your grade book, and follow any schoolwide procedures for reporting unexcused tardies to the attendance office. Check the excuse notes to verify them. If you need to talk to a student about being tardy, do so then, while the rest of the class is occupied. Following these procedures prevents the tardy student from getting attention or interrupting your lesson.

There should be corrective consequences for unexcused tardies. If your school does not have such a policy, develop your own and inform students of it on the first day of school. An example policy is below, although the severity of individual consequences will depend on how much authority you have:

Two unexcused tardies in a semester: family notification (notification occurs for each subsequent incident)

Four unexcused tardies: after-school detention

Six unexcused tardies: half-day in-school suspension

Exhibit 3.1
Record of Tardies: Reproducible Form

Teacher _____ Day _____ Date _____

Names

Excused or Unexcused?
If your tardy is excused,
attach the excuse slip from
the attendance office or a
note from the excusing teacher.

First Period

_____	Excused ❏	Unexcused ❏
_____	Excused ❏	Unexcused ❏
_____	Excused ❏	Unexcused ❏

Second Period

_____	Excused ❏	Unexcused ❏
_____	Excused ❏	Unexcused ❏
_____	Excused ❏	Unexcused ❏

Third Period

_____	Excused ❏	Unexcused ❏
_____	Excused ❏	Unexcused ❏
_____	Excused ❏	Unexcused ❏

Fourth Period

_____	Excused ❏	Unexcused ❏
_____	Excused ❏	Unexcused ❏
_____	Excused ❏	Unexcused ❏

Fifth Period

_____	Excused ❏	Unexcused ❏
_____	Excused ❏	Unexcused ❏
_____	Excused ❏	Unexcused ❏

Sixth Period

_____	Excused ❏	Unexcused ❏
_____	Excused ❏	Unexcused ❏
_____	Excused ❏	Unexcused ❏

Seventh Period

_____	Excused ❏	Unexcused ❏
_____	Excused ❏	Unexcused ❏
_____	Excused ❏	Unexcused ❏

Goal: Announcements and other housekeeping tasks will not take up too much time.

You want to begin instructional activities as soon as the period begins. Therefore, plan to spend no more than a minute or two on announcements and housekeeping. Activities that are not directly related to the subject of the class should be reserved for advisory or home-room periods.

Materials

Goal: You should have procedures for dealing with students who do not have materials or are otherwise unprepared.

This goal will:

- Ensure that a student who does not have the necessary materials can get them in a way that does not disrupt instruction.
- Establish penalties that will reduce the likelihood students will forget materials in the future.
- Reduce the amount of time and energy that you spend dealing with this issue.

First, make sure that you clearly communicate to students exactly what materials you expect them to have each day in your class (for example, two writing instruments, a binder with a divider, lined notebook paper, and the textbook). This information should be communicated verbally to students and in writing to students' families as part of a syllabus or letter that goes home on the first day of class. At the end of each period during the first week, remind students what materials they should have when they return to class on Monday.

Next, develop procedures that will allow a student who lacks any of the necessary materials to get what he or she needs to participate in the lesson *and* receive a mild consequence designed to reduce the probability that the student will forget materials again. For example, you might inform students that they should try to borrow the missing material from another student (a pencil or some paper) without involving you or interrupting instruction. Explain further that everyone who has their materials will gain 1 point toward their behavior or participation grade for the week. (See Chapter Two for proper application of this strategy.)

If it seems likely that there will be times when students need to go to their lockers to get materials, include procedures that minimize the teaching time you will lose to fill out hall passes. For example, you could inform students that if they have to go back to their locker for materials after class has begun, it will count as being tardy. Tell them that you will give them a hall pass that they must fill out for you to sign. That way, while the student is filling out the pass, you can continue with your other teaching responsibilities. Having the student fill out the pass reduces your involvement with this student from two or three minutes to only thirty seconds or so. Remember never to let more than one student at a time leave class to go back to his or her locker.

If you ask other teachers in your building how they deal with students who do not have materials, you will probably hear a wide variety of procedures. Some teachers just give away pencils and loan books without any penalty. Others impose a cost in the form of a point fine or other consequence. There is no one right answer; the important thing is to decide in advance how you will deal with this very common occurrence. If you aren't sure whether your planned procedure is fair or appropriate, ask your administrator for feedback. Some administrators, for example, may not want teachers to impose penalties, and there may be other limitations to policies regarding students without materials or tardiness.

It's important that during the first few days of class you inform your students how you will respond if they do not have their materials. For high-structure classes, you should start conducting a materials check daily: "As you are working on the challenge problem, I want to check that you came to class with all your materials. Put your spare pencil, your notebook, and your textbook on your desk. While you are working, I'll come around and check." If any students are missing one or more of the required materials, provide a gentle but firm reminder about the importance of being responsible for bringing their materials every day.

After the first couple of weeks, conduct intermittent spot checks of materials. Any students who do not have what they need should receive a minor corrective consequence (for example, losing 1 point from their participation grade), while students who have all their materials might receive 1 bonus point. If you plan to do this, be sure to inform students on the first day of class that you may conduct spot checks for the first few weeks of school.

When a student does come unprepared to class, do not get upset or frustrated; simply follow through consistently with the procedures you have implemented. Remember that you don't want these procedures to usurp too much of your instructional time. If you start feeling frustrated because you are spending too much time dealing with students who have forgotten materials, ask colleagues for ideas on how to streamline your procedures so that you can keep your focus on instruction.

Dealing with Students Returning After an Absence

Goal: Students who have been absent can easily catch up on missed assignments without greatly involving you.

An excellent way to deal with absent students is to set up two baskets in the classroom—one labeled "Absent, Missed Assignments" and one labeled "Absent, Due Assignments"—that you keep in a consistent location. Any time you give students an assignment or a handout, put that same material in a folder for any students absent that day. The folder should have the date and the class period clearly marked on it. Place these folders in the "Absent, Missed Assignment" basket.

Teach students that when they return after an absence, they should collect the folders for the dates they missed. This way, they can find out all the tasks they missed and get any handouts they might need without needing to interrupt you.

The basket marked "Absent, Due Assignments" can be used in two ways. When a student returns on Tuesday from an absence on Monday, he can turn in any assignment that had been due on Monday to the "Absent, Assignments Due" basket at the same time he is picking up the folder from the "Absent, Missed Assignments" basket. When the student completes the work assigned on Monday (the day he was absent), he will also return that work to the "Absent, Assignments Due" basket. A system like this will save you time and interruptions, but will work only if you keep the baskets up-to-date and remind students who return from being absent to collect what they missed and hand in anything that was due.

As a general rule, students should have the same number of days to complete a missing assignment as the number of days they were absent. Thus, the student who returns Tuesday from being absent on Monday would have until the next day to turn in the work assigned Monday and due on Tuesday. If the student did not return until Thursday, he would have until the following Tuesday, three school days following his return, to turn in his missing assignments.

Decide if you will allow students to make up assignments they missed as a result of unexcused absences. If you do not have a policy, ask your building administrator whether students should be allowed to make up missed assignments from unexcused absences. Defer to his or her judgment.

End of Class or Period

Goal: Your procedures for wrapping up the period will:

- Ensure that students will not leave the classroom before they have organized their own materials and completed any necessary cleanup tasks.
- Ensure that you have enough time to give students both positive and corrective feedback and to set a positive tone for ending the class.

Leave enough time at the conclusion of each class to ensure that things end on a relaxed note. How much time this entails will vary. For example, in a math class, one minute will probably be sufficient; in an art class, it may take up to ten minutes to get all the supplies put away and the room ready for the next class. Allow time for reminders about homework, upcoming tests, permission slips for field trips, and so on. Avoid trying to do all this in too brief a time, or you can inadvertently demonstrate a franticness and sense that you are somewhat disorganized and out of control.

> **Note**
>
> At the beginning of the year, plan to leave a little extra time at the end of class until you determine precisely how much time is needed for these wrap-up activities.

When students have finished organizing and cleaning up, give the class as a whole feedback on things they are doing well and things that may require more effort on their part. This is especially important during the first six weeks of school but is also useful intermittently throughout the school year: "Class, I want to let you know that the way you have been using class time demonstrates a high level of responsibility. You should be very proud of how well you are all functioning as a group. One thing that a few people need to manage more effectively is remembering homework. Tomorrow you have a science assignment due. Make a decision right now when you are going to work on that assignment."

Dismissal

Goal: Students will leave the classroom when you dismiss them and not by the bell.

On the first day of school, and periodically thereafter, remind your students that they are not to leave their seats when the bell rings. Explain that the bell is the signal to *you* and that you will excuse the class when things are reasonably quiet and all final tasks have been completed. If you let students run for the door when the bell rings, it sets a precedent that your instructional control ends then. By reserving the right to excuse the class, you can judge whether you should excuse the whole class at once or by rows or table clusters. As a general rule, higher-structure classes should be excused by rows, and lower-structure classes can be excused as a group. However, if you excuse as a group, let the students know that if they rush out of the room or crowd the door, you will start excusing them by rows.

The beginning and ending of class periods play major roles in setting the climate of the classroom. Opening and dismissal routines that are welcoming, calm, efficient, and purposeful demonstrate to students that you are pleased to see them and that you care so much about class time that not a minute will be wasted. Calm and efficient dismissal brings organized closure and sets a tone for your class for the following day.

Task 5: Design Effective, Efficient Procedures for Assigning, Monitoring, and Collecting Student Work

An all-too-common frustration for teachers is dealing with students who do not complete assigned work. The problem is often compounded by the fact that students who do not complete assignments will not achieve mastery of skills they need to complete future assignments. In addition, without seeing their work, you will be unable to track your students' progress. If you can increase the likelihood that students will complete their assignments, students will learn more and you will be less frustrated. This task addresses procedures for managing student work. Implementing well-designed and organized strategies for assigning, monitoring, and collecting student work will (1) let students know that you put a high value on their completing work, (2) prompt more responsible student behavior regarding assigned tasks, and (3) help you effectively manage student work without taking unreasonable amounts of time (Lynn, 1994).

If you are new, find out what policies your school has before you start implementing your own homework policies. Check with the administration, your department chair, or a colleague to see what rules are already in place. High schools often create schoolwide policies on late work and makeup work, and may have standing rules on assigning work. Some schools are also implementing a policy to monitor when other classes assign major projects like term papers so that they do not overlap. This enables your students to focus more on one class at a time, instead of potentially having to turn in three big projects in a week.

There are five major areas related to managing student work for you to consider (see Figure 3.6). The rest of this section gives some considerations and suggestions for each area.

Assigning Class Work and Homework

The first step toward greater student work return is to create a system that allows students to track their assignments. Students should have a consistent place to look (for example, on a board or an assignment sheet) to find out what their assignments are. It is not enough simply to tell students what their assignments are or to write them out during the lessons. These methods do not create the necessary permanent place for students to check when they need to find out what they should be working on or may have missed. If there is no set place where students can check what their assignments are, a student who forgets an assignment will have no choice but to ask you or another student for the information. When assignments are left on the board or recorded on an assignment sheet, the student can easily check to determine what he needs to do.

In keeping with this, also teach students to keep their own records of assigned work, so that when they get home, they will know what they need to do. If you decide to put assignments on the board, teach students to copy the homework assignments onto a sheet that they

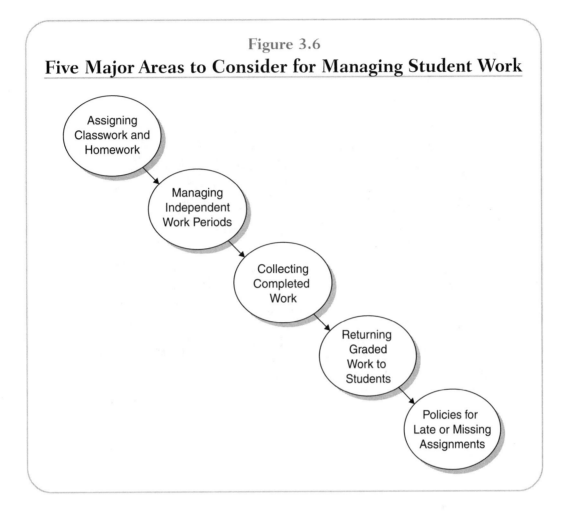

Figure 3.6
Five Major Areas to Consider for Managing Student Work

- Assigning Classwork and Homework
- Managing Independent Work Periods
- Collecting Completed Work
- Returning Graded Work to Students
- Policies for Late or Missing Assignments

keep in a consistent place in their notebook. If you give out a weekly assignment sheet, students should be taught to keep the assignment sheet in a consistent place in their notebooks. Be specific: tell students exactly how and where they should record the information. Show them an example and, especially at the beginning of the year, monitor whether they are following through—for example: "Class, we have a couple of minutes before the bell. Open your notebooks to the page immediately after the divider for this class. I want to see that you have the weekly assignment sheet in the correct place."

If you give both short-term daily assignments and long-term assignments (for example, a term paper), make sure both assignments are noted. Daily reminders about a long-term task will help students remember that they should be working on the task on an ongoing basis, not putting it off to the last minute. This is also an opportunity to remind students what part of the assignment they should have completed at any given time: "Remember that your projects are due in one week, so by Monday you should have your outline and your first draft completed."

Figure 3.7 shows how you might use board space for recording assignments.

A permanent record of daily assignments is especially useful if you have determined that your students need a high-structure classroom management plan. It is essential, then, to establish a way for a student to find out what assignments were missed during an absence. Refer to Task 4 for more information on how best to approach this.

Figure 3.7
Sample of Assignments on the Board

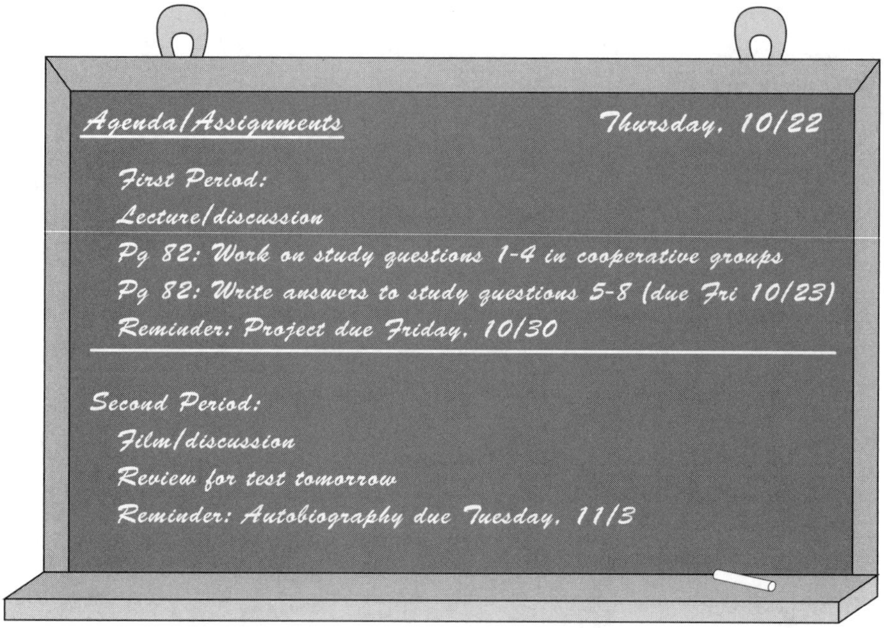

Agenda/Assignments   *Thursday, 10/22*

First Period:
Lecture/discussion
Pg 82: Work on study questions 1-4 in cooperative groups
Pg 82: Write answers to study questions 5-8 (due Fri 10/23)
Reminder: Project due Friday, 10/30

Second Period:
Film/discussion
Review for test tomorrow
Reminder: Autobiography due Tuesday, 11/3

Note

Another helpful tool if students are struggling with their reading is *REWARDS (Reading Excellence: Word Attack and Rate Development Strategies)* (grades 4–12) and *REWARDS Plus* (grades 6–12), by Anita Archer, Mary Gleason, and Vicky Vachon (2005).

While helping students keep track of their assignments in a particular place, also monitor their study habits. Just as you should encourage them to progress on long-term projects instead of doing them all at once, you should watch to see which specific students are more likely to let work go unfinished. Encourage them particularly to stay on top of their assignments, specifically encouraging them for any successes.

Managing Independent Work Periods

The following information will give you a basic approach to effectively setting up independent work periods.

Be sure that any work you assign can be done independently by all your students. If you assign students tasks that they cannot complete, you set them up to fail. When students have to do work that is beyond their ability, they may do the work and fail because they can't understand it, or just avoid doing the work at all. Either way, the student fails. Over time, a lot of students tend toward the second option because when they do nothing, they may look tough or bored rather than stupid or helpless. The following ideas are steps you can take to ensure that all of your students are capable of completing the independent work assigned them:

> **Note**
>
> If your school does not have a study skills curriculum, you might want to suggest that your staff consider *Advanced Skills for School Success* by Anita Archer and Mary Gleason (2003). This is a study skills program for grades 7 to 12 that is designed in four modules. Each module addresses one area of school performance that is of immediate use to students in meeting school demands: school behaviors and organization skills, completion of daily assignments, effective reading of textbooks, and learning from verbal presentations and participating in discussions.

- Modify assignments for the lower-performing students in the class. For more information on modifying instruction for meeting the needs of lower-performing students, see *Interventions: Collaborative Planning for High Risk Students* (Sprick, Sprick, & Garrison, 1993).

- Provide alternative assignments for some of the students.

- Work with a few students in a small group and do the assignment together while the rest of the class works independently.

- Have students work in pairs or cooperative groups to help each other. (Do not overuse this strategy or your higher-performing students may get tired of assisting others.) Consider setting up the groups—who works with whom—to avoid having clusters of low-performing students choose to work together and be unable to perform the required tasks.

Schedule independent work times in a way that maximizes on-task behavior. The timing of independent work periods within a class can have a significant impact on the degree to which students will stay focused on their work. Below are a few considerations:

- Schedule small, standard periods of time for students to work independently. There is no magic rule about how long students can stay focused, though having students work on the same task for more than thirty minutes without some variation typically results in high rates of off-task behavior.

- Plan for independent work periods that occur at the end of the day to be shorter than the independent work periods during classes that occur at the beginning of the day.

- Create immediate accountability during independent work time. Walk between the desks and follow the students' progress, particularly keeping an eye on those most likely to become distracted.

Develop and present to students a clear vision of what you want student behavior during independent work times to look and sound like. Keep in mind that if you do not clarify and teach exactly what you want from students, some will likely assume that behaviors such as chatting in groups or moving about the room are acceptable during independent work times. Once you have a vision of the behaviors you want to see and those you don't, teach students to meet those expectations. (This suggestion is covered in detail in Chapter Four.)

Provide guided practice on tasks and assignments, working with students in a teacher-directed activity for the first 10 to 50 percent of an assignment. When teaching a math lesson, for example, you might first review previously taught concepts, then introduce the new concept, work through the first several exercises with students, and finally let students work on the remainder of the assignment independently or in groups. If there were thirty problems in the assignment, you might lead students through the first six: "Watch me do the first two problems on the overhead, and copy what I do." Then demonstrate and explain. At the end of the explanation, tell the students, "On the next two problems, I'll do the first part and you do the second part."

Demonstrate the first part, and let students do the second part; correct the problems, and answer questions from students or reteach based on student mistakes. Then let all students do two problems while you monitor student performance: "Now do the next two problems on your own. Stop when you finish problem 6, so we can correct." Model or have individual students demonstrate the correct answer, answer any questions, and provide additional instructions. If students are doing well, you could assign the remainder of problems as independent work. If many students are having problems, continue to work through them together until you are sure the students understand.

Guided practice increases the chance that students will understand what they need to do in order to complete their tasks successfully. It has the further advantage of creating behavioral momentum. That is, if you guide students through the first part of a task, a portion of that task is already completed by the time you say, "Now do the rest of the assignment on your own." Without guided practice, when you say, "Start work on your assignment," students are faced with a blank piece of paper. For many people (and not only students!), the hardest part of doing assigned tasks is getting started. Guided practice increases work completion because it ensures that tasks are begun before the independent part of the class period starts. The structure level your group management plan calls for should determine how often you use guided practice. The more structured your classroom environment, the longer you should guide the work before letting your students work independently.

Develop a system that allows students to get their questions answered during independent work periods. When students have a question about how to do something, they will often feel that they cannot continue with their work until the question is answered. If you have not structured a way for students to get the necessary help, you will have higher rates of off-task behavior. For those independent work periods in which you are available to answer questions, develop and teach your students to use some kind of a visual signal when they need assistance. You might have students put an upright book (other than the book they need for the assignment) on the corner of their desk (Figure 3.8).

Another way students can indicate they need assistance is to write their name on the board along with the question or problem number with which they need help. In this way, if several students have a question on the same problem, you can gather those students together and provide assistance one time instead of helping each person individually: "Sandra, Mark, and Dani, if you'd like to come up to my desk, we can look at problem 5."

None of these suggestions requires students to raise their hands when they want help. The problems with the traditional hand-raising procedure are that (1) it is physically difficult to

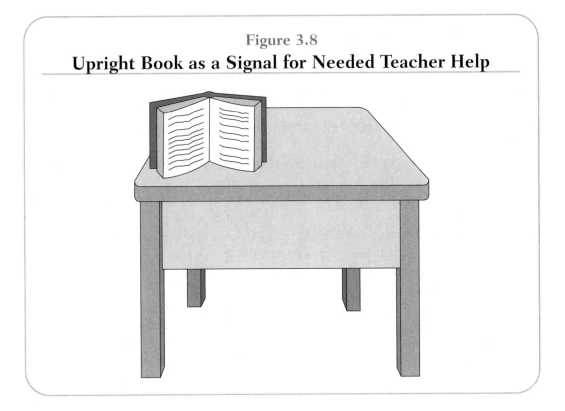

Figure 3.8
Upright Book as a Signal for Needed Teacher Help

keep a hand in the air for the three to five minutes it may take you to respond; (2) the student is necessarily off-task while waiting for your help; and (3) hand-raising tends to draw more attention to a student, which may discourage some students from asking for help. With the open book signal (or some variation), students can be trained to use their signal unobtrusively, mark the question or problem that has them confused, and continue working on other problems.

For independent work times that you are not immediately available, you will have to devise and teach students to use strategies for asking and helping each other. Be sure that students understand that this is appropriate only to get needed help, not to chat. This is something to implement gradually, and under supervision, until you feel your students are responsible enough to continue assisting each other on their own.

Collecting Completed Work

Give some thought early on to what method you will use to collect homework. Whenever possible, collect the work personally from each student: "Class, put your homework on the upper-right-hand corner of your desk. While you are working on the challenge problem on the overhead, I will come around and collect it." The biggest advantage of this procedure is that you know immediately if students have not completed the work (and your students will know you know). If a student does not have his or her homework, take that moment to reemphasize that work completion is an important aspect of responsible behavior in your class. Do not accept excuses, but let the student know that she will need to speak to you later. It is important to doubly use this time by having your students work on a current project while you collect their completed assignments.

Because this allows you to give students immediate feedback about their work, it is most effective in a classroom that is using a high-structure plan. This does have the drawback of being time-consuming for you. If you require only a low- or medium-structure classroom management plan, you may prefer a less hands-on way of collecting homework and monitoring completion.

Having students turn in their work, having a student helper collect it, or having the work turned in to a basket are all less time intensive, but lack the advantage of personal contact that your collecting the work has. Even if they don't see a grade for a day or two, seeing you take the completed work and knowing you have it, instead of knowing you'll get it eventually, is a much more powerful reminder of the value of their work. If you are not directly collecting student work in your classes and you have been unhappy with the percentage of completed work, experiment with directly collecting your students' work. You may find the rate of completion will improve.

Consider having students check off completed tasks. If you give students a daily or weekly assignment sheet or have them use an assignment notebook, consider adding a place for students to check that they have completed a task. Another option is to display a wall chart (similar to the reproducible form shown in Exhibits 3.2 and 3.3) on which students can check off completed tasks. This is *not* an official record and does not take the place of your grade records. It is simply an opportunity for students to put closure on their tasks. It is also a quick way for them to verify whether they are on top of their assignments. You should, however, make sure it is not used by any students to show off or brag about their marks.

Teaching students to use a check-off procedure can also give you an opportunity to teach them about self-reinforcement. Encourage them to tell themselves they have been responsible when they check off each completed assignment.

Returning Graded Work to Students

Just as students are expected to be on time turning in their work, you must be timely with grading it and returning it to them. For simple homework and in-class assignments, return it the next day whenever possible. This will keep students actively aware of their progress and allow them to work on problem areas when the tasks are still relatively fresh in their mind. In addition, timely return gives students a chance to learn what they are doing wrong before moving to more advanced work, which often builds on the previous work

Since you expect a reasonable level of neatness from your students on their written work, you must hold yourself to the same standard. Anything that is complex or difficult to communicate should be covered in person, not in a note you write in the margin. Legibility is essential as well. Feedback serves no purpose if students can't read it.

It is vital that grades be kept as confidential as possible. Do not post the grades on the checksheet or anywhere else public. Your students will find out about each other's grades quickly enough without your help. Respect the fact that some of your students will not want to share their grades or may be embarrassed. Put letter grades on the back pages of assignments, or return work face down. To facilitate the latter, write each student's name on the back of the papers where you can see it.

Exhibit 3.2
Completed Assignments Checklist

Class Period _____   Week of _____

Directions: When you turn in an assignment, put your initials in the space next to your name under that assignment.

Name

_____								
_____								
_____								
_____								
_____								
_____								
_____								
_____								
_____								
_____								
_____								
_____								
_____								
_____								
_____								
_____								
_____								
_____								
_____								
_____								

Exhibit 3.3
Completed Assignments Checklist

Class Period _____   Week of _____

Directions: When you turn in an assignment, put your initials in the space next to your name under that assignment.

Name

_____								
_____								
_____								
_____								
_____								
_____								
_____								
_____								
_____								
_____								
_____								
_____								
_____								
_____								
_____								
_____								
_____								
_____								
_____								
_____								
_____								
_____								
_____								
_____								
_____								

Finally, do not waste class time by having students wait while you return graded work. Have them do some in-class work or talk about the assignment you are returning. This would be a perfect time to address problems that most of your students had trouble with or to answer questions that were raised by the work.

An extra procedure for classes needing high structure. In addition to ensuring that all students receive regular and ongoing feedback about their current grade status, you may consider giving the class feedback on the quality of their homework as a class. If you want to increase the rates of homework completion, you might use a wall chart or an overhead to track the percentage of the class that returns any given assignment. This gives you the opportunity to reiterate on a daily basis the importance of taking responsibility for completed homework. Divide the number of completed assignments by the number of your students, and chart the number so your students can see over time how many of them are finishing their homework.

In addition to emphasizing the importance of responsibility, this procedure may create some healthy peer pressure as the students will see the effect their completion of homework has on the whole class. If you need to give them a further incentive, you can tie a percentage of completion to a reward: when they reach a certain completion percentage, they can have a period of free time or a day without homework.

Late or Missing Assignments

The last major consideration regarding management of student work is how you will deal with late and missing assignments. Some teachers choose to have no penalty for late work: students can hand in anything at any time. Other teachers do not allow students to turn in any assignment late: a late assignment receives zero points. Some form of middle ground between these two extremes is probably the best option. When there is no penalty, some students will turn in everything late, possibly even handing in all assignments on the last day of the term. If students are allowed to do this, it is unfair to you (you should not have to stay up all night at the end of every grading period) and to the students (they can learn that they do not really have to pay attention to due dates). An extreme "if it's late, it's a zero" policy does not take into account that an occasional late assignment is likely for even the most responsible student. Exhibit 3.4 shows a sample policy that might be implemented by a high school science teacher.

In most classrooms, a large percentage of a student's time will be spent working on written work. The way you manage assignments and work periods will have a big impact on how responsible students will be for managing and completing their written tasks. If you effectively manage student work, they will be more likely to complete their work, thus giving them the practice they need on essential instructional objectives. In addition, when students complete their work, you will be able to track whether they are achieving mastery of those objectives and judge whether additional instruction is necessary (McLean, 1993).

Note

The details of and criteria used in a policy will reflect the decisions of the individual teacher. The important point is to develop a policy that works for you and to inform students and their families about the policy at the beginning of the term or year.

Exhibit 3.4
Sample Late Assignments Policy

- Any assignment that is turned in late will receive an immediate 10 percent penalty (for example, a 100-point lab will have 10 points deducted from whatever score you earn).

- No assignment will be accepted beyond one week late.

- Students who have more than _____ late or missing assignments will have their families informed.

- No more than four late assignments will be accepted during the quarter.

After taking the time to develop the policies and procedures you plan to use for managing student work, you should be able to summarize this within a syllabus that you provide students on the first day of class. Chapter Seven has a syllabus template and an example of a syllabus that include the policies and procedures covered in this chapter.

In Conclusion

The day-to-day operation of your class may make the difference between success and failure for many of your students. It is one thing to have a plan and an entirely different thing to follow that plan on a day-to-day basis. Taking advantage of these procedures, laying them out for your students, and sticking to them will help your students succeed and will also help you maintain a better classroom environment. Each of the items in this chapter should be summarized for students on your comprehensive syllabus. A clear syllabus will be a cornerstone of your curriculum. With a proper syllabus and frequent reference to the policies contained within, your students will not be able to complain they were unaware of something when it has clearly been presented to them on more than one occasion.

Organization Self-Assessment Checklist

Use this worksheet to identify which parts of the tasks described in this chapter you have completed. For any item that has not been completed, note what needs to be done to complete it. Then transfer your notes to your planning calendar in the form of specific actions you need to take (for example, "September 5, finish arranging desks in the classroom").

✔	Task	Notes and Implementation Ideas
☐	*Arrange the schedule of activities for each class period so that it maximizes instructional time and responsible behavior.* I have evaluated my schedule by listing the subjects I teach and the length of class periods. Then I listed typical activities and the amount of time those activities take. I have used this information to: • Arrange my daily schedule to include a reasonable balance of teacher-directed, independent work, and cooperative group activities; • Arrange my daily schedule so that no one type of activity (for example, teacher-directed, independent work, or cooperative group) lasts for too long a period of time; and • Schedule independent work and cooperative group activities to immediately follow teacher-directed tasks. I have identified and taken steps to address those times of the class or day when students are more likely to misbehave, such as: • Last hour of day • Last five minutes of class	
☐	*Arrange the physical space in your classroom so that it promotes positive student-teacher interactions and reduces disruptions.* I have arranged the physical space in my classroom in such a way to create a comfortable and functional space. I have achieved this by: • Arranging desks in my classroom so that I can easily circulate about the room; • Arranging desks in my classroom to optimize the most common types of instructional activities students engage in and to reflect the level of structure my students require; and • Arranging desks so they are not near high-traffic areas so that disruptions caused by activity in high-traffic areas will be kept to a minimum.	

Organization Self-Assessment Checklist (*continued*)

❑	*Decide on a signal you can use to immediately quiet your students and gain their full attention.* I have identified an age-appropriate attention signal to use that has both auditory and visual components so that I can gain my students' full and immediate attention at any time during class. I have taught my students this signal and how to respond to it.

❑	*Design efficient, effective procedures for beginning and ending the class period.*
	
	I understand that setting procedures for beginning and ending class allows me to use class time more efficiently, and communicates to students that time in my class will not be wasted.
	
	1. I have identified how I will begin class and the school day in a way that makes students feel welcome and has them going immediately to their seats to work on a productive task.
	
	2. Students will be instructionally engaged while I take attendance.
	
	3. I have set up procedures for dealing with tardiness that will ensure that tardy students will not disrupt class or greatly involve me.
	
	4. I will not waste valuable class time by spending more than a minute or two on announcements and housekeeping tasks.
	
	5. I have procedures for dealing with students who do not have necessary materials or are otherwise unprepared that:
	  • Ensures students can get needed materials in a way that does not disrupt instructions;
	  • Establishes reasonable penalties to reduce the likelihood the students will forget materials in the future; and
	  • Reduces the amount of time and energy I have to spend dealing with this issue.
	
	6. I have identified how I will deal with students returning after an absence so that they can easily find out what assignments they have missed and get any handouts and returned papers in a way that does not greatly involve me.
	
	7. I have developed procedures for wrapping up at the end of the school day or class period that:

- Ensures that students will not leave the classroom before they have organized their materials and completed any necessary cleanup tasks; and

- Ensures that I have enough time to give students both positive and corrective feedback and set a positive tone for ending class.

8. I have developed dismissal procedures that ensure that students will not leave the classroom until they have been dismissed by me (not by the bell).

Design efficient, effective procedures for assigning, monitoring, and collecting student work.

I understand that implementing well-designed and organized strategies for assigning, monitoring, and collecting student work will let students know that I put a high value on their completing work, prompt more responsible student behavior regarding assigned tasks, and help me effectively manage student work without taking unreasonable amounts of time.

I have designed procedures for assigning class work and homework that ensure that students can easily find out information about the tasks they have been assigned.

As I set up my independent work periods, I will make sure that:

- I only assign independent work that I know *all* students can do independently.

- The independent work times will be scheduled at a time, and in a way, that maximizes on-task behavior (see Task 1).

- I have a clear vision of what I want student behavior to look and sound like during independent work times, and I have made that vision clear to my students.

- I will arrange to provide guided practice on tasks and assignments, working with students in a teacher-directed activity for the first 10 to 50 percent of an assignment, that I expect students to do independently.

- I have a visual signal for how students can get questions answered during independent work periods, and have taught them this signal.

I have developed procedures for students to check off completed tasks.

I have developed procedures for how I will return graded work to ensure that it is returned in a timely, legible, and confidential fashion.

I have designed efficient and effective procedures for dealing with late and missing assignments.

Organization Peer Study Worksheet

With one or more of your colleagues, work through the following discussion topics and activities related to the tasks in Chapter Three. If necessary, refer back to the text to get additional ideas or for clarification. (See the Vision Peer Study Worksheet in Chapter One for suggestions on structuring effective discussion sessions.)

Task 1: Arrange the Schedule of Activities for Each Class Period So It Maximizes Instructional Time and Responsible Behavior

    A. Have all group members share their daily schedule and explain the balance they have established among teacher-directed instruction, independent student work, and cooperative group activities.

    B. As a group, identify those times or events during the day or class that are likely to produce more irresponsible student behavior and discuss how each of you might proactively address those times and events to reduce misbehavior.

Task 2: Arrange the Physical Space in Your Classroom So That It Promotes Positive Student-Teacher Interactions and Reduces Disruption

    A. Arrange for the group to visit each group member's room, one at a time. When the group is in a particular room, have group members give feedback on the arrangement of desks, the use of bulletin board space, and the general effectiveness of (or potential problems with) the way the room is arranged.

Task 3: Decide on a Signal You Can Use to Immediately Quiet Your Students and Gain Their Full Attention

    A. Have each group member share what he or she has decided to use for an attention signal and get feedback from the other group members.

    B. As a group, discuss how you will provide positive and corrective feedback to students regarding how they respond (or don't respond) to the signal.

Task 4: Design Efficient, Effective Procedures for Beginning and Ending the Class Period

    A. For each of the following designated areas, have all group members explain their procedures. Give each other feedback and help each other problem-solve any areas that have proven difficult to address.

        • Before and immediately after the bell rings

        • Taking attendance

        • Dealing with tardy students

        • Dealing with students who come to class without necessary materials

        • Dealing with students on their return from an absence

        • Wrapping up at the end of the day or class period

        • Dismissal

Organization Peer Study Worksheet *(continued)*

Task 5: Design Efficient, Effective Procedures for Assigning, Monitoring, and Collecting Student Work

A. Have individual group members explain the procedures they use for managing the following aspects of student work. Give each other feedback.

- Assigning class work and homework
- Collecting completed work
- Keeping records and giving students feedback about their performance and progress
- Setting up independent work periods
- Dealing with late or missing work

Chapter Four

Expectations

Plan to teach students how to be successful

The school and teacher effectiveness literature has consistently shown that successful teachers are very clear with students about exactly how they expect them to behave during the school day (Kame'enui, Carnine, Dixon, Simmons, & Coyne, 2002; Cotton, 1999). Many teachers think that by developing classroom rules and classroom procedures, they have prepared everything they need to orient students to their classroom. Rules and procedures are certainly essential, but they do not provide details on what behaviors are expected and not expected of students in each type of classroom activity (Baer, 1999). You want your students to behave one way during lectures, a different way during independent work periods, and still a different way during cooperative group activities. If you don't know or don't communicate behavioral expectations to students, then the students have to guess at what constitutes responsible behavior. The problem with this is obvious when you consider the most common student misbehaviors:

- Talking too much or too loudly or about the wrong things
- Demanding attention by following the teacher around or by calling out to the teacher
- Doing math when they should be working on science or socializing when they should be cleaning up
- Doing work together that they should do on their own, or copying another student's work, or copying source materials without giving credit
- Wandering around the room or sharpening pencils when they are supposed to be listening to the teacher
- Monopolizing classroom discussions or not participating at all
- Disrupting lessons or sitting and doing nothing during work periods

You can avoid most of these problems by clearly defining for yourself and then communicating to your students how you expect them to behave during each activity and transition that occurs during the typical class period. If you do not, your students won't know whether their behavior is acceptable. For example, are they allowed to sharpen their pencils during cooperative group times, ask other students for help during a work period, or ask you questions while you are taking attendance?

Keep in mind that the answers to these kinds of questions will be different for different teachers. The important thing is that you know what *your* answers are. That is why the first two tasks in this chapter are designed to help you specifically define your behavioral expectations for students during major classroom activities (for example, teacher-directed instruction, independent seat work, class discussions, cooperative group work) and common transition times (switching from one subject to another, getting textbooks open to a particular page, correcting papers). The foundation for completing the tasks is the CHAMPs acronym, which itself reflects the major issues that affect student behavior problems (Sprick, Garrison, & Howard, 1998; McCloud, 2005):

C—Conversation

H—Help

A—Activity

M—Movement

P—Participation

The issues incorporated in CHAMPs and the basic questions to be addressed for each issue are included within Task 1. The CHAMPs acronym has been used successfully by many high school teachers to clarify expectations. Some teachers are understandably concerned that their students may consider the CHAMPs acronym to be too elementary. To accommodate this concern, this chapter also introduces a more sophisticated acronym, ACHIEVE:

A—Activity

C—Conversation

H—Help

I—Integrity

E—Effort

V—Value

E—Efficiency

The basic questions to be addressed for each issue within this acronym are included in Task 1. Samples and blank templates for both CHAMPs and ACHIEVE are included to assist you in deciding which model to use and to facilitate your planning for the first day of school.

Defining your expectations with precision is critical if you hope to have a positive and productive classroom. However, defining expectations alone is not sufficient. You also have to effectively communicate your expectations to your students. Thus, the third task in this chapter has to do with designing lessons to teach students the expectations you have defined. Teaching expectations is the first step in a three-step process for effectively communicating expectations to students: teaching expectations, monitoring student behavior during activities and transitions, and giving students feedback about their implementation of the expectations (National Research Council, 2000). This three-step process is summarized in Figure 4.1. (Detailed information about how to apply this three-step communication process is presented in Chapters Seven and Eight.)

The three tasks described in this chapter are designed to ensure that you will be ready for the first day of school with clear expectations and lessons for teaching those expectations to students.

At first glance, this may seem too elementary for high school students. However, think about effective high school or college coaches. Coaches start the first practice by going over the basic expectations: "Attend every practice and game if you are not physically sick." Successful coaches drill their athletes in the sport's fundamentals throughout a season, teaching and reteaching the basics as necessary. If students need instruction to know how to function as a member of a basketball team, then it is reasonable to assume they need instruction on how to function responsibly in a chemistry class (Bell, 1998; Sprick, Sprick, & Garrison, 1993; Paine, Radicchi, Rosellini, Deutchman, & Darch, 1983).

The three tasks presented and explained in this chapter are:

> **Note**
> Even if you are starting this program partway into the school year, it is critical that you attend to the tasks in this chapter. Clarifying and teaching expectations is especially useful for any activities and transitions during which student behavior has been consistently problematic.

Task 1: Define clear and consistent behavioral expectations for all regularly scheduled classroom activities.

Task 2: Define clear and consistent behavioral expectations for the common transitions, both within and between activities, that occur during a typical school day.

Task 3: Develop a preliminary plan, and prepare lessons for teaching your expectations to students.

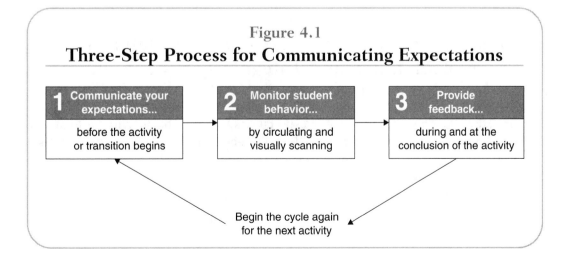

Figure 4.1

Three-Step Process for Communicating Expectations

1 Communicate your expectations...	**2** Monitor student behavior...	**3** Provide feedback...
before the activity or transition begins	by circulating and visually scanning	during and at the conclusion of the activity

Begin the cycle again for the next activity

Immediately following the explanations of the tasks in this chapter is a Self-Assessment Checklist, designed to help you determine which (or which parts) of the tasks you have done and which you still need to do. The chapter ends with a Peer Study Worksheet, which presents a series of discussion questions and activities that can be used by two or more teachers who want to share information and collegial support as they work to improve their classroom management practices.

The focus of this chapter is on student behavior in individual classrooms. However, one other related area needs to be addressed: student behavior in the school's common areas. Although this important consideration is not specifically covered in this program, students need to know the behavioral expectations for common area settings (hallways, cafeteria, restrooms, bus waiting areas, buses, assemblies) and with substitutes. If your school has not clarified schoolwide expectations for them, ask your principal what you should teach your students about responsible behavior in these settings. For more information on defining and teaching behavioral expectations for common area settings, you may want to preview one or more of the following programs:

Sprick, R. S. (1994). *Cafeteria Discipline: Positive Techniques for Lunchroom Supervision* [Video]. Eugene, OR: Pacific Northwest Publishing. *Cafeteria Discipline* provides guidance to a school's staff in how to organize the cafeteria, teach students appropriate cafeteria behavior, and train supervisors to circulate, praise good behavior, and correct misbehavior.

Sprick, R. S. (2004). *START on Time! Safe Transitions and Reduced Tardiness* [Multimedia program]. Eugene, OR: Pacific Northwest Publishing. *START on Time!* supplies information on how to develop and implement procedures for supervising halls and restrooms as a unified staff, teach students appropriate hallway behavior, and dramatically reduce tardiness.

Sprick, R. S., Sprick, M. S., & Garrison, M. (2002). *Foundations: Establishing Positive Discipline Policies* [Video]. Eugene, OR: Pacific Northwest Publishing. *Foundations* guides a school-based leadership team to involve the entire staff in implementing a proactive and positive approach to managing student behavior. This three-volume set teaches data-driven decision making, how to set priorities, and how to increase student and staff motivation.

Task 1: Define Clear and Consistent Behavioral Expectations for All Regularly Scheduled Classroom Activities

The first step in defining your behavioral expectations for classroom activities is to make a list of the major types of activities your students will engage in on a daily (or regular) basis. Your list might include topics like these:

Opening/attendance routines   Class meetings
Teacher-directed instruction, lecture   Tests/quizzes

Discussion	Labs/stations
Independent work	Peer tutoring sessions
Cooperative groups	Cushion activities

The idea is to identify specific activities or categories of activities for which you will have different behavioral expectations. For example, you may choose not to list teacher-directed instruction and discussion as different items if your expectations for student behavior are exactly the same in both. However, you would list them as two separate items if you require students to raise their hand before speaking during teacher-directed instruction but allow students to speak up whenever they wish as long as they do not interrupt anyone else during discussions. You will likely have the same classroom activities, and thus the same set of expectations, among classes within the same subject area (for instance, the same activities for all foreign language sections) but different expectations for other subjects you teach, such as an English class.

Exhibit 4.1 is a reproducible "Classroom Activities List" form. Stop now, and use it to list your major classroom activities. Note that you may have different expectations for different subjects you teach.

Once you have identified your major classroom activities, either the CHAMPs or the ACHIEVE acronym can serve as your guide to developing behavioral expectations for students. Below is an explanation of each term of the acronym and some of the things that you will strive to clarify for students for each different instructional activity. Later in this task, you will find reproducible worksheets for CHAMPs and ACHIEVE, respectively, that you can use to clarify your expectations. Pick either CHAMPs or ACHIEVE as an approach; using both might be too much of a good thing!

CHAMPs guides you in clarifying the following:

C—Conversation	Under what circumstances, if at all, can students talk to each other during the activity? If they can talk during this activity, with whom can they speak, about what, and for how long?
H—Help	How do students get their questions answered during the activity? How do they get your attention? What should they do while they are waiting for your help?
A—Activity	What is the task or objective? What is the end product?
M—Movement	Can students move about? If so, for what reasons? Do they need your permission? What routes should they take?
P—Participation	What does the expected student behavior look or sound like? How do students show they are fully participating? What behaviors would indicate they are not participating?

Exhibit 4.1
Classroom Activities List: Reproducible Form

Teacher: _____ School Year: _____

List each major activity or category of activity that will occur during a typical day in your classroom. Create a separate item for every activity or category during which you will have *different* behavioral expectations. Note that you may have different expectations for different subjects you teach.

Subject 1: _____

Major Activities
- _____
- _____
- _____
- _____
- _____
- _____

Subject 2: _____

Major Activities
- _____
- _____
- _____
- _____
- _____
- _____

Subject 3: _____

Major Activities
- _____
- _____
- _____
- _____
- _____
- _____

ACHIEVE guides you in clarifying the following:

A—Activity What is the activity that is being defined? (A lecture or a cooperative group, for example.)

C—Conversation Under what circumstances, if at all, can students talk to each other during the activity? If they can talk during this activity, with whom can they speak, about what, and for how long?

H—Help How do students get their questions answered during the activity? How do they get your attention? What should they do while they are waiting for your help?

I—Integrity What are your expectations regarding students doing their own work and avoiding copying work or plagiarizing sources? When is collaboration appropriate or inappropriate?

E—Effort What does appropriate student work behavior during the activity look or sound like? How do students demonstrate their full participation? For classes needing high structure, identify under which circumstances, if any, students can move about during the activity. For example, can they get up to sharpen a pencil?

V—Value How will participation in this activity be of value to students? Explain to your students how their efforts will contribute to their success in your class.

E—Efficiency What tips or suggestions can you give students for getting maximum benefit from this activity?

The details are important. The more specific you can be in your own mind about exactly what you expect from students, the more clearly you will be able to communicate those expectations to your students. In addition, the more specific your expectations are, the more consistent you are likely to be in enforcing them (Deno, 1985). For example, Exhibit 4.2 sets out a simple method for explaining noise levels appropriate to a classroom setting. You may choose to post these levels in your room as a memory aid to students and use them when describing appropriate volume levels for talking and working.

Exhibit 4.2
Levels of Conversation

Level 0	Silence
Level 1	Whisper
Level 2	Soft conversation
Level 3	Presentational
Level 4	Outside

When defining your behavioral expectations, pay close attention to the level of structure your students need. The greater the level of structure your students require, the more tightly you will need to define your expectations to reduce the probability that students will make irresponsible behavioral choices. For example, with a class needing high structure, you should have narrowly defined guidelines about when and how it is acceptable for students to sharpen their pencils (for example, okay during independent work but not okay during teacher-directed instruction). For a class needing only low structure, it is reasonable to have a broad guideline that permits pencil sharpening at any time.

Also keep in mind that it's always easier to lessen highly structured procedures gradually than to try to implement more structure because students are making poor choices. So if students need high structure, it is probably advisable not to allow student-to-student talking during work periods at the beginning of the year. Two or three weeks into the year, after you've had a chance to see how your students typically behave, you might revise your expectations: "Class, starting today, if you have a question and I am not available, you can quietly ask the person next to you, get the question answered, and then get right back to quiet, independent work."

Exhibit 4.3 is a reproducible template of a CHAMPs classroom activity worksheet, and Exhibit 4.4 is a reproducible of an ACHIEVE classroom activity worksheet. Make multiple copies of whichever form you decide to use. Then document your behavioral expectations by filling out one worksheet for each major type of activity you identified. The completed worksheets will provide the content for your lessons to teach your students about your behavioral expectations. (Specific information on teaching your expectations is covered in Chapters Seven and Eight.)

> ## Note
>
> Immediately following the CHAMPs and ACHIEVE classroom activity worksheet templates are completed examples showing CHAMPs and ACHIEVE expectations for a variety of classroom activities (see Exhibits 4.5 to 4.12). These completed examples have been provided as models only; there is no intent to imply that you should use the expectations included on them.

Exhibit 4.3
CHAMPs Classroom Activity Worksheet: Reproducible Template

Activity: _____

CONVERSATION

Can students engage in conversation with each other during this activity?

If yes, about what?

With whom?

How many students can be involved in a single conversation?

How long can the conversation last?

HELP

How do students get questions answered? How do students get your attention?

If students have to wait for help, what should they do while they wait?

ACTIVITY

What is the expected end product of this activity? (This may vary from day to day.)

MOVEMENT

Can students get out of their seats during the activity?

If yes, acceptable reasons include:
Pencil	Restroom
Drink	Hand in/pick up materials
Other	

Do they need permission from you?

PARTICIPATION

What behaviors show that students are participating fully and responsibly?

What behaviors show that a student is not participating?

Exhibit 4.4

ACHIEVE Classroom Activity Worksheet:
Reproducible Template

Achieve—To succeed in something!

Activity (for example, lecture, labs, independent work, tests, cooperative groups)

Conversation

Can students talk to each other?

If so, about what?

To whom?

How many can be involved?

How long should conversations last?

Help

How should students get questions answered during this activity?

How should students get your attention?

Integrity

What are your expectations for students working together, quoting sources, and so forth? In other words, define what you consider to be, for example, cheating or not cheating, plagiarizing or not plagiarizing.

Effort

What behaviors would demonstrate active participation?

What behaviors would demonstrate a lack of participation?

Value

How would active participation be of benefit for students?

Efficiency

Can you provide tips to increase student productivity?

Exhibit 4.5
Completed CHAMPs Activity Worksheet: Example 1

Activity: **Teacher-directed instruction**

CONVERSATION

Can students engage in conversation with each other during this activity? No.

If yes, about what?

With whom?

How many students can be involved in a single conversation?

How long can the conversation last?

HELP

How do students get questions answered? How do students get your attention?
Raise their hand.

If students have to wait for help, what should they do while they wait?
Keep hand raised, wait quietly.

ACTIVITY

What is the expected end product of this activity? (This may vary from day to day.)
Working on tasks and activities presented by the teacher. Verbal and written responses to teacher-presented tasks.

MOVEMENT

Can students get out of their seats during the activity?   Yes

If yes, acceptable reasons include:
Pencil   No   Restroom   Yes
Drink   No   Hand in/pick up materials   Only if directed by teacher
Other

Do they need permission from you?   Any leaving of seat must have permission.

PARTICIPATION

What behaviors show that students are participating fully and responsibly? Looking at teacher. Raising hand with something to say. Answering questions when called on or signaled to. Looking when teacher directs. Writing as directed by teacher.

What behaviors show that a student is not participating?   Talking to another student. Getting out of seat without permission. Looking somewhere other than where directed. Not following teacher directions. Not raising hand. Not answering when signaled.

Exhibit 4.6
Completed CHAMPs Activity Worksheet: Example 2

Activity: **Group activity**

CONVERSATION

Can students engage in conversation with each other during this activity? Yes, up to level 3. (So just those involved can hear you.)

If yes, about what? The assignment they are working on.

With whom? Only students they are working with.

How many students can be involved in a single conversation? Those assigned to the activity with you.

How long can the conversation last? Throughout activity, until signal is given.

HELP

How do students get questions answered? How do students get your attention? Put out sign that says, "I need help, but I'm still working."

If students have to wait for help, what should they do while they wait? Students will continue working on the rest of the assignment.

ACTIVITY

What is the expected end product of this activity? (This may vary from day to day.) Working on tasks and activities presented by the teacher. Verbal and written responses to teacher-presented tasks.

MOVEMENT

Can students get out of their seats during the activity?   Yes

If yes, acceptable reasons include:

Pencil   Yes   Restroom   Yes
Drink   No   Hand in/pick up materials   Yes, only relating to this assignment.
Other

Do they need permission from you?   Any movement must be assignment related.

PARTICIPATION

What behaviors show that students are participating fully and responsibly? Looking at paper or others in group. Writing or doing what task requires. Talking only with those in group. Staying with group until finished.

What behaviors show that a student is not participating?   Not working with group. Not writing or doing what task requires. Talking with others outside of group. Leaving group before finished.

Exhibit 4.7
Completed CHAMPs Activity Worksheet: Example 3

Activity: __Individual written tests__

CONVERSATION

Can students engage in conversation with each other during this activity? No.

If yes, about what?

With whom?

How many students can be involved in a single conversation?

How long can the conversation last?

HELP

How do students get questions answered? How do students get your attention?
Put out sign that says, "I need help, but I'm still working," if it's an individual test.

If students have to wait for help, what should they do while they wait?
Student will continue working on the rest of the test.

ACTIVITY

What is the expected end product of this activity? (This may vary from day to day.)
Working on written test. When finished with test, sit quietly and read.

MOVEMENT

Can students get out of their seats during the activity?   No

If yes, acceptable reasons include:
    Pencil   No   Restroom   No
    Drink   No   Hand in/pick up materials   No
    Other

Do they need permission from you? Any leaving of seat must have permission.

PARTICIPATION

What behaviors show that students are participating fully and responsibly?
Looking at paper. Writing or doing what task requires. Not talking. Not leaving seat for any reason.

What behaviors show that a student is not participating? Talking to another student. Getting out of seat. Not looking at paper. Not working on task.

Exhibit 4.8

Completed CHAMPs Activity Worksheet: Example 4

Activity: Individual seatwork

CONVERSATION

Can students engage in conversation with each other during this activity? Yes, level 2 only.

If yes, about what? If a student has a question about work assigned.

With whom? Only students they sit next to.

How many students can be involved in a single conversation? Only two students.

How long can the conversation last? Only about a minute, then back to silent work.

HELP

How do students get questions answered? How do students get your attention? Put out sign that says, "I need help, but I'm still working," and mark question for when the teacher gets to you.

If students have to wait for help, what should they do while they wait? Student will continue working on the rest of the assignment.

ACTIVITY

What is the expected end product of this activity? (This may vary from day to day.) Help another student to do an assignment.

MOVEMENT

Can students get out of their seats during the activity?   Yes

If yes, acceptable reasons include:

Pencil   Yes   Restroom   Yes, after signing out.
Drink   Yes, as long as it doesn't create a line.   Hand in/pick up materials   Yes
Other

Do they need permission from you? Only for the restroom.

PARTICIPATION

What behaviors show that students are participating fully and responsibly? Looking at paper. Writing or doing what task requires. Talking only under above circumstances.

What behaviors show that a student is not participating? Talking outside above circumstances. Talking during movement. Wandering around the room. Looking somewhere other than at work. Not doing task.

Exhibit 4.9

ACHIEVE Classroom Activity Worksheet: Example 1

Achieve—To succeed in something!

Activity (for example, lecture, labs, independent work, tests, cooperative groups)

Lecture, Q&A

Conversation

Can students talk to each other? No, unless called on.

If so, about what?

To whom?

How many can be involved?

How long should conversations last?

Help

How should students get questions answered during this activity? Raise your hand and wait to be called on. Ask questions about anything you don't understand.

How should students get your attention?

Integrity

What are your expectations for students working together, quoting sources, and so forth? In other words, define what you consider to be, for example, cheating or not cheating, plagiarizing or not plagiarizing. If you get behind in notes, look at a neighbor's paper or raise your hand and ask me to repeat and slow down. All information in lectures is open for sharing.

Effort

What behaviors would demonstrate active participation? Sit up and act interested!!! Eyes on the presenter, overhead screen, board, handout or your own notes. Write note on material from board or screen.

What behaviors would demonstrate a lack of participation? No eye contact with presenter. Reading or writing something unrelated to this class. "Off the bus!" with no signal.

Value

How would active participation be of benefit for students? Lecture content will help you understand what is important in the textbook. Your lecture notes will help you study for tests and complete assignments successfully.

Efficiency

Can you provide tips to increase student productivity? Immediately put all handouts, lecture notes, and assignments in correct section of notebook. Be sure to write notes on what parts of the text are most important!! This is what will be tested.

Exhibit 4.10

ACHIEVE Classroom Activity Worksheet: Example 2

Achieve—To succeed in something!

Activity (for example, lecture, labs, independent work, tests, cooperative groups)

Cooperative groups

Conversation

Can students talk to each other? Yes —that's the whole idea!

If so, about what? Only the assigned task or questions.

To whom? Only with the members of your group.

How many can be involved? Three to four.

How long should conversations last? Until the task is completed or the time is finished. Watch the overhead timer.

Help

How should students get questions answered during this activity? Try to answer within the group.

How should students get your attention? If everyone in the group has the question, one member of the group can come and get me.

Integrity

What are your expectations for students working together, quoting sources, and so forth? In other words, define what you consider to be, for example, cheating or not cheating, plagiarism or not plagiarizing. Each person should contribute to the discussion or task completion. It is not fair to the other members to be passive.

Effort

What behaviors would demonstrate active participation? Talking to the group, listening, recording responses, looking at source material. Sit up, make eye contact.

What behaviors would demonstrate a lack of participation? Never talking, working on other assignments, not contributing ideas and work.

Value

How would active participation be of benefit for students? Some tasks will have a graded project. Other tasks will give you information or processes that will help you succeed with other assignments or tests and will deepen your understanding of the content.

Efficiency

Can you provide tips to increase student productivity? If your group gets right to work, you can have more time on the task and /or finish before the time is complete.

Exhibit 4.11

ACHIEVE Classroom Activity Worksheet: Example 3

Achieve—To succeed in something!

Activity (for example, lecture, labs, independent work, tests, cooperative groups)

Discussion

Conversation

Can students talk to each other? Yes, but only when you "have the floor."

If so, about what? Only about the topic under discussion.

To whom? To the group — no side conversations.

How many can be involved? One at a time — wait for logical pauses.

How long should conversations last? Evaluate if you are "playing Monopoly" — that is, monopolizing. Are you talking too much?

Help

How should students get questions answered during this activity? Ask any question any time.

How should students get your attention? If you cannot get the floor, raise your hand and I will "get you the floor."

Integrity

What are your expectations for students working together, quoting sources, and so forth? In other words, define what you consider to be, for example, cheating or not cheating, plagiarism or not plagiarizing.

If you are stating something you have heard or read, credit sources.

Effort

What behaviors would demonstrate active participation?

Sit up. Make eye contact with the person speaking. Join discussions verbally at least once per week.

What behaviors would demonstrate a lack of participation?

No eye contact. Never speaking. Not listening to what others are saying.

Value

How would active participation be of benefit for students?

The exploration of ideas during discussion activities will help prepare you for essay questions on unit tests and will help formulate your own understanding of the course content.

Efficiency

Can you provide tips to increase student productivity?

If you think of something to say about what someone said earlier, it is OK if you introduce what you have to say with something like, "Going back to what Jamal said earlier, I think . . ."

Exhibit 4.12
ACHIEVE Classroom Activity Worksheet: Example 4

Achieve—To succeed in something!

Activity (for example, lecture, labs, independent work, tests, cooperative groups)

Independent work

Conversation

Can students talk to each other? *Yes.*

If so, about what? *Only to get help on the assigned work.*

To whom? *Anyone close. Use a whisper or quiet conversational level.*

How many can be involved? *No more than three people total.*

How long should conversations last? *No more than a couple of minutes.*

Help

How should students get questions answered during this activity? *Ask another student or me.*

How should students get your attention? *Place an open book upright on the desk — facing away from you if it is not the book for this class. Keep working on other parts of the task.*

Integrity

What are your expectations for students working together, quoting sources, and so forth? In other words, define what you consider to be, for example, cheating or not cheating, plagiarism or not plagiarizing.

Do your own work. Help with a few questions is fine. Copying someone else's work is not okay.

Effort

What behaviors would demonstrate active participation?

Reading, writing, briefly asking or answering a question about some aspect of the task. If finished, you can read or work on tasks from other classes.

What behaviors would demonstrate a lack of participation?

Doing nothing, sleeping, doing work from another class before work on this task is complete.

Value

How would active participation be of benefit for students? *Time to work in class reduces the amount you must do as homework, and doing as much as possible in class will help you identify questions while I am available to help. All assignments have point values.*

Efficiency

Can you provide tips to increase student productivity?

Avoid being distracted, and when you complete one task or question, move immediately to the next. You can connect your mind to the task and get done in a fraction of the time it would require if you let your mind wander to other things.

Task 2: Define Clear and Consistent Behavioral Expectations for the Common Transitions, Both Within and Between Activities, That Occur During a Typical School Day

In between the activities that take place during the class period, there are also transitions, or times when students make a transition from one task to another during an activity (for example, in a math lesson, you present teacher-directed instruction and then have students get out their math books to work independently). Transitions are often problematic in terms of student behavior, and poorly managed transitions are troublesome because of their potential for student misbehavior and because they end up consuming valuable instructional time (Dawson-Rodrigues, Lavay, Butt, & Lacourse, 1997). When you clearly define and communicate your expectations for transitions, you will have well-managed and efficient transitions.

As with classroom activities, the first step in defining behavioral expectations for transitions is to list the major transitions that typically occur during any given class period (see the reproducible transitions list form in Exhibit 4.13). Be sure to identify all the specific transitions and categories of transitions for which you will have different behavioral expectations. A list of transitions might include the following:

- Before the bell rings
- After the bell rings
- Getting out paper, pencil, and writing the heading on your paper
- Getting a book out and opening to a particular page
- Moving to and from locations such as lab stations
- Putting things away (clearing their desks)
- Handing in work (for example, after an in-class assignment or a quiz)
- Trading papers for corrections
- Cleaning up after project activities
- Leaving the classroom at the end of the class period
- Handing things out (for example, an assignment sheet or art supplies)
- Handing things back (graded papers, for example)
- Opening and dismissal routines (expectations for these transitions were discussed in Chapter Three)

Teachers of specialized subjects such as music, art, physical education, and technology are likely to have types of transitions not listed above. Special education teachers with a self-contained classroom will have a greater variety of transitions during the day than a general education teacher, as they may have the same students all day, and have additional transitions involving students who are in general education classes part of the day.

Exhibit 4.13
Transitions List: Reproducible Form

Teacher: _____ School Year: _____

List each common transition and category of transitions that will occur during a typical week. Create a separate item for every transition (or category) during which you will have different behavioral expectations. If you teach different subjects during the day, think about whether there are some transitions that may occur in that subject, but not in the other subjects you teach. If so, list transitions for each subject separately.

Subject 1: _____

Transitions
- _____
- _____
- _____
- _____
- _____
- _____

Subject 2: _____

Transitions
- _____
- _____
- _____
- _____
- _____
- _____

Subject 3: _____

Transitions
- _____
- _____
- _____
- _____
- _____
- _____

Once you have your list of transitions, use the CHAMPs acronym as a guide for defining your behavioral expectations for the important issues. If you are using ACHIEVE, the full acronym is too involved for every transition. Therefore, if you are using the ACHIEVE acronym to clarify instructional expectations, the transition worksheets that follow do not use the acronym. Make copies of the reproducible CHAMPs transition worksheet template (Exhibit 4.14) or the ACHIEVE transition worksheet template (Exhibit 4.15) for all of the transitions on your list. Be thorough: remember that the more detailed you are, the more clearly you will be able to communicate your expectations to students and the more consistent you are likely to be in implementing your expectations. (Information on teaching expectations to students is covered in Task 3 in this chapter and in Chapters Seven and Eight.)

Following the CHAMPs and ACHIEVE transition worksheet templates are examples for a variety of transitions (see Exhibits 4.16 to 4.24). These completed examples are included as models only, and are not meant to imply that the expectations on them should be your expectations.

Level of structure and expectations for transitions. The more structure your class requires, the more specific and tightly orchestrated you need to make your expectations for transitions. For a low-structure class, you probably don't need to specify the routes students are to take to get to lab stations. For students needing high structure, include the expectation that students need to take the most direct route and keep their hands, feet, and objects to themselves so they do not disturb students who are working at their seats.

Exhibit 4.14

CHAMPs Transition Worksheet: Reproducible Template

Transition:

CONVERSATION

Can students engage in conversations with each other during this transition?

If yes, clarify how (so that they are keeping their attention on completing the transition).

HELP

How do students get questions answered? How do students get your attention?

ACTIVITY

Explain transition. What will be different afterward (for example, change in location, use of different materials)? Include time criteria (how long it should take).

MOVEMENT

If the transition itself does not involve getting out of seats, can students get out of their seat for any reason during the transition?

If yes, what are acceptable reasons?

If the transition itself involves out-of-seat movement, can a student go elsewhere, for example, to sharpen a pencil?

PARTICIPATION

What behaviors show that students are participating in the transition fully and responsibly?

What behaviors show that a student is not participating appropriately in the transition?

Exhibit 4.15

ACHIEVE Transition Worksheet: Reproducible Template

ACHIEVE Transition Expectations

Transition: _____

Describe the transition. What will be different after the transition?

How long should this transition require? Be specific.

What behaviors would indicate a student is participating?

What behaviors would indicate a student is not participating in this transition?

Exhibit 4.16
CHAMPs Transition Worksheet: Example 1

Transition: Getting a book out and opening to a particular page —for example, for guided practice on problems during a math lesson

CONVERSATION

Can students engage in conversations with each other during this transition? Only if a student needs to ask to look on with a neighbor's book because he or she does not have his or her book in the desk.

If yes, clarify how (so that they are keeping their attention on completing the transition). If a student needs to look on with a neighbor, he or she can quietly whisper the request to the neighbor and can quietly move his or her chair so they can both see.

HELP

How do students get questions answered? How do students get your attention? Raise hand.

ACTIVITY

Explain transition. What will be different afterward (for example, change in location, use of different materials)? Include time criteria (how long it should take). Teacher will tell (and write on the board) the book and the page number. Within 10 seconds, all students will have the book open to the correct page and should be waiting quietly. If a student does not have the book, they can ask to look on with a neighbor.

MOVEMENT

If the transition itself does not involve getting out of seats, can students get out of their seat for any reason during the transition? No.

If yes, what are acceptable reasons?

If the transition itself involves out-of-seat movement, can a student go elsewhere, for example, to sharpen a pencil?

PARTICIPATION

What behaviors show that students are participating in the transition fully and responsibly?
As soon as the instruction is given, students will open the book quickly and quietly and will wait for further instruction to be given.

What behaviors show that a student is not participating appropriately in the transition?
Asking, "What page?"
Talking (other than asking quietly to share book).
Wasting time (for example, looking for book in messy desk or playing).

Exhibit 4.17
CHAMPs Transition Worksheet: Example 2

Transition: Getting out supplies (paper/pencil, etc.)

CONVERSATION

Can students engage in conversations with each other during this transition? No.

If yes, clarify how (so that they are keeping their attention on completing the transition).

HELP

How do students get questions answered? How do students get your attention?
Raise their hand.

ACTIVITY

Explain transition. What will be different afterward (for example, change in location, use of different materials)? Include time criteria (how long it should take).
Teacher will tell (and write on the board) what supplies are needed. Within 10 seconds, all students will have the supplies out and should be waiting quietly.

MOVEMENT

If the transition itself does not involve getting out of seats, can students get out of their seat for any reason during the transition? No.

If yes, what are acceptable reasons?

If the transition itself involves out-of-seat movement, can a student go elsewhere, for example, to sharpen a pencil?

PARTICIPATION

What behaviors show that students are participating in the transition fully and responsibly?
As soon as the instruction is given, students will get out supplies quickly and quietly and will wait for further instruction to be given. They will be prepared for this by making sure they have supplies in the morning.

What behaviors show that a student is not participating appropriately in the transition?
Asking, "What do we need?"
Talking
Wasting time (looking for supplies in a messy bag).

Exhibit 4.18
CHAMPs Transition Worksheet: Example 3

Transition: Handing in papers (tests, etc.)

CONVERSATION

Can students engage in conversations with each other during this transition?
Yes, level 2 only.

If yes, clarify how (so that they are keeping their attention on completing the transition).
Conversation is only for the purpose of saying, "excuse me," "thank you," and "please."

HELP

How do students get questions answered? How do students get your attention?
Raise their hand.

ACTIVITY

Explain transition. What will be different afterward (for example, change in location, use of different materials)? Include time criteria (how long it should take).
Students will pass their papers to the next person and so on in the direction the teacher indicates. Last person at the back row will come forward collecting papers from the other rows and giving papers to teacher. Collecting papers should take no longer than 30 seconds.

MOVEMENT

If the transition itself does not involve getting out of seats, can students get out of their seat for any reason during the transition? Yes.

If yes, what are acceptable reasons? Only the last person in the back row to bring papers forward.

If the transition itself involves out-of-seat movement, can a student go elsewhere, for example, to sharpen a pencil? No.

PARTICIPATION

What behaviors show that students are participating in the transition fully and responsibly?
Students will collect papers from the person next to them, making sure the papers don't fall on the floor. Talking only as above. Paying attention so everyone gets the papers in quickly.

What behaviors show that a student is not participating appropriately in the transition?
Talking without reasons given above. Throwing papers to the next person. Getting up and collecting papers from each person in your row. Not paying attention, so others don't get their papers in.

Exhibit 4.19
ACHIEVE Transition Worksheet: Example 1

ACHIEVE Transition Expectations

Transition: <u>Beginning the class</u>

Describe the transition.
Students will come in from the hallway to the classroom. Students may sharpen pencil or get necessary supplies. When the bell rings, student will sit at assigned seat immediately and begin warm-up activity.

How long should this transition require? Be specific.
No more than length of passing time.

What behaviors would indicate a student is participating?
Moving directly to the desk. Sharpening a pencil or getting other necessary supplies. Talking quietly at your desk with another student until the bell rings and work is begun on the warm-up activity.

What behaviors would indicate a student is not participating in this transition?
Moving around the room without a purpose. Continuing to move in the room after bell has signaled the beginning of class. Not working on warm-up activity. Talking loudly, yelling, or continuing to react to a situation that occurred outside the classroom in the hallway.

Exhibit 4.20
ACHIEVE Transition Worksheet: Example 2

ACHIEVE Transition Expectations

Transition: <u>Ending the class</u>

Describe the transition. What will be different after the transition?
Students will prepare for departure from the class. Students will have all materials cleaned up and put away and will be seated in assigned seats prior to the bell ringing to end the period. The instructor will dismiss the class.

How long should this transition require? Be specific.
No more than 3 minutes.

What behaviors would indicate a student is participating?
Cleaning up or putting away any materials used during the class. Moving directly to the desk. Asking me a quick question or making an appointment to see me. Talking quietly at the desk with another student until the teacher signals for attention.

What behaviors would indicate a student is not participating in this transition?
Staying at a station. Talking without moving. Leaving materials out. Going to someone else's desk.

Exhibit 4.21
ACHIEVE Transition Worksheet: Example 3

ACHIEVE Transition Expectations

Transition: <u>Getting a book out and open for teacher instruction</u>

Describe the transition. What will be different after the transition?
Students will have their books out and open to the page written on the board so I can provide instruction.

How long should this transition require? Be specific.
No more than 30 seconds..

What behaviors would indicate a student is participating?
Getting their book out and open on their desk. If they did not hear the correct page, they can look at the board —I always write the page. If they do not have a book, they go and get a classroom copy from the back of the room and fill out a "borrow card." They do not need to ask permission to do this..

What behaviors would indicate a student is not participating in this transition?
Delaying getting the book, asking what page, distracting another student from getting his or her book, distracting me from starting instruction after 30 seconds.

Exhibit 4.22
ACHIEVE Transition Worksheet: Example 4

ACHIEVE Transition Expectations

Transition: <u>Moving to lab stations</u>

Describe the transition. What will be different after the transition?
Each student will move from his or her desk to the appropriate lab.

How long should this transition require? Be specific.
One minute

What behaviors would indicate a student is participating?
Moving directly to the lab station. Checking the syllabus if they do not remember which station they are assigned to be in for the quarter. Asking me a quick question or making an appointment to see me. Sharpening a pencil or getting other necessary supplies. Getting immediately to work on the lab activity.

What behaviors would indicate a student is not participating in this transition?
Staying at a desk, talking without moving, going to someone else's lab station, asking me which station they are assigned to, moving to the station, but not getting immediately to work.

Exhibit 4.23
ACHIEVE Transition Worksheet: Example 5

ACHIEVE Transition Expectations

Transition: _Moving into cooperative groups or back to lecture_

Describe the transition. What will be different after the transition?
Students will move their desks from lecture (desks in rows) to cooperative groups, or from cooperative groups back to lecture.

How long should this transition require? Be specific.
No more than 1 minute.

What behaviors would indicate a student is participating?
Moving his or her desk, chatting with other students, giving me attention when the signal is given.

What behaviors would indicate a student is not participating in this transition?
Not moving, moving into the wrong position, not ceasing to talk when the signal is given.

Exhibit 4.24
ACHIEVE Transition Worksheet: Example 6

ACHIEVE Transition Expectations

Transition: _Preparation for a test_

Describe the transition. What will be different after the transition?
Each student will immediately put everything away except a writing instrument and blank paper.

How long should this transition require? Be specific.
Fifteen seconds

What behaviors would indicate a student is participating?
Clearing _everything_ from the desk except writing materials. Sharpening a pencil or getting a pencil from the back of the room.

What behaviors would indicate a student is not participating in this transition?
Leaving a text, notes, or sweatshirt on the desk. Moving about the room as others start the test. Talking after the test period begins—which is at the _beginning_ of this transition.

Task 3: Develop a Preliminary Plan and Prepare Lessons for Teaching Your Expectations to Students

As important as it is for you to define for yourself exactly how you expect students to behave during various classroom activities and transitions, identifying expectations alone is not enough. If students are going to be able to meet your expectations, you also need to communicate those expectations to students clearly and thoroughly (Deno, 1985; Martin, 1989). Effectively communicating expectations can be accomplished through the three-step process introduced earlier in this chapter (and shown in Figure 4.1).

> **Note**
> Detailed information on the second and third steps in the communication process—monitoring student behavior and giving students feedback on their implementation of the expectations—is presented in Chapters Seven and Eight.

The first step in the communication process is teaching your expectations to students. To do this effectively, develop a preliminary plan for how you will teach students and then prepare lessons that you will use to teach them. The remainder of this task addresses those two issues.

Develop a preliminary plan for how you will teach your expectations. Your plan for how you will teach your expectations should reflect answers to these three basic questions:

- How detailed do your lessons need to be?
- How long do you anticipate having to actively teach the lessons?
- What is the best way to organize the content?

When answering these questions, you need to consider the complexity of the expectations you have defined, your own teaching style, and the age and sophistication of your students. For example, in settings with mature and responsible students (a class that needs only a low-structure behavior plan), it may be sufficient to simply verbalize your expectations on the first day of school, provide short verbal reviews on the second and third days, and thereafter use only occasional reminders. With difficult students (a class that needs a highly structured management plan) or in a setting with dangerous chemicals or equipment, you should probably plan to teach your expectations using visual displays, demonstrations, and perhaps even actual practice every day for at least the first ten days of school.

If a verbal presentation alone will work with your students, you may not need to prepare any lessons; you can just have your CHAMPs or ACHIEVE worksheets handy. However, when you anticipate that repeated teaching will be necessary, vary the instructional approach you use to keep students' attention (Kame'enui, Carnine, Dixon, Simmons, & Coyne, 2002; Stone, 2002). If you believe your class will need high structure, plan on preparing lessons that have maximal variety and include student involvement so that you reduce the probability that students will get bored and ensure that students will fully understand the expectations.

Another consideration when developing your teaching plan is how you will organize the content for students. You may not want to actually use the CHAMPs or ACHIEVE acronym when teaching your expectations. However, one advantage of using the acronym is that it can be a useful way to communicate that there is consistency regarding what students have to know to behave responsibly (Chance, 1998; Kame'enui & Simmons, 1990). Although the specific expected behaviors might be different between, say, cooperative groups and teacher-directed instruction, students will learn that the issues you consider to be important (conversation, help, integrity, effort, value, and efficiency) are the same from one activity or transition to another; that is, you have definite thoughts about each of those categories. Without the acronym as an anchor, students may feel cast adrift among hundreds of unconnected expectations. Another advantage of using either the CHAMPs or ACHIEVE acronym is that the content is already neatly organized for you; all you have to do is use the worksheets that you completed to help you clarify your expectations.

> **Note**
>
> Regardless of whether you use the CHAMPs or ACHIEVE acronym with your students, you should use it when defining your expectations to ensure that you cover all important aspects of student behavior.

One final advantage is that if either acronym has been adopted schoolwide, students come to expect each teacher to clarify how these expectations will be defined for each class. Using the acronym, lesson preparation for students can be as simple as writing your expectations in bold letters on the worksheet itself, then reproducing a transparency of each activity sheet. More ideas for visual displays of your expectations are provided later in this chapter.

Prepare lessons for teaching your CHAMPs or ACHIEVE expectations. Preparing these lessons in addition to academic lessons may seem overwhelming. However, the amount of time required to clarify your expectations fully is slight in comparison to the time you will have to spend correcting misbehavior throughout the year if you do not.

As you begin to prepare lessons, keep in mind that you will teach the lesson for a particular activity or transition immediately before it occurs. Also keep in mind that the two main components that must be included in all lessons on expectations are presenting the expectations to students and verifying that students understand the expectations. Depending on what you determined when you developed your teaching plan, you may also want to include the following elements as part of your presentation:

> **Note**
>
> When developing your plan for teaching expectations (that is, deciding how detailed your lessons will be, anticipating how many days you will actively teach the expectations, and choosing how you will organize the content), it is better to overplan than underplan. Err on the side of more lessons and more detailed lessons than you might need because it is always easier to condense (or eliminate) some of what you have than it is to scramble to create new lessons once school has started.

- Some kind of textual or graphic visual display (for example, overhead transparency, flip chart, flip notebook, bulletin board)
- Actual demonstrations of the expected behaviors (by you, by students)
- Opportunities for students to practice and rehearse the expected behaviors

Given the amount of detail involved with most classroom expectations (which you may have noticed when you completed your CHAMPs or ACHIEVE worksheets), it is important that you structure your lessons so that they inform but do not overwhelm or intimidate students. Following are brief discussions of the various means of embellishing the way you present (explain) your expectations.

Visual displays. Using a visual display as part of your presentation of expectations has several advantages. It can be used to summarize key expectations and make the lesson more graphic for students. A visual display represents a permanent record of the expectations to which students can refer if they have any questions. It also provides a concrete object to which you can draw students' attention, both when you are explaining the expectations and as a prompt during an activity should students not be following them. If you decide to use a visual display, you will have to make further decisions about which to use.

Among the most useful of the many forms for presenting visual displays of your expectations are overhead transparencies, flip charts, notebook flip charts, and bulletin boards:

• *Overhead transparencies.* Immediately prior to an activity or transition, put the transparency on the overhead and use it as the focus for a short lesson on how students are expected to behave. If you do not otherwise need the overhead projector, you can leave the transparency showing during the activity or transition. You can use overhead transparencies regardless of how you have decided to organize your lesson content. That is, you could create transparencies on which you list your expectations, or on which you have placed a T-chart of "Looks Like/Sounds Like." A particularly simple solution is to make transparencies of the various worksheets you completed as part of Task 1.

> **Note**
>
> You can use either a full-size flip chart or a notebook flip chart (Figure 4.3), which is a large three-ring binder that can be set up on the teacher's desk or a file cabinet. In order to find the page for a particular type of activity quickly, plan to have tabs staggered as in the transparency example in Figure 4.2.

You can effectively use overhead transparencies for major activities and transitions by simply writing your expectations in bold letters on the activity or transition worksheet and then keeping a transparency of each worksheet handy. Then you can place a tab on each sheet that indicates what the transition is (Figure 4.2). By staggering the tabs on the right-hand side of each of these transparencies, when the transparencies are in a stack within a file folder, you can have immediate access to each sheet without having to sort them physically. To teach your expectations before an activity or transition begins, you can simply pull the appropriate transparency and present them.

• *Flip charts.* On each page of the flip chart, put the expectations for one activity or transition (Figure 4.3). (Again, you can organize the content in any way that is comfortable for you—with the CHAMPs or ACHIEVE acronym, as a T-chart, or simply as a list of major expectations.) Keep the flip chart in a location that all students can see easily. As you are about to begin a particular activity or transition, flip to the page for that activity or transition and have students follow along as you describe the activity or transition and what your expectations for student

Figure 4.2
ACHIEVE Transparencies with Tabs

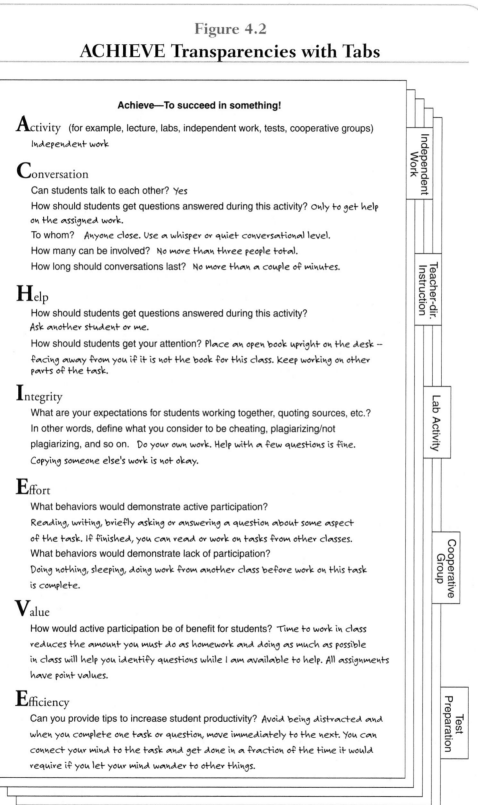

Achieve—To succeed in something!

Activity   (for example, lecture, labs, independent work, tests, cooperative groups)
Independent work

Conversation
Can students talk to each other? Yes
How should students get questions answered during this activity? Only to get help
on the assigned work.
To whom?   Anyone close. Use a whisper or quiet conversational level.
How many can be involved? No more than three people total.
How long should conversations last? No more than a couple of minutes.

Help
How should students get questions answered during this activity?
Ask another student or me.
How should students get your attention? Place an open book upright on the desk —
facing away from you if it is not the book for this class. Keep working on other
parts of the task.

Integrity
What are your expectations for students working together, quoting sources, etc.?
In other words, define what you consider to be cheating, plagiarizing/not
plagiarizing, and so on. Do your own work. Help with a few questions is fine.
Copying someone else's work is not okay.

Effort
What behaviors would demonstrate active participation?
Reading, writing, briefly asking or answering a question about some aspect
of the task. If finished, you can read or work on tasks from other classes.
What behaviors would demonstrate lack of participation?
Doing nothing, sleeping, doing work from another class before work on this task
is complete.

Value
How would active participation be of benefit for students? Time to work in class
reduces the amount you must do as homework and doing as much as possible
in class will help you identify questions while I am available to help. All assignments
have point values.

Efficiency
Can you provide tips to increase student productivity? Avoid being distracted and
when you complete one task or question, move immediately to the next. You can
connect your mind to the task and get done in a fraction of the time it would
require if you let your mind wander to other things.

Independent Work

Teacher-dir. Instruction

Lab Activity

Cooperative Group

Test Preparation

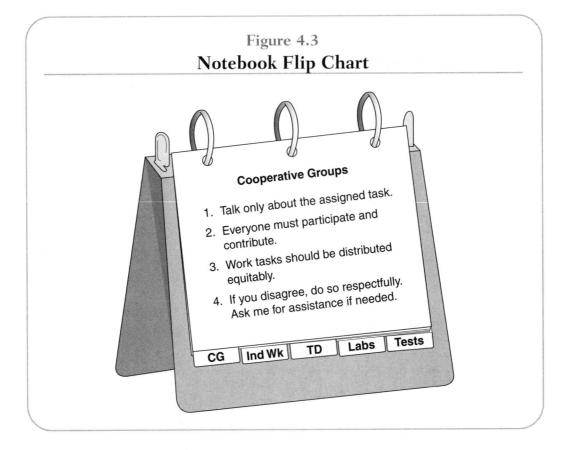

Figure 4.3
Notebook Flip Chart

Cooperative Groups

1. Talk only about the assigned task.
2. Everyone must participate and contribute.
3. Work tasks should be distributed equitably.
4. If you disagree, do so respectfully. Ask me for assistance if needed.

| CG | Ind Wk | TD | Labs | Tests |

behavior are. When you get to the point that you no longer have to review your expectations with students, you can simply flip the chart to the correct page and point to the list of your major expectations for that activity or transition.

There are other options for organizing the content of your expectations. One is to simply list the three or four main expectations you have for each activity or transition. This option might be appropriate if you have students who need only a low-structure management plan. Another possibility is to organize your expectations into T-charts of "looks like/sounds like" descriptors. Exhibit 4.25 shows a sample T-chart for teacher-directed instruction and class discussions that might be used by a history teacher who conducts interactive lessons involving frequent discussion opportunities. T-charts are appropriate for classes needing medium to high structure because of the amount and nature of detail they provide.

Visual displays, whether they are on overhead transparencies, flip charts, notebook flip charts, or bulletin boards, can include text only, graphic icons only, or some combination of text and graphics. Again, the decision will depend on the complexity of your expectations, the age and sophistication of your students, and, to a lesser extent, how you have chosen to organize the content of your expectations.

Demonstrations. Some aspects of behavioral expectations may be clearer to students if they are demonstrated. One way to do this is for you to model (that is, act out) both positive and

Exhibit 4.25
T-Chart Sample

Expectations for Teacher-Directed Instruction and Discussions

Looks Like:	Sounds Like:
• Eyes on speaker, overhead, or your own notes	• Only one voice at a time can be heard
• Everyone looks as if they are listening to the speaker	• Presentation voice is used when you are the speaker
• Hands raised before speaking	• Questions and comments from the speaker relate to the lesson
• Notes being taken on essential points	• No other noise than writing or turning a page of your notes if you are not the current speaker
• Everyone in seat except speaker	
• If someone disagrees, she or he raises hand to become the speaker—no non-verbal expressions of disagreement	• All verbal participation sounds respectful—even when you are disagreeing

negative examples of what you expect. For example, when teaching students what active participation during independent work periods should look and sound like, you might want to model the right way and the wrong way for students to demonstrate participation (McLeod, Fisher, & Hoover, 2003). You can even ham it up a bit. If you use modeling, it's a good idea to provide a couple of positive models, that is, the right ways to demonstrate participation. Then give the negative models, showing the most likely wrong ways students might misbehave. End by briefly reprising the positive models. By beginning and ending with positive models, you reduce the chance that students will mistakenly view the negative models as the way to do things.

You may also wish to involve students when modeling expectations. Students at all school levels enjoy participating in role-play situations, in which student volunteers demonstrate one or more aspects of the expectations. The advantage of involving students in role-playing is that they become more actively involved in the lesson. Ask for a couple of volunteers, and have them demonstrate a positive model of one or more aspects of your expectations. Then, unless you think they will act irresponsibly, have the students demonstrate one or more negative examples. Just as when you model the expectations, be sure the students' final role plays demonstrate positive examples.

Verification. Regardless of exactly how you teach your expectations, you should probably ask students a few questions about them before you start an activity or transition. The answers students give (or fail to give) will help you determine whether you have adequately explained the essential information. If students can answer your questions, you are probably ready. If they seem unsure or are unable to answer the questions at all, go over the information again more thoroughly. Plan on reteaching the expectations until students know what you expect of them.

Do not ask for volunteers to answer the questions. Students who do not know the answer are unlikely to volunteer, so you will not get accurate information about whether all students understand the expectations. A more effective approach is to ask the question first, give everyone time to think, and then assign individual students to answer. The questions should be very specific and use similar wording from the teaching phase—for example, "Everyone, get ready to answer a few questions. During the time we will be working in cooperative groups, can you choose to work on an independent project? If so, what are the reasons? [Pause] Jared, please answer."

Level of structure and lessons to teach expectations. The greater the level of structure needed in your classroom, the more detailed you are going to have to be when teaching your expectations, and the more time you should plan to spend explaining and reviewing your expectations. If your expectations are relatively simple and your students relatively sophisticated, it might be enough to tell them the expectations before an activity begins. If your expectations are complex or students are less mature, your lessons should be more involved—perhaps using the CHAMPs or ACHIEVE acronym, visual displays, modeling, practice, and verifying student understanding. The goal is to ensure that your lessons communicate to students exactly what behaviors you expect from them.

In Conclusion

Your students will never know what you expect of them until you find a way to communicate it to them. Once your students understand what you expect them to achieve, you will be a big step closer to helping them in that success. Making sure that your expectations are achievable and well communicated are the first two steps in making this happen. When it does, you will find yourself working with your students instead of working against them.

Expectations Self-Assessment Checklist

Use this worksheet to identify which parts of the tasks described in this chapter you have completed. For any item that has not been completed, note what needs to be done to complete it. Then transfer your notes to your planning calendar in the form of specific actions you need to take (for example, "September 30, finish listing major classroom activities").

Task	Notes and Implementation Ideas
Define clear and consistent behavioral expectations for all regularly scheduled classroom activities.	
I have made a list of the major classroom activities and/or categories of activities that will take place during a typical day for which I have different behavioral expectations.	
For each activity (or category), I have defined in detail my behavioral expectations for students using the CHAMPs acronym. For each activity (or category), I have considered the level of class structure my students need as I addressed the following issues/questions:	
Conversation	
• How much and what type of conversation among students is allowed?	
Help	
• How are students to request help, and what should they do while they are waiting for help?	
Activity	
• What is the activity, task, or assignment students will be engaged in? What is its purpose? What is the expected end product?	
Movement	
• How much and under what circumstances can students move about?	
Participation	
• What student behaviors show active and responsible participation, and what student behaviors show lack of appropriate participation?	
For each activity (or category), I have defined in detail my behavioral expectations for students using the ACHIEVE acronym. For each activity (or category), I have considered the level of class structure my students need as I addressed the following issues and questions:	

Expectations Self-Assessment Checklist (*continued*)

Activity
- What is the activity that is being defined?

Conversation
- Under what circumstances can students talk to others, how long, and with whom?

Help
- How do students get their questions answered? How do they get my attention? What should they do while they're waiting for help?

Integrity
- What are my expectations regarding students' own work? When is collaboration appropriate or inappropriate?

Effort
- What does appropriate student work behavior during the activity look or sound like? How do students demonstrate full participation?

Value
- How will participation in this activity be of value to students?

Efficiency
- What tips or suggestions can I give students for getting the maximum benefit from this activity?

Define clear and consistent behavioral expectations for the common transitions, both within and between activities, that occur during a typical school day.

I have made a list of the common transitions and categories of transitions (within and between activities) that will take place during a typical day.

For each transition (or category), I have defined in detail my behavioral expectations for students using the CHAMPs acronym. For each transition (or category), I have considered the level of class structure my students need as I addressed the following issues and questions:

Conversation
- How much and what type of conversation is allowed?

Help
- How are students to request help, and what should they do while they are waiting for help?

Activity

• What is the transition and its purpose? What will be different after the transition? How long should the transition take?

Movement

• If the transition does not involve movement, how much and under what circumstances can students move about? If the transition does involve movement, are there any restrictions to student movement?

Participation

• What student behaviors will show active and responsible participation, and what student behaviors will show lack of appropriate participation?

For each transition (or category), I have defined in detail my behavioral expectations for students using the ACHIEVE acronym. For each transition (or category), I have considered the level of class structure my students need as I addressed the following issues and questions:

• Describe the transition. What will be different after the transition?

• Specifically, how long should this transition require?

• What behaviors would indicate a student is participating?

• What behaviors would indicate a student is not participating in this transition?

Develop a preliminary plan, and prepare lessons for teaching your expectations to students.

Based on the needs of my students, I have developed a preliminary plan to teach my CHAMPs or ACHIEVE expectations for activities and transitions. In developing my plan, I considered the following questions:

• How detailed do my lessons need to be?

• How long do I anticipate having to actively teach the lessons?

• What is the best way to organize the content?

Based on my plan, I have prepared CHAMPs or ACHIEVE lessons that I will use at the beginning of the school year to communicate behavioral expectations to students. In developing my plan, I considered the following:

• Visual displays

• Demonstrations

• Verification

• Level of structure and lessons to teach expectations

Expectations Peer Study Worksheet

With one or more of your colleagues, work through the following discussion topics and activities related to the tasks in Chapter Four. If necessary, refer back to the text to get additional ideas or for clarification. (See the Vision Peer Study Worksheet in Chapter One for suggestions on structuring effective discussion sessions.)

Task 1: Define Clear and Consistent Behavioral Expectations for All Regularly Scheduled Classroom Activities

A. Have all group members share their list of major classroom activities or categories of classroom activities. As a group, help each person identify whether he or she has omitted any important activities from the list.

B. Have group members share their CHAMPs or ACHIEVE expectations worksheets for classroom activities. As a group, give individuals feedback on the clarity and thoroughness of their expectations. (Group members do not have to agree with each other's expectations; their feedback should focus on whether the expectations are specific and detailed enough that lessons for students could be taught from them.)

Task 2: Define Clear and Consistent Behavioral Expectations for the Common Transitions, Both Within and Between Activities, That Occur During a Typical School Day

A. Have all group members share their list of common transitions or categories of transitions. As a group, help each person identify whether he or she omitted any important transitions from the list.

B. Have group members share their CHAMPs or ACHIEVE expectations worksheets for transitions. As a group, give individuals feedback on the clarity and thoroughness of their expectations. (Group members do not have to agree with each other's expectations; their feedback should focus on whether the expectations are specific and detailed enough that lessons for students could be taught from them.)

Task 3: Develop a Preliminary Plan and Prepare Lessons for Teaching Your Expectations to Students

A. Have all group members share their ideas for lessons on communicating expectations. In particular, discuss the decisions you have made regarding the answers to the following questions and issues about your lessons:

- Do you plan to use the CHAMPs or ACHIEVE acronym with your students?
- Will you use visual displays within your lessons on expectations?
- Will you use modeling and role playing within your lessons?
- Will you have students practice some of the expectations?
- Will you verify students' understanding of expectations prior to beginning activities?
- Share any samples of visual displays, ideas for modeling or role playing, and so on.

B. Discuss how many days of repetition of these lessons you anticipate at the beginning of the school year. Identify strategies that will reduce the probability that students will get bored with whatever repetition is likely to be required.

Chapter Five

Rules and Consequences

Plan to respond consistently to student misbehavior

In this chapter you will create and apply procedures to address misbehavior. This chapter has only three tasks: developing a set of rules, designing consequences for violations of those rules, and preparing a lesson to introduce these rules and consequences on the first day of school.

A system of rules and consequences provides specific information about what behavior is acceptable and what is not (Metzger, 2002). Unacceptable behavior leads to consequences. Consider an interstate highway. Simply telling people they need to drive safely isn't specific enough to provide guidance or clear enough to be enforceable. Therefore, most jurisdictions identify a specific speed deemed appropriate, and that speed is posted and enforced.

Posting rules and enforcing consequences does not guarantee compliance, but it does help manage the frequency and intensity of misbehavior. To return to the driving metaphor, assume the posted speed is 70 miles per hour, but it is reduced to 60 miles per hour through an urban area with a lot of on and off ramps. Without posting that speed, some drivers would continue at 70 miles per hour simply because they were unaware of the increased risk in the urban setting. The posted speed limit provides those drivers with the information they need to be compliant. Of course, some drivers will exceed that speed, but if they drive at 80 miles per hour in the 70 miles per hour zones, they may slow to 70 miles per hour in the 60 miles per hour zones. Thus, the posted rules reduce the number of drivers exceeding the limit and reduce the magnitude of the misbehavior of other drivers. In addition, once the drivers know the rules, the presence of a police car on the side of the road or in the next lane prompts careful following of the rules, which is why teacher monitoring of student behavior is also important (it is discussed in detail in Chapter Seven).

The most important and basic concept of this chapter is that preplanning your response to misbehavior will make your corrections more effective. This is true for both early-stage misbehavior and more chronic rule violations. By developing and mentally rehearsing the application of corrective consequences to various misbehaviors, you reduce the probability that you will be rattled, frustrated, or upset by student misbehavior (Spaulding, 1978).

The three tasks in this chapter are:

Task 1: Identify and post three to six classroom rules that will be used as a basis for providing positive and corrective feedback.

Task 2: Develop a plan for correcting early-stage misbehaviors.

Task 3: Develop consequences for committing rule violations.

Task 1: Identify and Post Three to Six Classroom Rules That Will Be Used as a Basis for Providing Positive and Corrective Feedback

Posted classroom rules communicate to students that you have specific expectations. Therefore, your rules should provide objective descriptions of the specific behaviors you expect from students and inform them that certain behaviors are unacceptable and will result in corrective consequences (Malone & Tietjens, 2000; McLeod, Fisher, & Hoover, 2003). Because these rules should serve as the basis for implementing consequences for the most frequent misbehaviors, you must develop them in such a way that if students follow the rules, the most likely misbehaviors will not occur. This means that before you develop your classroom rules, you need to identify the misbehaviors that you think are most likely to occur. Think about your grade level and the typical developmental level of students in your class. Also consider your schedule, routines, procedures for managing work, and so on. Once you have classroom rules, you need to teach students what the rules are and how they can demonstrate that they are following those rules (Mendler & Curwin, 1999).

Decide who will help develop the rules. The first decision is whether you are going to develop the rules yourself or work them out with your students. This decision is really a matter of style and expediency; both teacher-designed and student-designed rules have high correlations with teacher effectiveness (Emmer, Evertson, & Worsham, 2002). An advantage of student-developed rules is that the process itself may give students a greater sense of ownership in the classroom. The disadvantages include the following: having no rules in place for the first day of school, difficulty keeping track of multiple sets of rules if you teach more than one class, and students not coming up with the rules you feel you need to have an orderly classroom. If you have not involved students in rule development before, it is best to design the rules yourself. However, if you like the idea of involving students and have been successful with the practice in the past, you certainly should feel free to continue doing so. Here is a sample set of rules:

1. Come to class every day that you are not seriously ill.
2. Arrive on time with paper, pencil or pen, textbook, and notebook with a divider for science.
3. Keep hands, feet, and objects to yourself.

4. Follow directions the first time they are given.

5. Stay on task during all work times.

You should have no more than six rules. If you have too many rules, students will not be able to keep track of them. In addition, a long list of rules sets a negative and adversarial tone when you present them to the students. You do not have to have a rule for every possible misbehavior that might occur—only those that are the most likely to occur, such as off-task behavior, minor disruptions, or not having materials.

State the rules positively. Positively stated rules communicate both high expectations and an assumption of compliance, and they set a positive tone. One or two of your rules may be impossible to state positively, for example: "No food or drink in the computer room." If this is the case, one or two negatively stated rules is acceptable, but make sure that the majority of the rules are stated positively.

Rules should be specific and refer to observable behaviors. Given that rules will be enforced with the application of consequences, you need to have rules that describe specific behaviors, not attitudes, traits, or conclusions. "Arrive on time with all of your materials" is specific and observable. "Be responsible" is not. "Stay on task during all work times" is observable. "Always do your best" is not. Nonspecific rules like "Be responsible" can have different meanings to different people and will create strife if you enforce a behavior you found to be irresponsible that your class did not.

Your classroom rules should be different from your Guidelines for Success, which are more global goals. For example, an exhortation like "Do Your Best" is something you want students to strive toward rather than a rule. It is too broad, subjective, and open to interpretation to be a rule that has consequences tied to it. That is, while you may have a discussion with a student about your perception that she is not doing her best, you are not going to impose penalties on her for not doing so. Rules must be specific because infractions of those rules have consequences. The rules are specific behavioral expectations that you will enforce with reasonable consequences. Guidelines for Success are more like beacons pointing your students toward the lifelong traits you wish to inspire in them.

Plan to teach your rules using positive and negative examples. The best way to help students understand your rules is to demonstrate specific examples of behavior following and not following the rules. Through the use of these positive and negative examples, you can teach students to understand your interpretation of the rule and how you will make judgments about whether a particular behavior breaks a rule. Students may not know what "irresponsible" looks or sounds like. This may require teaching some things that you feel are unnecessary, but it is better to overteach than to underteach. You might sit at a desk and show your students what you think not paying attention looks like to contrast it with what paying attention looks like. This can help make a concept that might be abstract concrete and easily understood. It might even make it fun.

Rules must be applicable. The rules you post must be applicable throughout the period. For example, "Keep hands, feet, and objects to yourself" can apply throughout the entire class period. "Raise your hand before speaking" may apply only to teacher-directed instruction, and you would not expect students to do this if you are having them work in cooperative groups. Therefore, "Raise your hand before speaking" should not be posted as a rule, but it may be taught as one of the CHAMPs or ACHIEVE expectations specific to teacher-directed instruction. A rule that may not apply to the entire class period, such as, "Arrive on time with all your materials," can be kept if there is no portion of the class period that invalidates it.

Although "Arrive on time with all your materials" focuses only on the beginning of class, it is a rule that affects the entire class period. If you believe a rule like this is important to have posted, include it on your list.

Be aware that if you are allowing students to help develop classroom rules, you will have to guide the group in coming up with a manageable number of positively stated rules. Some groups of students will tend to develop a laundry list of negatively stated rules. Thus, you may want to start by having the class brainstorm possibilities, then state each in positive terms (if possible), and then select a set of three to six that are the most important.

Post the rules in a prominent, visible location. Certainly include the rules in your syllabus, but posting them creates even more of a sense of permanence and importance. Posting also enables you to point to them whenever they are discussed and allows you to be brief in some of your reminders about minor violations. For example, if during a teacher-directed portion of a lesson, students are getting restless and off-task, you can give a quick reminder as you point to your rules, such as, "Class, Rule 5! Please stay focused on the lesson."

When you have to speak to an individual student about a rule violation, point or refer to the rules as you speak to him or her. The act of orienting the student's attention to the rules reduces the sense of negative personalization—that you are attacking the student—and implies the act is simply the teacher enforcing the classroom rules. In addition, the act of indicating the rules decreases any intense eye contact between you and the student. This make-eye-contact, break-eye-contact pattern can also reduce the possibility that the student will argue with you about the rules.

Task 2: Develop a Plan for Correcting Early-Stage Misbehaviors

Early-stage behaviors are those that are not yet a pattern. Once a particular misbehavior has become habitual, it is past the early stage and is more difficult to correct. Student violation of a rule at the beginning of the year and any other time it appears that students are violating a rule because they may not understand it is early-stage misbehavior. This must be dealt with differently from when a student is knowingly or intentionally violating a rule.

This task includes a list of potential corrective consequences for early-stage misbehaviors. For an early-stage misbehavior, the correction must be instructional more than being a consequence or punishment (Lovitt, 1978; Sponder, 1993). To return to the speeding analogy, if the speed limit on a stretch of highway is changed, the highway patrol on that section of highway probably would not issue tickets on the first day of the new law; rather, they would issue warnings for a period of time. Once the highway patrol was certain that the new speed limit was widely known, they would begin to ticket normally. In the next task, information will be provided on the type of consequences you might use when the students know and understand the rules and should receive a consequence that comes with a cost—the type of consequence drivers receive for exceeding the speed limit on a section of highway in which the speed limit has been posted and in force for more than a week or two.

The basic rule for early-stage misbehavior is to try the easy solution first. In general, the easiest correction strategies are simply to give the student information about what he or she should be doing at that moment. If you try a simple correction strategy and it works, the problem is solved. If the misbehavior continues over a period of days or weeks, then you are no longer working with an early-stage problem, and you will need to look at the situation more systematically and analytically.

What follows is a series of correction strategies that are appropriate for early-stage misbehaviors. These are especially useful in the first week of school, when you get a new student, or when a new behavior occurs that is not covered by your classroom rules. If you take the time to familiarize yourself with these strategies, you will be prepared to respond effectively when faced with an early-stage misbehavior.

Proximity

The proximity correction strategy is based on the same rationale as having highway patrol officers on the roadways. Most people, even those who tend to exceed the speed limit, are more likely to follow the speed limit when a police officer is near. In the classroom, proximity simply involves moving to where the misbehavior is. The misbehavior is likely to cease as you get near, because your proximity will prompt the students to stop exhibiting the misbehavior and start exhibiting the desired behavior. The more you move throughout your room in unpredictable ways, the better able you will be to correct misbehavior through proximity (Marzano, 2003).

For example, if you are presenting a lesson and a couple of students begin talking to each other rather than listening to you, you might start walking over to that part of the room while continuing to present the lesson. If the students quit talking while you are on the way, continue the lesson from where you are, and then move to a different place in the room or back to the front. After a few minutes, make eye contact with the students who had been talking. The eye contact after they are behaving appropriately communicates that you notice and acknowledge the appropriate behavior and is less potentially embarrassing to the students than a public compliment.

Ideally, proximity can work both passively and actively. The previous example shows how moving around the class can actively prevent misbehavior. Moreover, if your students are aware of your tendency to patrol the class or move about during your lessons, then they will be much less likely to misbehave, given the chance that you may be nearby.

Gentle Verbal Reprimand

To use a gentle verbal reprimand is simply to go over to the student or students engaged in misbehavior and quietly tell them what they should be doing at that moment. For example, if the two students in the previously described scenario did not stop talking as you moved in their direction, you might say to them, without drawing undue attention, "Johanna, Alexander, if you have something to say, you need to raise your hand and wait to be called on."

Effective verbal reprimands have the following features:

- They are short. They cause only a brief interruption in the lesson.
- They are given when you are physically near misbehaving students, not from across the room.
- Their tone and content are respectful.
- They are clear and unequivocal.
- They state the expected behavior rather than accusing the student of misbehavior.
- They are given in a way that creates the impression of privacy. They should be heard without making the students feel they are on display and without making the rest of the class feel a secret is being told.

Discussion

Sometimes you may need to talk with a student about misbehavior in a way that is more detailed and lengthy than a reprimand. For example, if a student makes a disrespectful comment as you are presenting a lesson, you may want to have a talk with the student about the importance of treating others with respect. Discussions are usually best if they occur at a neutral time. There are several reasons that having a discussion immediately after a misbehavior tends to be ineffective: you leave the rest of the class waiting; you give the misbehaving student immediate attention that can be affirming; the student may be defensive; and you are likely to be somewhat frustrated or angry at that moment. It is far more effective to wait until later, when the class is engaged in independent work, or even after class and then privately speak with the student. During your meeting, be sure to discuss with the student better ways that he or she could handle similar situations in the future.

Family Contact

An important and potentially effective early-stage correction procedure is family contact. When making contact with the family regarding misbehavior, keep the following suggestions in mind:

- Provide an objective description of the behavior, not a judgment about the student.
- Suggest that it would be useful if the family discussed the behavior with the student and communicated the expectation that the student will behave more responsibly in the future.
- Avoid implying that the student should be punished at home or that the family should make the student behave.
- Create a sense that you and the family can work as partners in helping the student reduce misbehavior and succeed in your class.

Be aware that it is also important to have positive, or at least neutral, contact with the family so that when they hear from you, it isn't always about the child's problem behavior.

Humor

Humor can be a powerful and effective way to respond to misbehavior, especially with older students. Consider a situation in which a student makes a sarcastic comment on the second day of school as the teacher is presenting a lesson. A quick-witted teacher might be able to respond to the student's comment in a way that will make the student himself laugh, and a tense moment can be diffused. This must not involve sarcasm or ridicule on the part of the teacher. The sensitive use of humor will bring people closer together; sarcasm or ridicule will make a student angry and hostile that you have made a joke at his expense.

If you do use humor in response to a misbehavior, plan on talking to the student later to make sure that he understands that his behavior was not acceptable and that you expect him to behave more responsibly in the future. In addition, you can check to see that you did not embarrass him with your humorous comment. For example, you could say something like:

Thomas, you made a comment in class today, and I made a joke out of it. I want to make sure that I did not embarrass you with what I said. I owe it to all of my students to treat them as respectfully as I expect them to treat me. If I ever do anything that feels disrespectful to you, please come and talk to me about it. Now, I need to ask that in the future, you raise your hand when you have something to say in class and that you make an effort to keep your comments respectful. I appreciate humor in the classroom, and I'm sure that you will be someone who will not only contribute to our lessons, but also help us to see the humor in our class as well. Thanks for taking the time to talk to me. I look forward to seeing you tomorrow.

Restitution

The goal of restitution is for a misbehaving student to learn that if her behavior causes damage, she needs to repair that damage. For example, if a student is rude to a guest speaker, she should be required to apologize to the guest speaker in writing, on the telephone, or in person. If you use this strategy, try to make it clear to the student that what you are asking her to do (in this case, apologize to the guest speaker) is not punishment but reparation—an attempt to repair any damage that might have been done on her part.

Conclusion

Whichever correction strategy you use to respond to an early-stage misbehavior, be sure that when the students who engaged in the misbehavior behave responsibly, you give them positive feedback. Students need to see that you notice positive behavior more than negative behavior (McLeod, Fisher, & Hoover, 2003; Ridley & Walther, 1995). Also, remember that if one or more of these strategies do not solve the problem quickly, you will need to develop and implement an intervention plan that is based on a more thoughtful analysis of the misbehavior (see Task 3).

Task 3: Develop Consequences for Committing Rule Violations

When you are sure that students understand your rules, plan to move from informative early-stage corrective techniques to consequences that impose a penalty for breaking a rule. If you do not plan in advance what your response will be, there is a high probability that you may inadvertently reinforce misbehavior (Lovitt, 1978).

If you developed the classroom rules with your students, this step should involve student input as well. If you developed your rules by yourself, you can decide whether to involve students in determining consequences. Either way, give a lot of thought to what the consequence for each rule violation should be. Identify what should happen if a student does not arrive on time with all materials. Identify what an appropriate consequence would be for tardiness or speaking out of turn, for example (Ma & Willms, 2004).

The following suggestions can help you choose and implement effective corrective consequences, which will help the student learn that engaging in misbehavior has a cost associated with it. There is a complete list of possible corrective consequences at the end of this task.

Plan to implement the corrective consequence consistently. If corrective consequences are going to reduce purposeful or habitual misbehavior, they must be implemented consistently. When you implement a corrective consequence only some of the time, the consequence, no matter how severe, is not likely to change the behavior. In fact, it may even make things worse than if there were no consequence at all. Any time a student is able to violate a rule and not receive the designated consequence, he is likely to feel a great sense of satisfaction. Getting away with misbehavior can be great fun, and the student may find he likes to see how frequently he can engage in the behavior and not get caught.

Teachers tend to implement corrective consequences based on an accumulation of misbehavior. Teacher emotion instead of a series of rules controls classroom consequences. What the student got away with five times might be the last straw the sixth time, but the consequence will seem to come from out of the blue to the student. While this is understandable behavior on the part of the teacher and can happen to anyone, it will not create a disciplined environment in your class. To change purposeful or habitual misbehavior, you need to define specific behaviors that are not acceptable and then implement corrective consequences for them every time, regardless of how you feel about the behavior at the time.

Your goal here is to develop clear expectations of what behaviors are unacceptable so that you can be consistent with your students. If you are concerned about disruptions, specify the precise behaviors you consider disruptive and connect the concept of disruption to one of the positively stated rules. As always, be sure to identify positive examples of nondisruptive behavior and class participation.

Make sure the corrective consequence fits the severity and frequency of the misbehavior. When deciding on the corrective consequence that you will implement, make sure to choose one that matches the severity of the problem (Wolfgang & Glickman, 1986). Choose a consequence that fits even the mildest example of the rule violation. All too often, teachers pick a consequence that is so harsh they are unwilling to implement it when the occasion arises. For example, a teacher who says, "Now, LaVona, stop that because I do not want to have to give you a detention," is demonstrating inconsistency. In this case, she is letting the student get away with it, but in some cases she may not. The consequence should be mild enough that you will be comfortable implementing it every time a student exhibits an irresponsible behavior. When determining the severity of a consequence, err on the side of making consequences too mild, because you may not follow through if the consequence is too harsh.

Whatever corrective consequence you choose, plan to implement the consequence in the same way for all the behavior within that category and with any student who violates that rule. In other words, if you have decided to deduct a point, all disruptive acts should result in a loss of 1 point. Do not create a situation in which some disruptive acts cost 1 point and some cost 3 points. You will find yourself having to explain why you feel the acts are of different severities and deserve different penalties. If you decide to use time owed as a consequence for a student who tends to be disrespectful, have each infraction equal the same amount of time owed (for example, fifteen seconds owed after class). Do not issue fifteen seconds in some instances and several minutes in others. Again, if you err on the side of consequences that are too mild, you are much more likely to follow through than if the consequences are too harsh. Also, keep in mind that a student may exhibit the behavior several times, and if the consequence is fairly severe, say a detention, you probably cannot assign several detentions to the same student in one class period. But if the student is disruptive three times, you can impose fifteen seconds for each incident.

Plan to implement the consequence unemotionally. Some students have learned that there is a high probability that they can make adults frustrated, hurt, or angry. For some students, this is virtually an invitation to do so as often as they can. If you get angry when correcting a student, your anger may reinforce the student's misbehavior. When a student is seeking a sense of power, seeing an adult frustrated or exasperated can be highly satisfying. For this student, getting an adult angry on a regular basis can provide a huge sense of power and control. You must strive to implement corrective consequences unemotionally so your reactions do not give any students the idea that they can have power over you by misbehaving.

Plan to interact with the student briefly at the time of the misbehavior without arguing. When any student breaks a rule, your interaction with that student should be brief: simply state the rule and the consequence. A common mistake is to explain and justify. The student may ask you for such information. Resist doing so. Any explanations should already be self-evident from your instruction or can be analyzed in a later conversation with the student. Sometime during the first few days of school, let the students know that if anyone ever wants to speak to you about something they think is unfair, they can make an appointment to see you before or after school. Once you have made this clear, if any student tries to argue, simply remind him that he can make an appointment to see you; then resume teaching. It is imperative not to let your students draw you into explaining your actions, consequences, or reasoning. That transfers the power to them and lets them know that they can disrupt class by misbehaving and making you explain yourself.

Although keeping interactions brief may be a difficult habit to get into, you will find that it allows you to keep your focus where it belongs: on teaching and providing positive feedback to all students who *are* meeting your expectations. Remember that the frequency of your positive feedback must far outweigh your negative feedback. Think about the consequence you plan to use for a targeted misbehavior. If you cannot imagine implementing that consequence without lengthy explanations or negotiations at the time of the misbehavior, consider a different consequence.

> **Note**
>
> *Never* use a corrective consequence that humiliates or ridicules the student, and avoid using academic tasks as corrective consequences (such as extra math homework or writing an essay).

The following pages contain descriptions of effective corrective consequences that can be implemented in a high school classroom. Each description includes a brief explanation of the consequence and how to use it. When using corrective consequences, be sure to assign them consistently and calmly, interacting with the student as briefly as possible (Orange, 2005).

Loss of Point

If you use the behavior grading procedures presented in Chapter Two, you have already set your class up so that certain infractions result in the loss of a point. In this system, each student starts the beginning of the week with a preestablished number of points—say, 15 out of a total weekly possible of 20. Then during the week, each singled-out example of positive behavior will add a point to the student's total and each rule violation will subtract a point from this total.

One of the biggest difficulties for high school teachers, as compared to elementary teachers, is that there are relatively few corrective consequences that the teacher can implement. One advantage of behavior grading is that you now have a mild corrective consequence that can be implemented consistently for low-level misbehavior that would otherwise be absent from your menu of possible consequences.

Here are some reminders of the essential features that are described in detail in Chapter Two:

- Check with your administrator to determine if this system can be a component of the academic grade or if it must remain separate.
- Each time an infraction occurs, inform the student of the infraction and the loss of a point.
- Make sure that all students get feedback on the total number of points they earned for the week.

Time Owed

When a student misbehaves and you have to intervene, some of your time is wasted. Therefore, a reasonable corrective consequence is to have the student lose time from an activity he or she values (for example, waiting fifteen seconds after the rest of the class has been dismissed). Time owed is an appropriate and effective corrective consequence for misbehaviors that occur frequently (such as disruptions, talking during lessons, name calling, or disrespectful behavior) because of its compounding nature.

Although fifteen seconds might sound almost silly, it is actually a pretty long time for an adolescent who wants to be in the hall talking with friends between classes. The brief nature of the consequence also allows it to be assigned more than once in a class. If the immediate corrective consequence was several minutes, you could not issue it to any student more than once a class. You may need to establish a policy that if the maximum of time owed is reached, another penalty will be issued, such as detention. For example, you could inform students in advance that each time you have to remind a student about a rule violation, he or she will owe fifteen seconds, but at the fourth infraction, you will make a parental contact and assign an after-school detention.

It is important that the time not be paid in such a way that it interferes with the student's time with another teacher. If keeping students after class for more than one minute would delay a student getting to his or her next class promptly, you should plan not to keep any student for more than one minute.

Finally, you must decide what to have the student do while paying this time owed. As a general rule, you should have the student do nothing. For a first offense, you may wish to use the time to discuss the misbehavior and ways the student could behave more responsibly in the future. Do not do this regularly, however, as the one-on-one interaction time with you may become reinforcing to the student and actually serve to perpetuate the misbehavior.

Time-Out

Many people think that the purpose of time-out is to send the student to an aversive setting. This is not the case. The actual purpose is to remove a misbehaving student from the opportunity to earn positive reinforcement. The goal is to communicate to the student that if he engages in a misbehavior, he will not get to participate in the interesting, productive, and enjoyable activities that will continue without him. The obvious implication here is that instruction and classroom activities need to be interesting, productive, and enjoyable. Following are descriptions of two different types of time-outs that some high school teachers have implemented effectively. Of course, if you think these procedures seem unlikely to be effective with your high school students, you should follow your instinct and utilize another consequence.

Time-out in class. In this option, you establish an area in a low-traffic part of your class-room. It can be as simple as having a chair off to the side of the room. Let students know that if you ask them to go to this "time-out area," you are doing it instead of sending them out of the classroom. Also let students know that if they go quietly to this area and complete their time-out without further disruption, they can rejoin the class and there will be no additional consequences. However, make sure students understand that if they refuse to go, disrupt others on the way, or continue to disrupt the class, you will have no choice but to remove the student from class and write a disciplinary referral. If you are concerned that your students may view this consequence as too elementary, consider using a sports example such as hockey: if a player breaks a rule, there is a time-out in the penalty box.

Time-out in another class. For students who are likely to misbehave during an in-class time-out (for example, a student may try to get other students to laugh at her while she is in time-out), it may be necessary to assign the student to time-out in another class. To do this, you need to find a teacher with a room near yours who has a class with fairly mature students.

A student who misbehaves in your room would be sent to the classroom of the other teacher, who should have a prearranged spot for a time-out student—for example, a chair in a low-traffic area of the class—and should have already warned his or her class to ignore the student when he enters. The time-out teacher should not be required to stop teaching class or interact with the misbehaving student. The idea behind this procedure is simply that the student is less likely to show off for students in a class he does not know.

Restitution

Restitution, which was presented as a correction strategy for early-stage problems in Task 2, can also be effective with chronic misbehaviors if they involve damage to property or social relationships. If a student engages in behavior that causes damage, a logical consequence is that the student has to repair the damage. For example, if a student writes on desks, a logical consequence is for the student to spend some time cleaning them. (You may not be able to have the student use chemicals such as a disinfectant, but he can certainly use water, a sponge, and a little effort.) When restitution is used with ongoing misbehavior, the amount of the restitution should increase with successive instances. Thus, if a student wrote on a desk, you might have him wash the desk. If he did it a second time, you would have him wash his desk and several others.

Detention

Detention is usually a schoolwide system that involves assigning a student to spend an estab-lished amount of time (forty minutes, for example) in a nonstimulating setting. Most schools that use detention have their detention periods after school, before school, or during lunch. When it is used as a schoolwide procedure, any teacher can assign any student detention. Detention is often structured so that the students are required to do academic tasks during the detention period. One problem with detention is that students may find it reinforcing if they are assigned to detention with friends. Like any other corrective consequence you try, keeping records can be helpful. If you are repeatedly assigning the same student to detention across a period of time, then this corrective consequence is not working for that student, and you should modify your correction plan accordingly.

Demerits

Demerits are negative points that, when accumulated, result in a negative consequence or the loss of a privilege. They can be used to soften a predetermined consequence that might otherwise be overly harsh for a single misbehavior. For example, if the consequence for talking in class is after-school detention (which would be rather harsh for a single instance), the teacher is likely to respond to that behavior inconsistently, sometimes ignoring the behavior and sometimes threatening ("If you keep talking I am going to have to give you a detention") and then finally giving the detention. The use of demerits might allow the teacher to set up a more consistent policy. The teacher might tell students that each time he has to speak to a student about talking in class (or any other minor disruption), that student receives a demerit. If a student gets four demerits within a one-week period, he or she will receive an after-school detention. The teacher is much more likely to intervene every time there is disruptive behavior if he is only issuing a demerit instead of a detention.

If you can use the loss of a point consequence or the fifteen seconds time owed after-class consequence (or both), you probably do not need to use the demerit system as well. However, if you cannot use either of these corrective consequences, demerits can be an adequate way to consistently correct mild misbehavior.

Office Referral

Referring a student to the administration should be used only in cases involving the most severe misbehaviors, that is, physically dangerous or illegal behaviors. If you think there may be other behaviors for which you might want to send a student to the office, discuss these circumstances with an administrator ahead of time, so that he or she can coordinate a plan for when the student is sent to the office.

In Conclusion

Classroom rules should be designed in advance to correct the most common misbehaviors. Your three to six rules should be specific, observable, and stated positively. Design the consequences that you will assign for violations of these rules. Clear rules and consistent corrective consequences will reduce, and eventually eliminate, the majority of classroom misbehavior. Teaching your students these rules and consequences is fully addressed in Chapter Seven.

Rules and Consequences Self-Assessment Checklist

Use this worksheet to identify which parts of the tasks described in this chapter you have completed. For any item that has not been completed, note what needs to be done to complete it. Then transfer your notes to your planning calendar in the form of specific actions you need to take (for example, "August 25, finish identifying classroom rules that will be used as a basis for providing positive and corrective feedback").

Task	Notes and Implementation Ideas
Identify and post three to six classroom rules that will be used as a basis for providing positive and corrective feedback. I understand that posted classroom rules communicate to students that I have specific expectations. I have identified three to six positively stated rules that describe specific observable behaviors I expect students to exhibit and specific observable behaviors I expect them not to exhibit. In creating my rules, I have considered the following: • Who will have input into the rules • How I will teach my rules (for example, using positive and negative examples) • That rules will be applicable • Where rules will be posted (that is, in a prominent, visible location)	
Develop a plan for correcting early-stage misbehaviors. I understand that early-stage behaviors are those that are not yet a pattern and that corrective consequences should be more instructional than punitive. I have a repertoire of information-giving correction strategies to use with early-stage misbehaviors that includes: • Proximity • Gentle verbal reprimand • Discussion • Family contact • Humor • Restitution When implementing any early-stage correction strategy, I am careful to always treat students with dignity and respect.	

Rules and Consequences Self-Assessment Checklist (*continued*)

Develop consequences for committing rule violations.

I understand that I need to impose penalties for rule breaking when it is no longer an early-stage misbehavior. I know that if I do not plan in advance what my response will be, there is a high probability that I may inadvertently reinforce the misbehavior. I have used the following suggestions to help me choose and implement effective corrective consequences:

- The corrective consequence needs to be implemented consistently.
- The corrective consequence must fit the severity and frequency of the misbehavior.
- The consequence must be implemented unemotionally.
- I will interact only briefly with the student during the time of the misbehavior and consequence.

The following are potential corrective consequences I can use:

- Loss of point
- Time owed
- Time-out in class
- Time-out in another class
- Restitution
- Detention
- Demerits
- Office referral

Rules and Consequences Peer Study Worksheet

With one or more of your colleagues, work through the following discussion topics and activities related to the tasks in Chapter Five. If necessary, refer back to the text to get additional ideas or for clarification. (See the Vision Peer Study Worksheet in Chapter One for suggestions on structuring effective discussion sessions.)

Task 1: Identify and Post Three to Six Classroom Rules That Will Be Used as a Basis for Providing Positive and Corrective Feedback

    A. Have each group member share the classroom rules he or she has developed. As a group, give feedback to each individual.

    B. As a group, discuss the possible corrective consequences that would be reasonable to assign for various infractions of classroom rules.

Task 2: Develop a Plan for Correcting Early-Stage Misbehaviors

    A. Have all group members bring a list of the techniques they use to correct early-stage misbehaviors. Discuss the effectiveness, or lack of, for each item on each person's list. Encourage each group member to experiment with at least one technique that he or she has not used in the past.

Task 3: Develop Consequences for Committing Rule Violations

    A. Have all group members bring a list of the consequences they use to correct rule violations that are not easily corrected with early-stage techniques. Discuss the effectiveness, or lack of, for each item on each person's list. Encourage each group member to experiment with at least one technique that he or she has not used in the past.

Chapter Six

Motivation

Enhance students' desire to succeed

As you review the tasks in this chapter and consider student motivation (or lack of it), keep in mind the following concepts from Chapter One. First, the students' behavior will let you know what they are motivated to do and what they are not motivated to do. As necessary, you will have to work on increasing their motivation to engage in appropriate or desired behaviors or decrease their motivation to engage in inappropriate or undesired behaviors. Second, when trying to increase student motivation to behave appropriately, use procedures that address both intrinsic and extrinsic motivation. Third, remember that students' motivation to engage in any behavior will be related to the degree to which they value the rewards of that behavior and their expectation of succeeding at the behavior (Cameron, Banko, & Pierce, 2001; Laraway, Snycerski, Michael, & Poling, 2003).

Five tasks are presented and explained in this chapter:

Task 1: Present the desired tasks to your students in a manner that will generate enthusiasm.

Task 2: Implement effective instruction practices.

Task 3: Use every possible opportunity to provide each student with noncontingent attention.

Task 4: Give students positive feedback on their successes in a variety of ways.

Task 5: Plan to interact at least three times more often with students when they are behaving appropriately than when they are misbehaving.

Immediately following the tasks in this chapter is a Self-Assessment Checklist designed to help you determine which tasks or parts of tasks you have done and which you still need to do. The chapter ends with a Peer Study Worksheet. This worksheet presents a series of discussion questions and activities that can be used by two or more teachers who want to share information and collegial support as they work to improve their classroom management practices.

Task 1: Present the Desired Tasks to Your Students in a Manner That Will Generate Their Enthusiasm

Consider a sports coach who is particularly good at motivating her players. In addition to teaching the necessary skills, she brings a great deal of passion to her interactions with the players. Think about what an effective coach says to players during the game, after the team has won ("You did great, but don't get overly confident, because next week we face the Cougars and they may be even tougher than the team we just beat"), and after the team has lost ("Yes, we lost, but you played a great game and we can learn from the mistakes we made—we just need to work even harder next week"). The actions of an effective coach are designed to inspire the players and motivate them to try their hardest.

This task has four specific strategies you can use, alone or in combination, to increase students' intrinsic motivation. By presenting tasks and behaviors in a manner that will generate student enthusiasm, you can help push your students toward success (Hamre & Pianta, 2001; Stronge, 2002).

Explain How an Activity Will Be Useful to Students

Most people are more motivated to work on a task that has a clear and important purpose than one that seems like meaningless busywork. Therefore, whenever possible, tell your students why you assign the tasks you give them. For example, when presenting a new math skill, you might emphasize how the skill will help them solve certain types of problems. When discussing an important historical event, you might emphasize how the event has relevance to current events in the country being studied. If you are trying to get your class to work harder toward one of your Guidelines for Success, you can stress how following the guideline will help them be more successful individually and help make the whole classroom a better place for everyone.

Obviously your explanations need to be age appropriate. With high school students, it is imperative to communicate what the expected outcome will be and how the task will be useful. It may not be necessary to provide this kind of explanation for everything you ask your students to do, but you should plan on doing it fairly often, especially for classes that require more than the typical amount of work or have more inquisitive students.

Provide a Vision of What Students Will Eventually Be Able to Do

Students should be aware of the long-term benefits of full and active participation in your class. Each student who follows your directions and works hard at the tasks you assign should know what he will be able to do at the end of the year that he was not able to do at the beginning. The benefits may involve academic skills, study skills, social skills, or a mix of all three. Your long-range classroom goals (see Chapter Two) may provide examples to your students of what they will be learning. You can show your students at the beginning of the semester what they will be able to accomplish or understand once they have learned what you have to teach them.

Relate New Tasks to Previously Learned Skills

Whenever you introduce a new skill or topic, tell students how the new subject relates to those they have previously learned. Students should not feel that you are presenting hundreds of unconnected skills or concepts. They need to understand how what you ask them to do at any one time relates to what they are working on. In this way, students can see how what they have already mastered is useful in understanding new skills or topics. When you combine this strategy with the two previous suggestions, you will ensure that students have a continual sense of where they have been and where they are going. Relating new information to the old also helps students make connections to what they are learning and thus increases the likelihood that they will remember new information.

Rally Student Enthusiasm, Especially for Challenging Tasks

Many students will not find it easy to be motivated to do something new or hard. This is where you must make a point of emulating that highly motivating coach. Don't be afraid to give some variation of the "Win one for the Gipper" speech (a famous pep talk given by coach Knute Rockne to the Notre Dame football team before a particularly challenging game, made famous by the 1940 movie *Knute Rockne, All American* starring Ronald Reagan as George Gipp). A classroom example might resemble the following hypothetical speech given two days before a unit test in science:

> Class, in two days we have the unit test in science. This is a tough unit, but I know that you can do it; you can learn these important concepts. I want you to do three things in the next two days that will help you get a good score on this test. First, work to pay attention in class. We are going to be reviewing the essential information you have to understand in these next two days, so keep focused. Second, any time you don't understand something we are reviewing, speak up! There are no stupid questions. If you are unsure what to ask, just ask me to give more information, and I'll explain the idea again in a different way. Third, decide right now how much you are going to study tonight and how much are you going to study tomorrow night for this test. How many minutes are you going to study? Decide—right now! Now add fifteen minutes to that number. If you were thinking that you would study zero minutes, add fifteen minutes—so you will study at least fifteen minutes tonight and fifteen minutes tomorrow night. If you planned to study thirty minutes each night, make it forty-five minutes. Remember, the more you study, the more you learn, and the more you learn, the better you will do on this test!

Generating enthusiasm for the tasks you assign can enhance student motivation. Always encourage motivated behavior from your students. As self-help author Zig Ziglar once put it, "People often say that motivation doesn't last. Well, neither does bathing—that's why we recommend it daily."

Task 2: Implement Effective Instruction Practices

Effective instruction practices are an integral part of effective behavior management practices. A teacher who implements dull instruction, presents unclear tasks, or assigns work that is consistently beyond the ability of some of her students—even if she does everything else well in terms of behavior management—is likely to have some students who appear unmotivated, disruptive, or hostile. Effective instruction prevents a great deal of misbehavior, mostly because students who are highly engaged in meaningful tasks do not have time to misbehave (Skiba & Peterson, 2003). In addition, it can have a snowball effect—when students are successful, their sense of accomplishment can be so satisfying that they are more motivated to behave responsibly.

All teachers must learn to ask themselves whether a behavior problem might be due, at least in part, to an instructional problem. While it is beyond the scope of this program to provide comprehensive treatment of effective instruction (the topic is far too broad and complex), what follows are brief descriptions of some factors related to effective instruction that can significantly influence student behavior.

Teacher's Presentational Style

Teacher behavior can be a big factor in the behavior of students. Students are more likely to pay attention to a teacher who is dynamic, clear, humorous, and excited in class than to a teacher who is confusing, boring, or talks in a monotone. To understand how important a factor teacher presentation can be, you need only think back to how you felt about the interesting (as opposed to boring) teachers you had in high school or college.

Although some teachers are naturally better presenters than others, every teacher can and should strive to make presentations more interesting to students. A reasonable goal to set is to be a slightly better presenter every year. Look at the following suggestions, and pick one or two that you will practice and work to improve over the course of this year:

- Vary your tone of voice to avoid monotony.
- Vary the intensity of your presentation; do not always act excited or calm.
- Use humor; try to make at least some part of every lesson fun or funny.
- Clarify the lesson purpose. Make sure students know what they are supposed to be learning and why it's important.
- Clarify the information you present. Zero in on the key concepts students need to understand; the more direct you are, the better.

Actively Involving Students in Lessons

Don't talk too much at any given time. When you speak for more than a few minutes without getting students involved in some way, less motivated students will start to tune you out. Some simple strategies can keep students engaged, even during teacher-directed lessons:

- Ask questions.
- Initiate brainstorming sessions.
- Give students tasks to work on in pairs.
- Present small tasks for students to work on independently.
- Have students volunteer personal examples.
- Give mini-quizzes.
- Set up role-plays.
- Bring in visual aids.
- Present guided practice of tasks students will work on later.

Ensuring High Rates of Student Success

All students learn faster when they get predominantly correct answers—on both oral and written tasks. While it is true that students should be challenged with difficult tasks, it's also true that students will get discouraged over time when they constantly face tasks on which they make a lot of errors. You should try to provide clear enough instruction and frequent enough practice opportunities to ensure that students will get approximately 90 percent correct on most tasks (Kame'enui, Carnine, Dixon, Simmons, & Coyne, 2002).

In situations where you know that students are likely to make a high number of errors, plan to provide more teacher-directed instruction. You can do this whether you are working with students in small groups (while the others work independently) or with the whole class. Consider the following example involving a whole-class math lesson. Your original plans may call for about fifteen minutes of teacher-directed instruction and thirty minutes of independent work. During the teacher presentation portion, you realize that many students are confused and do not seem to understand. If you stick with your plan, many students are likely to make a lot of errors, and some will become discouraged. Several students may seek your help during the independent work period. Since many students are confused, a better approach would be to change your plan. Instead of giving thirty minutes of independent work, you might say, "Class, since this is such a difficult assignment, I am going to walk you through the first ten problems. Anyone who wants to work ahead may do so, but I invite anyone who is still confused to do them together with me. Watch me do item 1; then copy what I have done."

Providing Students with Immediate Performance Feedback

When students practice a task, they need to receive information on the parts of the task they are doing correctly and the parts they are doing incorrectly—and as quickly as possible. If you have students hand in an assignment on a new math concept, but you do not get their corrected papers back to them for a week or more, they will learn little. A student who is making mistakes needs to know it as soon as possible in order to learn from those mistakes and avoid imprinting them in memory. During an oral class exercise, you should provide this kind of performance information to students immediately. Feedback regarding correct and incorrect responses during guided practice in class also should be immediate. When you assign written tasks that are to be done independently, be sure to correct the papers within one or two days and then go over the corrected papers when you return them—for example: "Class, look at the papers I just handed back. Quite a few people had trouble with question 5. Let's look at why. When you do a problem like this, keep in mind that . . ."

Chapter One, Task 3 discussed the importance of high expectations on the part of the teacher. When high expectations are combined with effective instruction, students soon see that if they apply themselves, they can be successful.

Task 3: Use Every Possible Opportunity to Provide Each Student with Noncontingent Attention

It is imperative that you make an effort to provide every student with attention that is not contingent on any specific accomplishment (Alberto & Troutman, 2003; Chance, 1998). Contingent positive attention (as described in Tasks 4 and 5) involves interacting with and giving feedback to students when they have accomplished or demonstrated improvement on important behavioral or academic goals. Noncontingent attention involves giving students time and attention not because of anything they've done but just because you notice and value them as people. Ways of giving noncontingent attention include greeting your students when they enter your room, calling on students during class, and showing an interest in their thoughts, feelings, and activities.

The benefits of noncontingent attention for students should be obvious. Like all of us, they need to be noticed and valued—and when they feel noticed and valued, they are more likely to be motivated to engage in appropriate behaviors. The benefits to you include (1) feeling more connected to your students, (2) providing students with a model of pleasant supportive social interactions, (3) improving student behavior, and (4) making each day much more pleasant by improving classroom climate.

You may wonder how simply saying hello and making an effort to talk to students can improve their behavior. Vern Jones (Jones & Jones, 2004), a leading expert on student discipline and motivation, explains it as being akin to putting something in the bank. Each time you interact with a student and show an interest in him or her as a person, you make a deposit. When you have invested enough (that is, interacted enough so the student feels valued by you), the student is more likely to want to follow your rules and strive to achieve your Guidelines for Success. In addition, if you make enough deposits, there will be reserve capital for those times that you may have to make a "withdrawal" when a student misbehaves. Whether the withdrawal consists of a gentle reprimand, a discussion, or a consequence designed to help improve the student's behavior, the more you have invested in the student, the more likely he or she is to understand that you are trying to help him or her and may think, "Mrs. Jacobsen cares so much about me that she is taking the time to help me learn to be responsible. I want to do what she is asking me to do." When nothing has been invested, the student may feel that you are simply trying to control his or her behavior—for example: "Mrs. Jacobsen wants me to sit down and be quiet because she doesn't like me. Well, screw that! I'll do whatever I want, whenever I want! She can't *make* me sit down." Noncontingent attention helps build a spirit of cooperation between you and your students.

Showing an interest and acting friendly does *not* mean trying to be a friend or a peer to the student. You are the teacher, and you do not want to be so friendly that you seem to be an equal. You are the person in a position of authority and the one who needs to intervene if there are rule violations. However, as the one in authority, you want to communicate that you value and are interested in every one of your students as individual people (Hamre & Pianta, 2001).

The following are more detailed explanations of some ways to give your students noncontingent attention.

Greet your students. This is the simplest but perhaps most important way to provide noncontingent attention. As students enter your room first thing in the morning (or at the beginning of class), you can say such things as, "Hello, Jonathan. Good morning, Wachera. Francine, how are you today? You know, I'm tired this morning too. You and I may have to nudge each other to stay awake in class. Maria, Jacob, Tyrone, good to see you today." You may not be able to greet every student each day, but you should try to greet enough students each day that over the course of a week, every student will have been greeted.

You can also make a point of greeting your students when you see them in the hall. They may barely respond (some students will be self-conscious if they are with friends), but they will notice if you don't take the time to acknowledge them.

Show an interest in students' work. During independent work periods, when no one needs immediate assistance, go to individual students (or cooperative learning groups) and look at the student's work. Taking a moment to look at what a student is doing demonstrates that you are interested in the student and her work. Sometimes you may offer praise in this context; other times you can simply say something like, "I'm looking forward to reading this when you're finished, Tamai."

Invite students to ask for assistance. Occasionally ask individual students how they are doing in class. If anyone indicates that he or she is having trouble, arrange a time for that student to get some additional help from you. For those who say they are doing fine, let them know that if they ever have trouble, they should not hesitate to come see you. If you make an offer of assistance to every student in the first couple of months of school, you communicate that you are aware of them as individuals and that you are available to them.

Whenever time permits, have a conversation with a student or a group of students. Having a conversation demonstrates even more than just a greeting that you are interested in your students and their experiences and ideas. Brief social interactions create an emotional connection between you and your students, and they are not hard to do. For example, as three students enter your classroom at the beginning of the passing period, you can casually chat with them as you stand at the door and greet other entering students. You might talk quietly with a couple of students as you go down the hall. Find out about your students' individual interests and ask about them (for example, ask a student about her soccer game the previous evening). Periodically share something about yourself—for example, "My son played goalie for his team in college. What position do you play?"

Make a special effort to greet or talk to any student with whom you've had a recent interaction regarding a misbehavior. This kind of gesture on your part communicates that what happened before is now past and that you do not hold a grudge. It also lets the student know you are prepared for a fresh start. For example, if you had to talk to a student about being disruptive, that student should definitely be one of the students you greet the next day: "Aaron, good to see you. How are you doing?" A greeting in these circumstances decreases the probability that the student will misbehave in the next instructional activity.

Task 4: Give Students Positive Feedback on Their Successes in a Variety of Ways

Among the most important practices an effective teacher engages in is letting students know about their behavioral and academic progress and success. Giving positive feedback is a powerful way to encourage responsible behavior (Martens, Lochner, & Kelly, 1992). When done well, positive feedback confirms for students that they are on the right track and increases the probability that they will demonstrate the same behaviors in the future. This task discusses five hallmarks of effective positive feedback. If you incorporate these suggestions into the positive feedback you give your students, you can significantly increase the probability that your feedback will encourage and motivate students to behave more responsibly in the future (Lalli et al., 1999; Silva, Yuille, & Peters, 2000).

Feedback should be accurate. Effective positive feedback should be related to a behavior (or set of behaviors) that did in fact occur. When an individual receives positive feedback about something he or she did not actually do, the feedback is basically meaningless. If you comment to a student that his accuracy in completing math assignments is improving, you need to be sure that the student's accuracy is really improving. Before you note that a student demonstrated improved self-control by staying in her seat during an entire instructional period, be sure that the student did stay in her seat.

Feedback should be specific and descriptive. When giving positive feedback, be sure to tell students exactly what they did. That is, feedback should be information laden—confirming for a student what it was she did that was important or useful. If you want to let a cooperative group know they have done well, describe the specific behaviors that they exhibited. When writing a note regarding a student's paper, identify what specifically he did that contributed to the quality of the paper.

Specific descriptive feedback lets the student know which aspects of his or her behavior you are commenting on. Simply writing "Excellent work" at the top of a paper, with no other comments, does not give the student any information about what aspects of the paper led to your positive reaction. Was it the effective use of figurative language? The organization? The use of vocabulary? The creative use of the overall ideas? The use of topic sentences? The clarity of the descriptive language? The more detail you are able to give students, the more they will understand about your criteria the next time.

Following are some common mistakes teachers make when providing positive feedback. All of them can be avoided by providing specific descriptions of student behavior:

- *The Good Job syndrome.* It's easy for teachers to fall into a simple repetitive phrase that they use over and over and over to give positive feedback. There are two problems with this. First, most simple phrases such as "Good job," "Nice work," or "Fantastic" provide no specific information about what exactly the student did that was useful or important. Second, when a particular phrase is overused, it becomes background noise, and students will cease to notice it.

- *Making judgments or drawing conclusions about the student.* Be very cautious about stating or implying that a student is "good" or "smart" or "brilliant." When a student answers a difficult question, it can be tempting to say something like, "Allison, you are so smart." The problem is that a statement like this not only doesn't provide specific information about what the student did, but it may imply to the student that if she had not come up with that particular answer, you might not think of her as smart. It's far more effective to say, "Allison, you applied the formula, performed a series of computations, and came up with the correct answer."

- *Calling attention to yourself.* Some teachers praise by saying, "I like the way you . . ." Even when what follows this statement specifically describes the student's behavior, that initial phrase may inadvertently be taken by the student to mean that he or she should behave to please you. In fact, what you are working toward is for students to behave in particular ways because it will help them be successful learners. Another problem with an "I like the way you . . ." type of phrase is that some students might get the idea that you like them when they are good, and infer that you *don't* like them when they are not good. Keep the focus of your feedback on the student and what he or she did, not on your own likes and dislikes. The one exception is when a student does something particularly helpful to you. In that circumstance, feel free to let the student know that you appreciate his or her help. For example, if you drop some papers and a student helps you pick them up, it is reasonable and logical to say something like, "Thank you for helping me pick those up. I appreciate having such a thoughtful student."

Feedback should be contingent. The student behavior you provide feedback on should have some level of importance. That is, it should not be an overly simple behavior for the individual who demonstrated it. To understand why, imagine that someone you know and respect (for example, a favorite college professor, your minister, your boss) sees you drive into the parking lot and, as you step out of your car, comes over to you and says, "Excellent left turn into this parking lot! You used your turn signals, you checked your blind spot, and you controlled your speed as you pulled into the parking space to ensure that you did not scratch the car on either side of you."

This feedback may be accurate, but it is also at best meaningless and at worst insulting. It implies that these driving behaviors are something special, when making a left turn into a parking lot and a successful turn into a parking space is what's expected of all drivers. You'd probably wonder why the person was being so gushy and excited about something that you had done successfully many times before. There's a good chance this meaningless feedback would reduce your respect for that person.

Three major circumstances contribute to positive feedback being contingent. The first is when the feedback occurs while someone is learning a new skill or behavior. When you were learning to drive, your driving instructor may have given you positive feedback similar to the statements in the previous example. The difference is that because you may have driven only once or twice before, your instructor's praise was probably not at all insulting or meaningless; it provided specific and descriptive confirmation of what you did correctly (Alberto & Troutman, 2003).

Feedback is also contingent when it refers to a behavior that requires effort—whether or not it is a new behavior. For example, imagine that you have been making a concerted effort to increase your helpfulness around the house (because your partner has been carrying more than his or her fair share). If your partner expresses gratitude for the extra help or shares appreciation that the household chores are more equally divided, that positive feedback is not likely to be meaningless or insulting to you. The behavior isn't new or particularly complex, but it does take effort to change a bad habit. Feedback that acknowledges one's efforts is likely to be valued and can lead to maintaining or increasing the frequency of the behavior in the future.

The third circumstance in which positive feedback will be contingent is when it concerns a behavior about which the individual is proud. For example, think about a time when you handed in a paper on which you felt that you had done an especially good job. Chances are that when you got the paper back, you looked at the score and then went through the paper page by page to see if the instructor had written any comments. Far from being seen as meaningless or insulting, positive comments in these circumstances are welcome, particularly if the instructor described which parts were well thought out or well written.

Feedback should be age appropriate. For obvious reasons, the way you give feedback to a kindergarten student will be different from the way you provide it to a high school student. For example, you can use more sophisticated vocabulary to describe behavior with older students. And in terms of being contingent, it is more appropriate to focus on advanced behaviors with older students. At the same time, be careful not to embarrass older students when providing positive feedback. High school students may feel a great deal of peer pressure to fit in or not stick out. Think about the thousands of messages students get that suggest that being good in school makes them a geek or a nerd. If you provide feedback in a way that embarrasses a student, it may actually *discourage* the student from behaving responsibly in the future. For example, many students will avoid behaving responsibly if they are praised in a way that results in their being accused of being the teacher's pet. If a student seems to be embarrassed when you give positive feedback, consider experimenting with one or more of the following suggestions:

- Use a quiet voice when providing feedback to individuals. If students feel you are making a public display of them, it may increase the possibility that they will feel embarrassed in front of their friends.

- Be brief. If you go on too long, accepting the praise graciously may be difficult for the student.

- Be somewhat businesslike. Simply state the positive behavior the student engaged in. If you sound too excited or pleased when you praise, it can make a student feel like a Goody Two-Shoes: "I pleased the teacher—yay."

- Avoid pausing and looking at the student after you praise. A pause can seem to imply that you expect the student to respond, and this puts a student in a difficult position. Are you waiting for a smile or a thank-you? Smiling or saying thank you in front of peers can be socially embarrassing, especially to a student who has an image of being tough. Such a student will often make a smart-aleck comment or engage in misbehavior to reassert to peers how tough and bad she is.

Feedback should be given in a manner that fits your own style. There is no single good way to give positive feedback. There is plenty of room for individual style, even when you incorporate recommended techniques. A teacher who has a more buttoned-down personality can and should employ a more businesslike style of providing positive feedback. A teacher who tends to be excited and energetic may be somewhat more like a cheerleader when giving feedback. And a soft-spoken teacher's feedback will naturally be more soft-spoken than that of a more boisterous teacher. In most cases, if you are comfortable with your style of giving feedback, your students will be too. In fact, you probably only have to consider the preceding tips on age-appropriate and nonembarrassing feedback if your students are responding to your current style with embarrassment.

Level of structure and positive feedback. The greater the number of risk factors your class has, the greater your need is to manage student behavior by positive as opposed to punitive means. With a low-structure class, you may be able to get away with relatively low rates of positive feedback and still have students behave responsibly. This is certainly not recommended, but it is plausible. If your students come from relatively stable situations and families in which they receive encouragement, they may work hard and behave well without getting much positive feedback from you—although they will probably not feel much joy about it.

However, when students need higher structure (in classes with many risk factors), frequent positive feedback is essential. Without it, some students will not know exactly what you want from them. Furthermore, if students are trying to meet your academic and behavioral expectations and they do not receive any feedback that you notice what they have done, some of them will cease striving to meet the expectations, perhaps wondering, "I try to do what she wants and she never even notices. Why should I bother?" The greater the number of high-needs students, the greater the need for you to provide frequent, positive feedback in a skillful manner.

Students who respond negatively to positive feedback. Some students may respond negatively to a teacher's efforts to provide positive feedback. For example, shortly after being told that he is behaving responsibly, a student may exhibit the worst behavior he ever has in class.

The temptation here might be to withhold all future positive feedback or acknowledgment. Actually, this is a relatively common phenomenon for which there are several possible explanations. One reason a student may misbehave immediately after receiving positive feedback is that it embarrasses him. If you suspect this is the case, try modifying your feedback. See whether making the feedback more private, stating it in a more succinct and businesslike way, or eliminating pauses after you provide positive feedback results in the student reacting more positively.

The other reasons a student might behave this way tend to be more complex and hence harder to remedy. Perhaps the student is trying to maintain a tough image, or feels peer pressure to remain aloof, or does not know how to handle success appropriately. When you provide feedback to a student who has one or more of these issues, the feedback won't fit the student's self-image and can make her feel uncomfortable (that is, terrified by her own success). Exhibiting misbehavior helps a student like this get back to feeling like a troublemaker or a loser again. It may even be that the student does not believe she really is capable of being successful and feels the need to show you that the success was an aberration of some kind. In addition, the misbehavior takes some pressure off by communicating that you can't expect the student to be successful all the time. Regardless of the reason for a student's misbehavior after receiving positive recognition, you can try experimenting with one or more of the following suggestions:

• *Treat the misbehavior as a momentary interruption in the student's success.* The key is to refrain from communicating anger or disappointment. This can be tough. When a student falls apart after you acknowledge his success, it is natural to feel angry or disappointed. You may want to say something like, "Jamie, you were doing so well, and now you go and do this sort of thing. I just don't understand and I am very disappointed." A reaction like that may feed a student's negative attitude and would reinforce him in the wrong direction. It definitely takes the pressure off the student to continue to succeed: the teacher has once again seen the worst the student has to offer.

• *At a neutral and reasonably private time, talk to the student about his tendency to misbehave after getting positive feedback.* See if the student can give you any insights into why this occurs. Ask him if he has any suggestions about ways you can give him positive feedback that will reduce the chance that he will feel a need to misbehave afterward. Try experimenting with any reasonable suggestions the student makes. If the student cannot come up with any strategies for you to try, ask him what he thinks about some of the suggestions included here.

• *Be more private with (or otherwise modify the form of) the positive feedback you provide to the student.* The student may prefer to get a note rather than public praise. He may prefer to have you give the feedback at the end of the period rather than during it. He may prefer that you use a signal that only he knows (for example, scratching your forehead) to let him know he is behaving responsibly.

• *Switch from giving specific descriptive feedback to simply interacting with the student when she is behaving responsibly.* Say hello to the student as she enters class. If she is on task during independent work, don't specifically praise her, but do go over and ask if she has any questions or needs any help. If she has behaved responsibly in your class for the past several days, don't praise, but ask her if she would be willing to pass out some papers that need to be distributed to the class. At the end of the class, tell her to have a good day. This attention, given when she is behaving responsibly, may reinforce the appropriate behavior, even though you are not providing specific descriptive positive feedback.

If eliminating the positive feedback is successful (that is, the student handles the attention as long as no praise is included), continue to withhold praise for at least four weeks. If the student's behavior is improving, gradually introduce subtle praise. Once a week or so, make a matter-of-fact statement about something the student has done. Don't gush or in any way make a big deal of it; just make a comment—for example: "Thank you for getting that assignment in on time" or "That was a creative contribution you made to the cooperative group you were working with." If you see a downturn, back off and return to attention without praise. However, if the student is handling it, gradually increase the frequency of specific descriptive feedback you give the student.

Task 5: Plan to Interact at Least Three Times More Often with Students When They Are Behaving Appropriately Than When They Are Misbehaving

One of the most essential behavior management strategies is also perhaps one of the most difficult: making the effort to interact with every student more frequently (at least three times more frequently) when the student is behaving appropriately than when he or she is behaving inappropriately (Henderson, Jenson, & Erken, 1986; Martens, Lochner, & Kelly, 1992). To understand why this strategy is so essential, consider the following:

• Some students are starved for attention. Most teachers have direct experience with how demanding of attention some students can be, and most have seen the desperate lengths some students will go to for attention.

• For the student who is truly starved for attention, the form of attention may not matter. A reprimand for misbehaving may be just as satisfying of this student's need for attention as praise for behaving responsibly. In fact, it might be even more satisfying because the scolding will probably last longer and involve greater emotional intensity.

• With students who are starved for attention, *the behavior you pay the most attention to is the behavior you will get more of in the future.* That is, if you have more interactions with students when they are behaving appropriately, you will see an increase in positive behavior over time. If you have more interactions with students when they are behaving inappropriately, you will see an increase in negative behavior over time.

Your interactions with students are considered positive or negative based on the behavior the student is engaged in at the time you attend to him or her. If a student is off-task and you say, "Wanda, you need to get back to work or you won't complete your assignment," that would be considered a negative interaction—even if you made the request very pleasantly and your intention was to help the student. It is a negative interaction because the student was engaged in a negative behavior (being off-task) when you initiated the interaction. Some teachers mistakenly believe that if they are being nice to a student, it is a positive interaction, and if they are acting hostile or sounding angry, it is a negative interaction.

It's also important to realize that just because an interaction is considered negative, it does not mean it is wrong. It may, in fact, be the most useful way to get the student back on-task at the time. However, it is important to understand that unless you make an effort to interact with this same student when she is on-task, the student may learn that it is easier to get your attention (which may be what she wants) for being off-task than it is for behaving well. Remember that each time you give attention to a student, you may be reinforcing the behavior you are paying attention to—whether the behavior is positive or negative. Hence the recommendation that you make it your goal to pay three times more attention to students when they are exhibiting positive behavior than when they are exhibiting negative behavior.

This is not always easy. In fact, observational studies regularly show that most teachers pay significantly more attention to students' misbehavior than they do to students' positive behavior. In 1971, Wes Becker and Siegfried Englemann wrote about studies Becker had done with elementary-level teachers who had been reprimanding and reminding students about out-of-seat behavior during work periods. He encouraged the teachers to reprimand students more immediately and more consistently: "Don't miss a single student who gets out of their seat at the wrong time." The teachers assumed this would decrease the out-of-seat behavior. In fact, the number of students getting out of seat at the wrong times actually increased.

Becker called this phenomenon the *criticism trap*: although the teachers thought they were doing something effective (for example, reprimanding or issuing a consequence for an inappropriate behavior), the students who were starved for attention were getting out of their seats, at least in part, to get their teachers to look at and talk to them. The students' need for attention was satisfied when their teachers told them to get back in their seats—which they typically did, at least initially. This tended to reinforce the nagging on the part of the teacher because the students usually sat down when asked to do so. But before long, the students would realize, consciously or unconsciously, that they were not getting attention when they were doing what the teachers wanted, so they would get out of their seats again. The teachers would reprimand again, giving the desired attention, and the students were again reinforced for getting out of their seats. Although these studies were done at the elementary school level, the phenomenon can continue into the secondary level.

This quickly becomes a destructive pattern in which everyone gets what they want in the short run. That is, the student gets attention when he violates the teacher's expectations; the teacher gets momentary compliance each time he reprimands. However, when this cycle is allowed to continue, no one gets what they want in the long run. Over time, students behave less and less responsibly and the teacher gets more frustrated and more negative. The only real way out of the criticism trap is to have more interactions with students when they are behaving responsibly than when they are misbehaving.

If you think you have fallen into the criticism trap or believe that your ratio of positive to negative interactions with students is fewer than three to one, consider implementing one or more of the following suggestions for increasing positive interactions:

- Each time you have a negative interaction with a student, tell yourself that you owe that student three positive interactions.
- Identify specific times each day that you will give students positive feedback on some aspect of their individual behavior or class performance. For example, you might decide that at the beginning of each math period, you will compliment five or six students.
- Schedule individual conference times with students to compliment them on their performance.

- Make a point of periodically scanning your classroom, seeking out specific reinforceable behaviors for which you can acknowledge students.
- Identify particular events that occur during the day (for example, a student getting a drink of water) that will prompt you to observe the class and identify a reinforceable behavior.
- Make a point to reduce the amount of attention (time and intensity) a student receives for misbehavior and increase the amount of attention (time and intensity) the student receives when not engaged in misbehavior.
- Engage in frequent noncontingent positive interactions with the students.

Suggestions are provided in Chapter Eight on how you can periodically monitor your ratios of interactions to determine if you have fallen into the criticism trap. For now, just be aware that the behaviors you pay the most attention to are the behaviors that are likely to occur with the most frequency as the year progresses. Make a concerted effort to interact with every one of your students more frequently when they are engaged in positive behavior than when they are engaged in negative behavior.

Note

In addition to these suggestions on ways to increase the number of positive interactions with students, review Chapter Five for information on how to reduce negative interactions.

Level of structure and ratio of positive to negative interactions. The higher the level of structure you have determined to be necessary for your students, the greater the probability is that at least some of the students will be starved for attention. This means that you are likely to have some students who will try to get their attention needs met through misbehavior, which can lead to a pattern of frequent nagging and reprimanding—and the classic spiral into the criticism trap. Therefore, the greater your class's need for structure is, the more you need to make an effort to maintain positive interactions at a very high level. That is, this task is absolutely essential for classes needing high structure. Maintaining a three-to-one ratio of positive to negative interactions is also important with low-structure classes, but it is generally easier to do because there isn't as much misbehavior to which you need to respond.

In Conclusion

Motivating your students will often be challenging, but the rewards will be worthwhile. When you have a highly motivated class, you will see higher rates of on-task behavior; experience decreased disciplinary problems, fewer referrals, and less absenteeism; and find you have more lesson time to devote to the "good stuff." Different students must be reached on different levels, but if you are diligent, you will find a way to inspire each of your students. Make sure each student is aware that you are expecting his or her success because you know he or she *can* succeed. Make the same effort to reach each student on more than one level, motivating them externally and intrinsically. Inspire them, and you may just find that they return the favor.

Motivation Self-Assessment Checklist

Use this worksheet to identify which parts of the tasks described in this chapter you have completed. For any item that has not been completed, note what needs to be done to complete it. Then transfer your notes to your planning calendar in the form of specific actions you need to take (for example, "December 2, take time to reflect on how effective my instructional practices are").

✔	Task	Notes and Implementation Ideas
☐	*Present the desired tasks to your students in a manner that will generate enthusiasm.* I have identified specific ways I can present tasks to students that will generate enthusiasm and intrinsic motivation on their part. These include, but are not limited to: • Explaining how or why the task will be useful to students; • Giving students a vision of what they will eventually be able to do; • Relating new tasks to previously learned skills; and • Rallying the enthusiasm and energy of students, particularly when I ask them to do something difficult or challenging.	
☐	*Implement effective instruction practices.* I understand that instructional style has a significant impact on student behavior. I have identified one or two aspects of my presentation style that I will work to improve over the course of the year. I have made plans to improve my presentational style by: • Varying the tone of my voice to avoid monotony • Varying the intensity of my presentation so I am not always excited or always calm • Using humor • Clarifying lesson purpose • Clarifying information I have made plans to actively involve students in lessons. Following are strategies I can use: • Asking questions • Giving students tasks to work on in pairs • Presenting small tasks for students to work on independently • Giving mini-quizzes	

- Setting up role-plays
- Presenting guided practice of tasks students will work on later

I have made plans to ensure high rates of student success.

I have made plans to provide students with immediate performance feedback.

☐ *Use every possible opportunity to provide each student with noncontingent attention.*

I understand that there are many benefits to giving students noncontingent attention. I have considered how I will provide each of my students with non-contingent attention by:

- Greeting students
- Showing an interest in students' work
- Inviting students to ask for assistance
- Conversing with a student or group of students when time permits
- Making a special effort to greet or talk to any student with whom I've had a recent interaction regarding a misbehavior

☐ *Give students positive feedback on their successes in a variety of ways.*

I have made a plan to ensure that I am incorporating the following characteristics into the positive feedback I give students regarding their academic and behavioral performance:

- Accurate feedback
- Specific and descriptive feedback
- Contingent feedback
- Age-appropriate feedback
- Feedback given in a way that fits my personal style

I have considered the structure level of my class in determining how much positive feedback I need to give, realizing that high-structure classes need more positive feedback. I also realize that even low-structure classes have students who cease to try to meet expectations if they do not receive positive feedback.

If any student seems to be responding to my positive feedback with an increase in inappropriate behavior, I am prepared to make modifications to the feedback I am giving.

Motivation Self-Assessment Checklist (continued)

☐	*Plan to interact at least three times more often with students when they are behaving appropriately than when they are misbehaving.* I understand how important it is for me to interact with each of my students at least three times more when they are behaving responsibly than when they are misbehaving. I will watch for any tendency on my part to fall into the criticism trap. I realize that the higher the level of structure of my class, the more I need to make an effort to maintain positive interactions at a very high level.

Motivation Peer Study Worksheet

With one or more of your colleagues, work through the following discussion topics and activities related to the tasks in Chapter Six. If necessary, refer back to the text to get additional ideas or for clarification. (See the Vision Peer Study Worksheet in Chapter One for suggestions on structuring effective discussion sessions.)

Introduction

A. As a group, discuss the classroom implications and give examples of the following four concepts related to motivation:

- When a particular behavior occurs repeatedly, it demonstrates a level of motivation on the part of the individual to engage in that behavior; and when a particular behavior does not occur, it demonstrates a lack of motivation on the part of the individual to engage in that behavior.

- In most cases, when an individual engages in a particular behavior, it is prompted by a mix of intrinsic and extrinsic motivational factors.

- A person's motivation to engage in a particular behavior is affected by the person's proficiency at that behavior.

- Motivation can be thought of as the result of Expectancy × Value.

Task 1: Present the Desired Tasks to Your Students in a Manner That Will Generate Their Enthusiasm

A. Have each group member give a specific example of how he or she will use each of the following strategies to generate student enthusiasm and increase students' intrinsic motivation to engage in desired tasks or behaviors.

- Explaining how the task or behavior will be useful to students

- Giving the students a vision of what they will be able to do

- Relating the new task or behavior to previously learned skills

- Rallying student enthusiasm and energy for the task or behavior

- Other

Task 2: Implement Effective Instruction Practices

A. Have all group members identify one or two aspects of their presentational style to work to improve over the course of the year.

B. As a group, create a list of ideas beyond those suggested in this program for actively involving students in lessons.

C. As a group, discuss the relationship among course content, course objective, and course evaluation.

D. Have each group member describe what he or she will do to ensure high rates of student success.

E. Have each group member share the ways he or she gives students timely performance feedback.

Motivation Peer Study Worksheet (*continued*)

Task 3: Use Every Possible Opportunity to Provide Each Student with Noncontingent Attention

   A. Have each group member identify situations (for example, times of day or types of activities) in which she or he provides noncontingent attention to several or many students.

   B. Consider having group members pair up and observe each other for part of a day (for example, the first ten minutes of the day as students arrive) in order to give each other feedback on the quantity and quality of the noncontingent attention they provide their students.

   C. Discuss the feasibility and logistics of encouraging all staff members to make an effort to give individual students as much noncontingent attention as possible.

Task 4: Give Students Positive Feedback on Their Successes in a Variety of Ways

   A. Have each group member give specific positive and negative examples of positive feedback that reflects each of the following qualities:

   - Accurate

   - Specific and descriptive

   - Contingent

   - Age appropriate

   B. Have one group member describe a student who reacts poorly to positive feedback. As a group, discuss possible strategies.

Task 5: Plan to Interact at Least Three Times More Often with Students When They Are Behaving Appropriately Than When They Are Misbehaving

   A. As a group, discuss the concept of the criticism trap, and have individuals come up with specific examples from their experience where this may have been happening.

   B. Have each group member identify the specific strategies he or she will employ to ensure interacting at least three times more often with each student when the student is behaving responsibly than when the student is misbehaving.

Chapter Seven

Preparation and Launch

Pull it all together for the first day

In this chapter, you will make sure that your classroom organization is complete and that you can smoothly implement the first day of school. The three tasks in this chapter will help you build your class syllabus, prepare your class to make a positive first impression, and prepare and implement effective behavior management strategies on the first day of school.

Most students are somewhat apprehensive about their first day, and putting them at ease will go a long way toward influencing your relationship with your students for the coming year. Keep in mind that your students have a lot more on their mind than just your class. They are concerned that other students won't like them, that they may be ignored, that they will be noticed for the wrong reasons, or that their clothes may not look right. The more you do to help your students feel safe and comfortable, the greater the likelihood that they will feel a sense of appreciation and loyalty to you (Brophy, 1998; Stronge, 2002).

By following the steps in this chapter, you should be fully prepared for your first day of class and beyond. Your students will notice, too. They should leave their first class with you knowing that you are interested in them, that you care about them, and that you have high expectations for them. They should leave knowing that you will be firm and fair with them and believing that they can succeed in your class.

There are three tasks in this chapter:

Task 1: Finalize your classroom management plan, and prepare to communicate that plan to your students.

Task 2: Complete your preparations for the first day.

Task 3: Implement your plan for the first day of school.

Task 1: Finalize Your Classroom Management Plan, and Prepare to Communicate That Plan to Your Students

Review your implementation of the essential concepts from Chapters One through Six by comparing your plan against the syllabus template in Exhibit 7.1. Although you may not provide a handout to your students that includes this much detail, you need to know in advance what your procedures and policies are going to be (Baron, 1992; McLeod, Fisher, & Hoover, 2003). Use this template as a guide for designing the handout you will give to students on the first day of class. If you have followed each task in the preceding chapters, you should have much of this information already at hand. This template provides an example of how to organize and present it. As you put everything together and compare it to the syllabus, you may find some sections where you are uncertain of your policies or procedures. The template includes references to tasks from previous chapters where you can find information to help you design them. Following the template is Exhibit 7.2, a completed class syllabus for a highly structured class for ninth-grade students.

Exhibit 7.1
Syllabus Template

Teacher: _____

Classroom Goals
Write your classroom goals in the form of what students will be able to successfully do at the end of the year or semester. You can find more information on this topic in Chapter One, Task 5.

Guidelines for Success
Write your list of attitudes and traits that you feel will ensure your students' success. You can find more information on this topic in Chapter One, Task 5.

Classroom Rules
Outline the important student behaviors that will ensure your class runs efficiently. You can find more information on this topic in Chapter Five, Task 1.

Activities
Outline the activities that students will be engaging in during a typical week. You can find more information on this topic in Chapter Four, Task 1.

Grades
Grading scale: Outline the percentage cutoffs for A's, B's, and so on.
Relative value: Outline the relative weight of homework, quizzes, tests, papers, and behavior and effort on the final grade.
You can find out more information on this topic in Chapter Two, Tasks 2 to 4.

Classroom Procedures

Entering the classroom

Outline exactly what students should do from the time they enter the room until the bell rings for class to begin. You can find more information on this topic in Chapter Three, Task 4.

Tardy to class

Provide your definition of *on time* and *tardy,* and identify the consequences for being tardy. You can find more information on this topic in Chapter Three, Task 4.

Paper or pencil

Identify what students should have to write with. In addition, specify what a student should do if he or she does not have this and what, if anything, you implement as a consequence. You can find more information on this topic in Chapter Three, Task 4.

How to find out what the daily assignments are

Identify how you will assign work and how students will know what they are to do each day. Also define how they should keep track of what they need to do for homework and long-range assignments. You can find more information on this topic in Chapter Three, Task 5.

Turning in assignments

Identify where and how students turn in class work and homework. Specify if students are to check off completed work they have turned in. You can find more information on this topic in Chapter Three, Task 5.

Returning assignments to students

Detail your policies on how you will return completed work to your students. You can find more information on this topic in Chapter Three, Task 5.

Finding out grade status

Review your grading system, and explain whether you will give students a weekly grade report or if you expect them to track their grades themselves. Also identify when and how a student can approach you to discuss his or her current status in the class. You can find more information on this topic in Chapter Two, Task 4.

Student responsibilities after an absence

Outline what students will need to do when returning after an absence.

- How to find out what they missed

- How long they have to make up assignments

- What to do if they miss a test

You can find more information on this topic in Chapter Three, Task 5.

Syllabus Template (*continued*)

Late, missing, or incomplete assignments

Outline the maximum number of late assignments you will accept, along with penalties and time limits for late work. You can find more information on this topic in Chapter Three, Task 5.

Communication procedures with parents and families

Identify if you will have any regular communication with families that you initiate. Provide information on when, where, and how family members can get in touch with you.

Ending class

Specify how you will end class, any responsibilities your students may have, and how you will dismiss the students. You can find more information on this topic in Chapter Three, Task 4.

Consequences for Classroom Rule Violations

List the range of corrective consequences that you may assign if rules are violated. You can find more information on this topic in Chapter Five, Task 3.

Consequences for Code of Conduct Violations

Inform students that you must follow through with disciplinary referrals for violations of schoolwide rules including dress code, unexcused absences, threats, and so forth. Make sure to get this information from your principal or assistant principal.

Exhibit 7.2

Class Syllabus for a Ninth-Grade Remedial Reading Skills Class

Welcome to Expanding Academic Opportunities
Teacher: Mrs. Hernandez

By the end of this class, you will be able to:

- Read long multisyllable words.

- Understand what you read.

- Use strategies to analyze what you read such as:

   Paraphrasing

   Visual imagery

   Self-questioning

- Learn to use new vocabulary words.

- Read aloud smoothly and with expression.

- Write complete sentences and well-organized paragraphs.
- Take reading tests with confidence, and perform well on those tests.

Accomplishing this will require cooperation.

Think of this class like a sport such as basketball or track. You will have to work hard independently, but you will also have to work effectively with other students and with me.

Guidelines for Success

Winners make their own luck. They achieve.

It takes:

Preparation

Responsibility

Integrity

Dedication

Effort

to be successful!

Classroom Rules:

Winners know the rules and follow them:

1. Come to class every day that you are not sick.

2. Arrive on time with your own pencil and paper.

3. Keep hands, feet, and objects to yourself.

4. Follow directions the *first* time.

5. Stay on task during all work times.

Activities:

Winners participate and strive to ACHIEVE. The ACHIEVE approach will teach you exactly what you have to do in each type of classroom activity. For now, just be aware that each activity below will include very specific information for you about how to be successful in this class.

Large Group Activities

- Teacher-directed instruction.

Station Activities

- Partner fluency practice
- Mastery checks with teacher (Parents: Mastery checks involve each student reading to me so I can monitor progress. They will occur about every two weeks.)
- Partner vocabulary practice
- Computer practice
- Independent practice: Writing activities

Notice the word *practice*. These activities are practice for you to improve your skills, just like an athlete, dancer, or musician does.

Class Syllabus for a Ninth-Grade
Remedial Reading Skills Class (*continued*)

Grades:

Winners know that you have to keep score.

Your grades for each of the coming nine weeks will be based on the following:

1. 50 percent of your grade will come from your class participation and how well you follow the rules. There are 10 possible points per day, for a total of 450 points for the quarter.

   You will start each day with 8 points, which is 80 percent, or a low B.

   • Each compliment adds 1 point.

   • Each rule violation costs 1 point.

2. Your written work is worth a total of 30 percent.

3. Your performance on mastery checks is worth 20 percent.

Classroom Procedures

Entering the Classroom:

1. Be in the room before the bell rings.

2. Have your folder ready.

3. Begin work on the activity on the board or left on your desk.

4. Quietly work on this activity until I signal for your attention.

Tardy to Class:

If you are in the classroom before the bell rings, then you are on time. If you enter after the bell rings, then you are tardy and will lose 1 behavior point. In addition, all tardies are reported to the attendance office according to school policy.

Paper and Pencil:

If you do not have a pencil, I keep golf pencils and stubs available on my desk. Please return them when you are finished and donate pencils that you no longer intend to use. There is also extra notebook paper on my desk. Use it when you need to and replace it when you bring your own.

Daily Assignments:

Each of you will have a folder on the counter by the door. There will be a weekly assignment sheet in this folder every Monday. This sheet will outline the tasks you will work on during the week.

Turning In Assignments:

Turn in your completed work to the tray labeled "Period Two," which is on the counter by the door.

Returning Assignments:

Graded work will be returned to your folder.

Finding Out Grade Status in Class:
A grade printout will be placed in your folder every week. This will show your current grade in the class, any missing assignments, and a progress report showing your current reading level.

Your Responsibilities After an Absence:
Anytime you are absent, you will view a videotape of the large-group activities you missed. You will also need to complete independent practice and vocabulary assignments for the days you missed. You will have the same number of days to make up your work as the number of days you were absent. If you were absent on Monday and Tuesday, you will have to finish your makeup work and turn it in on Friday. *Always be in class if you are not seriously ill!*

Communication procedures with parents or guardians:
Show your weekly grade printout to a parent or guardian each week. You will get 3 bonus points for each week you return a weekly grade printout with a parent or guardian's signature.

Ending Class:
One minute before the end of class, I will ask you to return to your assigned seats for final announcements. You will be excused by rows, *after* the bell rings.

Consequences for Classroom Rule Violations
If you violate a rule, you may be assigned a consequence. Depending on the frequency and severity of the misbehavior, you may receive one or more of the following consequences:

- Loss of a behavior point
- Parental contact
- Change in seating assignment
- Time owed after class
- Detention
- Office referral

If you ever feel that the enforcing of rules and consequences is unfair, you have the right to make an appointment to discuss the situation. I will be as neutral as I can in hearing your complaints or comments.

Consequences for Code of Conduct Violations
If a student breaks a rule that is covered by the Code of Conduct in your student handbook (possession of illegal substances, abuse, etc.), I must refer the situation to the office for the administrator to make decisions on parental contacts, police involvement, and other matters. This is part of my job, and not my decision. If you violate a Code of Conduct rule, it will be handled out of class.

In addition to completing your classroom plan, give some thought to how you will communicate the plan to your students (Harlan, 2002). One easy way to accomplish this is to provide a comprehensive syllabus to students that they can keep in their notebook. Each day during the first week of school, teach some portion of the syllabus in detail. If you are concerned that this may be overwhelming to students, you might instead provide students a one-page overview on the first day of school and then one more page each day that follows for the first week. This way you will cover a small amount of information at a time, but still cover everything necessary before getting too far along in the class (Bell, 1998; Lovitt, 1978).

Task 2: Complete Your Preparations for the First Day

In this task, you will complete your unique preparations for the first day of school. This will include preparing a modified schedule for the first day, preparing a sign to help students find your room, preparing an activity for students to work on when they enter your room, and preparing an orientation handout for parents and guardians.

Develop a modified class schedule for the first day of school. In Chapter Three, Task 1, you developed a well-thought-out schedule for each of your classes. That schedule will need to be modified for the first day of school to ensure the inclusion of the unique tasks and activities that must occur on the first day. Your goal is to make it as close to a typical day as possible, while still including activities that will accomplish such important first-day functions as helping students feel comfortable; communicating your classroom goals, rules, guidelines, and expectations; communicating any schoolwide rules and expectations; and dealing with logistics such as distributing textbooks.

Before you create your first-day schedule, find out from your school administrator whether there will be any schoolwide activities such as assemblies or testing that you need to take into account. Be sure to schedule the first few minutes of the class period for going over your goals, classroom rules, Guidelines for Success, and other essential information from your syllabus. Other activities you may need to include are distribution of books, assignment of storage space, and otherwise getting your students settled in. Plan on allowing more regular time for each activity on the first day in order to acquaint students with how you do things. Chapter Three, Task 3 presents detailed information on how to introduce and communicate your expectations to students.

Exhibit 7.3 shows a sample first-day schedule as it might be posted on the board.

Exhibit 7.3
Sample First-Day Schedule

Ninth-Grade Science (Periods 1, 3, and 6)

10 minutes	Welcome, goals, and rules
10 minutes	Grading and homework
15 minutes	Activity to identify what you know about science (not graded!)
10 minutes	Tips on being successful in this class
5 minutes	Wrap-up and dismissal

Make a sign that identifies your room. Create an easy-to-read sign displaying your name, grade level, subject, and room number that you can place in the hall near your door to help students find your room. Be sure to put it in print large enough that students will be able to see the information from a distance; your students are likely to be self-conscious about looking as if they do not know what they are doing. A nice clear sign will keep them from having to go from door to door looking at room numbers or teacher names. Don't block the sign as you greet incoming students by the open door!

Prepare an initial activity for students to work on when they enter the room. Having an initial activity serves several important functions. First, it will give your students something to do while they wait for the bell to ring. This can reduce the self-consciousness that some students will feel if they don't have a friend in the class to talk to. Second, having an activity to work on will keep students who know each other from grouping together. Without an activity, students may become so engrossed in their own activities that when the bell rings, you will have to interrupt them and try to get them into their seats so that class can begin. Having students occupied with an activity gives you the added benefit of being able to focus on greeting all your students as they enter. Finally, this initial task communicates the expectation that when students are in your class, they will be actively engaged, not just free to do what they want (Paine, Radicchi, Rosellini, Deutchman, & Darch, 1983).

Choose any task that students can do independently—that is, with no assistance from you. Ideally it should be reasonably short and educational. Don't forget that students who enter the room first will have longer to work on the task than students who don't enter until just before the final bell. Exhibit 7.4 provides an example. Plan to have this or a similar activity on a sheet you can hand to students when they enter or visible on the board or overhead.

Prepare an orientation handout for parents and guardians. Your comprehensive syllabus may contain too much information for parents to review. You can pare it down onto a one-page handout that you ask students to share with their parents or guardian and have them sign and return it (see Exhibit 7.5). This could include your goals, the Guidelines for Success, grading information, and homework expectations. Also include information regarding how and when parents can contact you if they have questions, suggestions, or concerns. Be sure to let them know your preferred method, like e-mail, and a backup method, such as telephone during specific hours.

Although you are not likely to get all of these back, the fact that you make an effort to contact parents will be valued by families that are showing an active interest in their child's high school experience. To increase the likelihood that students will show this to a parent or guardian, you can offer bonus points for the form's return. For example, you could have something at the bottom of this page under where the parent signs that says, "Five bonus points if this signed form is returned by tomorrow, Tuesday, August 23; 4 points if returned by Wednesday, 3 points by Thursday, 2 points by Friday. One point will be given if this is returned at any time during the second week of school." This must also be clearly explained to the students so they are aware of their involvement in the process.

The procedures suggested in this task have been designed to completely organize the first class you spend with your students and help put your students at ease from the moment they arrive in your classroom. Implementing these procedures will help you head into your first day feeling confident, organized, and prepared to motivate your students toward responsible behavior.

Exhibit 7.4

Sample First-Day Worksheet

Welcome to Room 19, Mr. Jacobi's Science Class!

For my records, and to help you learn as much as possible from this class, please fill out this form while waiting for class to begin.

Name: _____

Name of Parent or Guardian: _____

Address: _____

Your Phone Number: _____

E-mail Address: _____

Please identify which type of classroom activity you think helps you learn most effectively:
Lecture [ ]   Hands-on Labs [ ]   Cooperative Groups [ ]   Independent Study [ ]

Explain why: _____

_____

_____

Identify two things for which you like to receive public praise and two things for which you would prefer to get feedback in a more private manner.

Public praise: _____

_____

More private feedback: _____

_____

Exhibit 7.5
Sample Letter to Parents

Dear Parents/Guardians,

Hi. My name is Mrs. Hernandez. I want to take this opportunity to introduce myself and to let you know that I am pleased and excited to have your child in my fourth-period Expanding Academic Opportunities class. I am providing the following information to you so you will know what my expectations are and how your child can be successful in my class. Please take the time to discuss the information here with your child. Although I am going over this information in class, discussing it with your child will be a meaningful way to increase understanding. If you have any questions or concerns, please feel free to contact me.

I believe that if we all work together, your child's success is certain!

The purpose of this class is to teach reading and writing skills that are needed for success in high school. My major goals are that by the end of the year, students will be able to:

- Read long multisyllable words.
- Understand what they read.
- Use strategies to analyze what they read such as:

    Paraphrasing

    Visual imagery

    Self-questioning

- Learn to use new vocabulary words.
- Read aloud smoothly and with expression.
- Write complete sentences and well-organized paragraphs.
- Take reading tests with confidence and perform well on those tests.

Classroom rules

These rules are designed to make sure that no student's behavior interferes with the learning of others. For violations of these rules, there will be minor penalties.

1. Come to class every day that you are not sick.
2. Arrive on time with your own pencil and paper.
3. Keep hands, feet, and objects to yourself.
4. Follow directions the *first* time.
5. Stay on task during all work times.

While I will enforce the rules when necessary, I will be putting more emphasis on teaching students how to be responsible for themselves. I will stress the following traits, which are called **Guidelines for Success.**

It takes: **P**reparation

Responsibility

Integrity

Dedication

Effort

to be successful!

Grading

Below is the information your student has been given about grades. Each Friday, I will provide each student with a weekly grade report that will show the current grade in the class as well as any missing assignments. Please check this on the weekend so that if the student is falling behind, we can all work on the problem in the early stages.

1. 50 percent of your grade will come from your class participation and how well you follow the rules.

   - There are 10 possible points per day, for a total of 450 points for the quarter.
   - You will start each day with 8 points, which is 80 percent, or a low B.
   - Each compliment adds 1 point.
   - Each rule violation costs 1 point.

2. Your written work is worth a total of 30 percent.

3. Your performance on mastery checks is worth 20 percent.

Contact Information

The students know that they can always ask me questions in class and can schedule an appointment to talk to me whenever they need help. If you want to contact me, my e-mail is Hernandez555@franklinHS.org. The best time to reach me by phone is during my preparation period (9:15 A.M. to 10:05 A.M.) or after school (3:15 P.M. to 4:15 P.M.) at 555–5555.

Thanks for your time. Please cut off the form below, sign it, and have your child sign that you have discussed this information. Have your child return the slip below for a few extra bonus points in the grade book.

Sincerely,

Mrs. Hernandez

We have discussed this information about how to be successful in Mrs. Hernandez's fourth-period class.

_____

Parent Signature

_____

Student Signature

_____

Date

Task 3: Implement Your Plan for the First Day of School

The first day of school is an important one for both you and your students. When it is managed well, students will leave your classroom thinking that you may expect a lot from them, but that you will be there for them while you push them. They should also leave with the feeling that your class will be exciting and fun, not intense or dreary. Your goal is to conduct each period on the first day of school in a manner that will make your students feel welcome and help them learn to behave responsibly from the beginning (Lewis & Sugai, 1999; Reddy, Rhodes, & Mulhall, 2003). The following strategies will help you succeed in doing just that.

Greet the students individually as they enter your room. Arrange to be near the door so you can greet each student as he or she enters. Ask the students their names and introduce yourself. Then instruct them to take their seats and start on the task you have prepared, like filling out the information form you hand them as they enter. Continue greeting other entering students. By the time the bell rings, all students should be in their seats and quietly working on the task. Being at the doorway sets an invitational tone and allows you to supervise the students in your room while also assisting in the supervision of hallway behavior.

Get students' attention as soon as the bell rings. Use your attention signal (raise your hand and say, "Class, your attention please"—see Chapter Three, Task 3) to get students to turn their focus to you. Although students will not yet know your signal, it is likely to be effective because students will be working quietly at their seats. If students look at you, thank them for their attention, and explain that whether or not they have completed their task, they should put their pencils down and turn their attention to you. If students fail to give you their attention, repeat the signal and wait with your hand up until everyone is quiet and looking at you. Even if this takes several minutes, which it should not, simply maintain the visual aspect of the signal and wait quietly. Resist the urge to shout at the students to get their attention. If you start shouting for your students' attention at the beginning of the year, having set that as a threshold you are likely to have to shout at them from then on.

Communicate the essentials in the first ten minutes. Once you have the full attention of all students, introduce yourself again and tell them one or two personal or interesting things about yourself, without going into great detail. Then describe your long-range goals for the year, both academically and behaviorally—for example:

> Thank you for giving me your attention. Please put your pencils down for now; you will be able to complete the form later in the period. My name is Mr. Younce [you may want to write your name on the board], and I will be your English teacher this year. Over the year we will get to know each other better, but for now I'll just tell you a couple of things about myself. I have two children of my own. They are both older than you: my daughter is twenty and my son is eighteen. My hobby is bicycling, and I have cycled as much as a hundred miles in a day. I look forward to getting to know you all this year.

Next, hand out your syllabus and explain to your students that this is a guide for how to succeed in this class. Let students know that you will be covering all this information in the next few days. Explain your major goals, your Guidelines for Success, and the classroom rules.

As you share this information, involve your students—for example: "Raise your hand if you have an idea about why I have a rule that says 'Stay on task'—regardless of the type of activity."

At the conclusion of this first ten minutes, students should have a preliminary sense of who you are, what will be expected of them, and what they will learn in your class. Do not spend more than ten minutes on this orientation. If you talk too much or provide too many details, many students will get overwhelmed or tune you out.

Teach your attention signal. Demonstrate the signal you used earlier to get your students' attention and tell them why the signal will be important:

> I appreciate how well all of you are keeping your attention on me while I'm speaking. During class when you are working at your seats, or in groups, or at one of the lab stations, there will be times when I need you to stop what you are doing and give me your attention. At those times, I will say, "Class, your attention please," while I am making this big circular motion with my arm. Then I will hold my hand in the air. When you hear me say those words or see me make that motion, stop whatever you are doing, stop talking, look at me, and raise your own hand. Raising your hand will help get the attention of other students who might not have seen or heard my signal. Stopping immediately when I give the signal is very important. There will be many times when we will all need to start an activity together. This way, even if each person is doing something different—working at their seats, at the lab stations, or at computers—I can give the signal and everyone will be quiet and paying attention within five seconds. Then we can begin the next activity, and no individuals or small groups will be wasting class time. I'm going to show you my signal one more time and do it for five seconds. This is how quickly I expect the whole class to be quiet and looking at me.

Then demonstrate the attention signal while counting five seconds.

Orient students to the posted first-day schedule and begin using the three-step process for communicating your expectations. Start by giving students a clear idea of what the class period is going to be like. Then for each activity throughout the class, use the three-step process for communicating expectations. This cycle, which was introduced in Chapter Four, is summarized in Figure 7.1 and then explained.

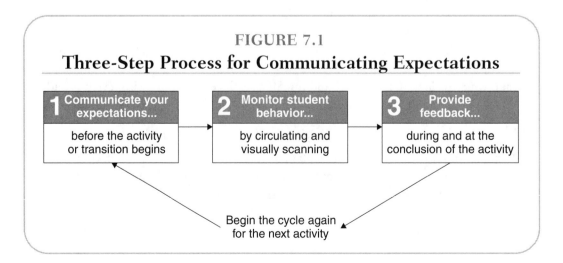

FIGURE 7.1

Three-Step Process for Communicating Expectations

1 Communicate your expectations...	**2** Monitor student behavior...	**3** Provide feedback...
before the activity or transition begins	by circulating and visually scanning	during and at the conclusion of the activity

Begin the cycle again for the next activity

Step 1: Communicate Your Expectations

The first step in this process is to teach students what your expectations are. Just before students engage in any activity or transition, you will use the lessons you developed (see Chapter Four, Task 3) to prepare students for what you expect during that activity or transition. It's important to note that you will teach your expectations for each particular activity or transition immediately before it occurs. You do *not* want to teach the expectations for more than one activity at a time (Brophy & Good, 1986; Sponder, 1993).

Be prepared to spend as much time as necessary at the beginning of an activity to ensure that students understand what is expected of them. If the lesson you have prepared (see Chapter Four) involves modeling or practicing a behavior, you will need to allow more time than if you are simply going to describe your expectations. For example, if you have scheduled a fifteen-minute teacher-directed instructional period, it is possible that on the first day, you may have to spend three to seven of those fifteen minutes explaining and modeling your expectations. In other words, be prepared to spend anywhere from 20 to 50 percent of the time scheduled for a given activity on teaching your expectations for that activity during the first days of class. Some teachers may feel that they do not have time to do this because there is so much content to cover; however, time spent teaching expectations early is time you will save in later weeks reviewing this information over and over.

Step 2: Monitor Student Behavior

The only way to track how well students are meeting your behavioral expectations is for you to monitor their behavior in some way (Deno, Espin, & Fuchs, 2002; Ysseldyke & Christenson, 1987). This is the second of the steps for effectively communicating your expectations. Two of the most useful and efficient ways to monitor student behavior during an activity or transition are to circulate among students and scan all parts of the classroom. These two basic but essential strategies will allow you to know exactly what is going on at all times. You can then use this information to help make sound decisions about the type and frequency of feedback you should provide students concerning their behavior. Circulating has another benefit. Your physical presence will reduce student misbehavior. It's human nature: your proximity makes the likelihood of getting away with something much lower, which in turn makes misbehaving much less attractive. The following provides more detail on circulating and scanning.

Circulating. Whenever you circulate through the classroom, do so in unpredictable patterns. Do not spend the majority of your time in any one part of the room, and do not move in patterns. If you do, your students will learn how long they have to misbehave before your attention turns to them. This is especially important during independent work periods and small group activities. Your proximity will communicate your interest in the students. It will also make clear that if someone chooses to engage in something other than the expected behaviors, you will be there to notice it. Obviously there are times (such as when you are teaching a small group or presenting to the class using an overhead) when circulating will be difficult. However, whenever possible, you should be moving about the room.

Visual Scanning. Regardless of what you and the students are doing, you should frequently visually scan the classroom. When you are circulating, don't look only at the students nearest to you, but visually sweep any place students are in the room. When you are conducting a classwide activity, visually scan the back rows and the front corners—those areas you are less likely to notice—just as you would regularly check your mirrors and "blind spot" while driving. When you are helping an individual student with work, periodically put your head up and look around the room. When you are working with a small group, look up from the group occasionally to find out what is going on with the rest of the class. This may seem obvious, but it is easy to become engrossed and forget to continue monitoring the rest of your class.

As you scan, look for any misbehavior that may require correction. If a student is engaged in misbehavior, go to the student and issue a gentle reprimand or assign an appropriate consequence. Also look for opportunities to acknowledge and encourage responsible behavior. If, as you scan, you notice that a student who often tends to be off-task is working hard, go to that student at the next opportunity and give him or her appropriate positive feedback. If a cooperative group is handling a conflict in a responsible way, go over to the group when there is a pause and congratulate them on the maturity with which they are handling themselves.

During independent work periods, you should also be looking for students who have signaled to you that they need assistance. If you ask students to use an open book signal for help (see Chapter Three, Task 5), you must show students that the signal will get your attention. If students find that you don't respond when they signal, they will stop using the signal and find less desirable ways to get your attention instead.

Monitoring techniques are a vital adjunct to communicating your expectations and are critical tools regardless of the type of classroom structure your students may need (Burnette, 1999). You must know what is going on in your classroom. A classroom that needs high structure, however, will require monitoring at all times, leading to the oft-heard line, "This class is so tough, you can't take your eyes off them for a second." Teachers with experience in highly structured classrooms understand that constant monitoring is essential.

Step 3: Give Students Feedback on Their Implementation of Expectations

The third step in the process of effectively communicating your behavioral expectations is giving students, both individually and as a class, clear information about the degree to which they behaved as expected for a particular activity or transition. Provide positive feedback when students are meeting expectations and corrective feedback (calmly, immediately, and consistently) when they are not. Positive feedback serves two vitally important functions: it gives students specific information about what they are doing correctly, and it gives them adult attention when they are behaving responsibly. Corrective feedback also serves two vitally important functions: it lets students know that you are monitoring their behavior, and it communicates that you are serious and consistent about your expectations for student behavior (Colvin & Sugai, 1988; Rosenshine & Stevens, 1986).

As you monitor students during an activity or transition, notice examples of students meeting your expectations and examples of students not meeting your expectations. Both represent opportunities for you to continue to teach students how to meet your behavioral expectations by giving them positive and corrective feedback.

Positive Feedback.   Here are a few quick tips on providing effective positive feedback. (More detailed information is outlined in Chapter Six.)

• *Give feedback that is accurate.* Do not provide positive feedback unless the individual or class has actually exhibited responsible behavior. When you tell a student that he has been responsible when he has not, you ruin your credibility and lead students to think, justifiably, that your positive feedback means nothing.

• *Give feedback that is specific and descriptive.* Tell the student or group exactly what they are doing that is responsible and important: "Alex, Maria, Travis, you are keeping your attention focused on your work. That is a very important part of being successful in this class." Avoid rote phrases like, "Good job," "Nice job," or "Well done."

• *Give feedback that is contingent.* Positive feedback provides useful information on important behaviors. Inform students how the positive behaviors they are demonstrating will contribute to their success and the success of the class. Also, praise students for demonstrating behaviors that are new or difficult: "Tanika, your comments in class today were insightful and contributed to the quality of class discussions. Thanks."

• *Give positive feedback immediately.* Immediacy is important because students need to know when they are doing something correctly. In addition, not getting any attention for meeting expectations will lead students who are starved for attention to demand attention through misbehavior. Positive feedback is most effective when it occurs immediately after the behavior you are trying to encourage.

• *Give positive feedback in a manner that fits your style.* The specific manner in which you give positive feedback does not matter. What is important is that you are specific and sincere. If you have a bubbly, happy personality, your positive feedback should be true to that form. If you are a more serious person, your positive feedback should be given in a more serious manner.

Corrective Feedback. When students exhibit behavior that does not meet your expectations for that activity, you *must* correct the inappropriate behavior. To give the most effective correction, consider each instance of not meeting expectations as an instructional opportunity. Consider a student's behavioral errors to be similar to errors he or she might make in math. Most math errors are a function of students' not fully understanding a particular concept or all the steps in a particular process. Effectively correcting those errors involves reteaching the concept or steps. If students fail to meet your behavioral expectations, you should first determine whether they understood what the expectations were or if they did not know how to meet them. If the answer to either of those questions is yes, then you will need to reteach what your expectations are and how your students can meet them. If the answer is no, then you need to provide corrective feedback.

Here are a few tips on providing effective corrective feedback. (More detailed information on using corrective feedback is provided in Chapter Five.)

• *Correct the misbehavior immediately.* When students are not meeting behavioral expectations, let them know *then*. Do not ignore it, and do not wait until the end of an activity. Ignoring can be an effective strategy for responding to chronic misbehavior that is designed to elicit attention. But when you are trying to establish your expectations at the beginning of the year, students may interpret ignoring as your not being really serious about your expectations.

• *Correct the misbehavior calmly.* Correcting misbehavior calmly shows students not only that you are serious and have high expectations, but that you are also completely in control and will not be rattled by their misbehavior. Emotional corrections are more likely to give power to the misbehavior and put you in a position of appearing controllable. Students may think that they can upset you with a certain behavior.

• *Correct misbehavior consistently.* For the first several days of instruction, correct most misbehavior with mild verbal reprimands that focus on the behavior, not the person. Simply restate what the students should be doing at the time. Always be direct. Saying something like "Tina and Adam, you should be working quietly on your lab notebooks at this time" is much more appropriate and effective than "Tina and Adam, you are so immature. I should not have to remind you that this is a work period, not a time to socialize."

• *Follow through.* When it becomes necessary to use a corrective consequence, it is imperative that you demonstrate that you will issue the appropriate consequence. If your students know that you will threaten consequences without actually issuing them, they will start to abuse the system.

Providing Feedback at the End of an Activity.   Early in the year, you should plan on ending each activity or transition by giving students feedback on how well they met your CHAMPs or ACHIEVE expectations as a class. When an activity or transition is finished and before the next activity begins, let the group know whether things went well and they behaved as expected, or whether they need to improve their behavior the next time that particular activity or transition occurs. When an activity goes perfectly, you have a wonderful opportunity to reinforce the class and begin establishing a sense of group pride: "Class, the way this work period went is exactly the way a lab activity of this type should go. Everyone followed safe lab procedures. Conversations at the lab stations were quiet, and all the conversations that I heard were focused on the lab activity. This is going to be a great class!"

If an activity does not go well, describe the specific behaviors that need to be different without pointing out individuals, and set a goal for the next time you have that activity: "Class, during the teacher-directed portion of the math lesson that we have just completed, there were several times that I had to remind people that if they had something to say, they need to raise their hand. Please remember that whenever anyone is presenting to the class, whether it is me or another student, there should be no side conversations. Tomorrow, I want you to remember: no side conversations and keep your attention focused entirely on whoever is speaking."

Avoid statements such as "Almost everyone remembered the expectation about talking only if you raise your hand and are called on." A statement of this type is *not* positive feedback; it only serves to get students wondering who did not meet the expectations.

Conclude the class period by orienting students to your end-of-class procedures (see Chapter Three, Task 4). Because this is the first day of school, allow plenty of time to end class. Review the materials your students need to bring the next day, and make sure they have any and all important papers to take home, such as the parent or guardian orientation letter. You want to create a sense of closure so that students will leave your classroom feeling comfortable, eager to return, and with the sense that you are interested in all of them.

The strategies presented in this task will help you get your first day of school off to the best start. Remember that the information you present and the atmosphere you establish on this day will yield valuable dividends throughout the school year.

In Conclusion

Careful planning can lead to a positive first day of class, which will set the stage for a productive year. In this chapter, you were shown how to pull everything together by developing a syllabus for your students that you can use to teach your organizational routines and procedures. A template was provided to assist you in this effort. The remainder of the chapter examined final details to consider before the first day and provided information on how to implement an effective and positive first day of school. Each of these steps will bring you closer to having a prepared, contained, and successful class.

Preparation and Launch Self-Assessment Checklist

Use this worksheet to identify which parts of the tasks described in this chapter you have completed. For any item that has not been completed, note what needs to be done to complete it. Then transfer your notes to your planning calendar in the form of specific actions you need to take (for example, "September 5, make a sign for the classroom").

Task	Notes and Implementation Ideas
Finalize your classroom management plan, and prepare to communicate that plan to your students.	
I reviewed and completed the essential tasks from Chapters One through Six. That is, I have . . .	
1. Developed and posted Guidelines for Success (Chapter One, Task 5)	
2. Created positive expectations for all students (Chapter One, Task 3)	
3. Reviewed the basic principles of behavior management (Chapter One, Task 1)	
4. Determined the level of structure for my class (Chapter One, Task 6)	
5. Outlined the activities students will engage in during a typical week (Chapter Four, Task 1)	
6. Decided on what basis I will give grades (Chapter Two, Tasks 2–4)	
7. Developed classroom procedures (Chapter Three, Tasks 3–5)	
8. Developed a regular daily schedule (Chapter Three, Task 1)	
9. Arranged the physical space in the classroom (Chapter Three, Task 2)	
10. Identified an attention signal (Chapter Three, Task 3)	
11. Developed beginning and ending routines (Chapter Three, Task 4)	
12. Identified and posted classroom rules (Chapter Five, Task 1)	
13. Defined and prepared lessons on behavioral expectations (Chapter Four, Tasks 1–3)	
I have decided how I will communicate my classroom plan to my students (for example, comprehensive syllabus).	

Preparation and Launch Self-Assessment Checklist (*continued*)

☐

Final preparations for the first day.

I understand that having my first day planned will help me spend more time with my students and put them at ease, and help me feel confident, organized, and prepared to motivate my students toward responsible behavior. Toward this end, I have:

- Developed a modified class schedule for the first day of school;
- Made a sign that identifies my classroom;
- Prepared an initial activity for students to work on when they enter the room; and
- Prepared an orientation handout for parents and guardians.

☐

Implementing your plan for the first day of school.

I understand that effective implementation of my plan for the first day of school will make my students feel welcome and help them learn to behave responsibly from the beginning. The following strategies will help me do that:

- Greeting students individually as they enter the room
- Getting students' attention as soon as the bell rings
- Communicating essential classroom information in the first ten minutes of the day (class)
- Teaching my attention signal
- Orienting students to the posted first-day schedule and using the three-step process for communicating my expectations
- Concluding the class period by orienting students to my end-of-class procedures

Preparation and Launch Peer Study Worksheet

With one or more of your colleagues, work through the following discussion topics and activities related to the tasks in Chapter Seven. If necessary, refer back to the text to get additional ideas or for clarification. (See the Vision Peer Study Worksheet in Chapter One for suggestions on structuring effective discussion sessions.)

Task 1: Finalize Your Classroom Management Plan, and Prepare to Communicate That Plan to Your Students

A. Have each group member bring in a completed syllabus. Discuss what parts of the syllabus template each group member included in his or her syllabus, which sections were omitted, and which sections were added that did not appear in the template. Discuss the rationale for those decisions.

B. Have each group member identify if there are any parts of the syllabus or their classroom procedures with which he or she is dissatisfied. If so, find out if other group members have suggestions. For example, if one member is not satisfied with her procedures for dealing with late work, other members could share their procedures and their summary of these procedures in their syllabi.

Task 2: Complete Your Preparations for the First Day

A. **Only if you have time,** have group members share what they have done in terms of final preparations for the first day of school. Specifically, individual members may want to share ideas for an initial activity that students can work on when they arrive and how they might deal with it if a student refused to work on the task.

Task 3: Implement Your Plan for the First Day of School

A. **Only if you have time,** have group members share their ideas and plans for displaying their first-day schedule, greeting students as they arrive, getting students' attention when the bell rings, communicating essential information in the first ten minutes, and teaching their attention signal.

B. Have group members discuss how they will begin to use the three-step process (of teaching, monitoring behavior, and giving feedback) to communicate behavioral expectations.

Chapter Eight

Implementation

Monitor and adjust your plan throughout the year

Through designing your management plan and implementing it on the first day of school, you have the potential for a wonderful classroom environment. This chapter offers suggestions on how you can adjust your plan throughout the year to maximize student responsibility, independence, and motivation. This process of monitoring and adjusting should begin on the second day of school and continue through the entire year (Nelson, 1996; Skinner & Belmont, 1993). The first month of school is critical. If you do not get your students onboard with your program and behaving responsibly from the start, it can be very trying to change negative behavior patterns later—but not impossible! From the second day forward, the most important adjustments will involve weighing how much class time is being spent teaching expectations and procedures as opposed to content (Marzano, 2003). This chapter offers ways to objectively monitor behavior, so you can better determine where adjustments to your plan are necessary.

During the first week, continue to use the three-step plan of communicating your expectations, monitoring student behavior, and providing feedback to the class. As the class demonstrates mastery, you may gradually use the cycle less frequently, providing more time for teaching the content of lessons.

Having a good plan is a means, not an end. You must be flexible enough to change that plan if necessary, analyzing your students' behavior to see what is working for them and what is not (Royer, Cisero, & Carlo, 1993). This chapter will prepare you to do that. You will periodically review your management plan, see the effects it is having on your students, and analyze it to determine if anything needs to be changed.

Immediately following the tasks in this chapter is a Self-Assessment Checklist, designed to help you determine which tasks you have done and which you will still need to do. The chapter ends with a Peer Study Worksheet.

The chapter has three tasks:

Task 1: Gradually decrease the amount of time spent teaching expectations, procedures, and routines.

Task 2: Mark on your planning calendar particular times that you will reteach your expectations.

Task 3: Collect objective data about classroom behavior, and adjust your management plan accordingly.

Task 1: Gradually Decrease the Amount of Time Spent Teaching Expectations, Procedures, and Routines

No matter how carefully you communicate your expectations on the first day, few students will know exactly how they are supposed to behave after just one day. Therefore, continue to implement the three-step process introduced in Chapter Four and reviewed in the previous chapter until students demonstrate they consistently meet your expectations. (See Figure 8.1 to review this cycle.)

Your students will internalize your expectations if you continue to use the three-step communication process for a couple of weeks. You should begin every activity with a brief lesson on the expectations, continue to monitor student performance, and provide feedback to both individual students and the whole class. Remember that your students will be hearing expectations from several other teachers, and they may get tired of hearing them. They may also get confused about details from teacher to teacher, as one may let them talk during independent work and others may not. Be sure to vary the format of your lessons so as to avoid student boredom (Fisher et al., 1980).

As the first month of school progresses, the lessons should become increasingly brief and focus mainly on any specific expectations that are not being met. When students seem to fully understand and remember expectations for an activity or transition, you can start to phase the lessons out (Meece, Blumenfield, & Hoyle, 1988). You might start introducing the activity or transition by letting students know that because they have been responsible you will

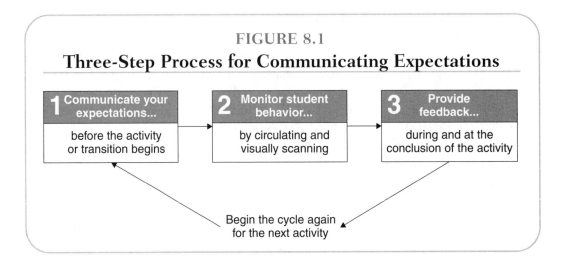

FIGURE 8.1

Three-Step Process for Communicating Expectations

1 Communicate your expectations...	**2** Monitor student behavior...	**3** Provide feedback...
before the activity or transition begins	by circulating and visually scanning	during and at the conclusion of the activity

Begin the cycle again for the next activity

not review your expectations: "Class, we are now going to have a twenty-minute work period for you to get going on the math assignment. Since we've done so well with this kind of work before, I don't think we need to review the expectations today. Please begin work on the assignment on the board."

Another option to consider is alternating lesson plans by teaching different expectations on different days. During a math lesson on Monday, you might present expectation lessons for the teacher-directed and cooperative group portions of class, and on Tuesday you might cover independent work and cooperative groups but not teacher-directed activities. If you rotate expectations in this manner, you will cover them all regularly without having to repeat yourself every day. Whenever a particular activity or transition has not gone as smoothly as you would like, plan to use the three-step process the next day to reassert your expectations. If the number of students who have not been meeting your expectations is more than five, plan on reteaching your expectations to the entire class from the beginning. Do *not* review them, but cover every step of your expectations again as if your class had never heard your class plans before. If only one or two students are having problems, use the three-step process with them as individuals. Figure 8.2 shows some slides from a PowerPoint Presentation created by Stanford Lewis, a teacher at Hillcrest High School in Dallas, Texas, for his high school band class. He presents a forty-slide presentation, "Discipline: A Management Guide," to his students on the first day of school and has them write down all the information from the slides. Because the information is presented in short bites, he can easily pull out a slide to go over expectations that need to be retaught.

By gradually reducing the length and frequency of your expectation lessons, you start spending more time instructing students. Before you stop, however, you should verify that your students fully understand your expectations (Covington, 2000). Evaluating this is covered at the end of this task. The second step in the communication cycle for expectations, monitoring student performance, must be maintained. As stated in Chapter One, if a class requires only a low-structure management plan, you can get by with less direct monitoring, but some level of monitoring is essential for classes of every structure throughout the year.

During the first several days of instruction, plan on giving students frequent feedback on how they are meeting expectations. This is the third step in communicating your expectations and might almost be an ongoing monologue during the activity. With classes needing low structure, you can begin to reduce the amount of positive feedback you give as soon as any activity has gone well for several consecutive days. The corrective feedback can be reduced to simply stating the name of a student who is not meeting your expectations. If two students are talking when they should be listening, you may be able to simply say the names of the two students, making brief eye contact, and then continue with your lesson. If you have a class with higher structure, plan to keep the frequency of positive feedback and the descriptive clarity of corrective feedback at a higher level for as long as the first month of school.

Verifying that your students understand what is expected from them. During the second or third week of school, you will need to determine whether your students really understand what you want from them (Assor & Connell, 1992). What you find will help you decide whether to continue actively teaching your expectations or begin tapering them off because students have mastered them. If you find that most of your students are able to accurately answer specific and detailed questions about your expectations (verbally or on paper), then you can begin to phase out the process. However, if you learn that a significant percentage cannot answer your questions, continue to conduct lessons on your expectations.

Making the effort to determine your students' understanding of your expectations by giving a quiz or conducting interviews will do more than provide you with information on

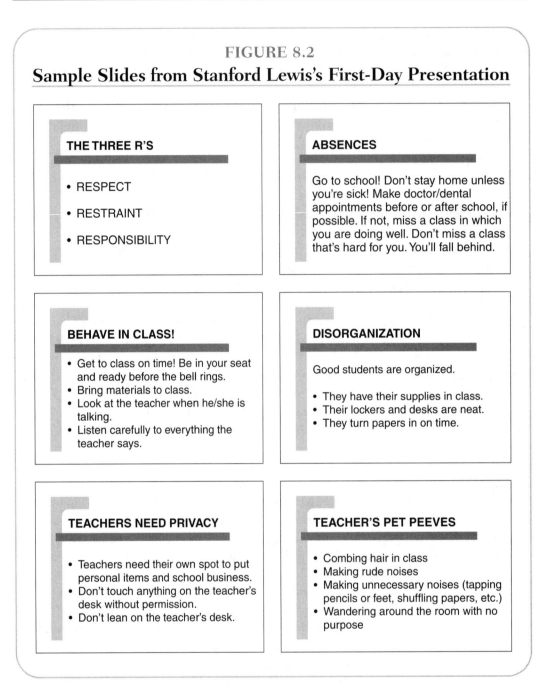

FIGURE 8.2

Sample Slides from Stanford Lewis's First-Day Presentation

THE THREE R'S

- RESPECT
- RESTRAINT
- RESPONSIBILITY

ABSENCES

Go to school! Don't stay home unless you're sick! Make doctor/dental appointments before or after school, if possible. If not, miss a class in which you are doing well. Don't miss a class that's hard for you. You'll fall behind.

BEHAVE IN CLASS!

- Get to class on time! Be in your seat and ready before the bell rings.
- Bring materials to class.
- Look at the teacher when he/she is talking.
- Listen carefully to everything the teacher says.

DISORGANIZATION

Good students are organized.

- They have their supplies in class.
- Their lockers and desks are neat.
- They turn papers in on time.

TEACHERS NEED PRIVACY

- Teachers need their own spot to put personal items and school business.
- Don't touch anything on the teacher's desk without permission.
- Don't lean on the teacher's desk.

TEACHER'S PET PEEVES

- Combing hair in class
- Making rude noises
- Making unnecessary noises (tapping pencils or feet, shuffling papers, etc.)
- Wandering around the room with no purpose

whether they fully understand your expectations. By being willing to take the time to do one or both of these, you further communicate to students the importance you place on them and their knowledge. The easiest and most reliable way to determine whether students understand your expectations is by giving a short written quiz. Later in this task is a sample of a quiz. If this seems too structured for your class, talk to your students to determine what they have retained from your lessons. The disadvantage to this is that unless you interview all of your students, you may fail to spot those who still do not know exactly what you expect. Unless you are able to interview all your students individually, consider the quiz instead.

Giving a quiz. A written quiz is a simple way to see how much information on your expectations your students are retaining. A major advantage of the quiz, as opposed to interviewing your students, is the relative speed with which you can see how well you are communicating your expectations. A disadvantage is that you are sampling knowledge of only some of your classroom procedures and routines.

Follow these directions for giving a quiz on expectations:

1. *Decide on a format for the quiz.* You can choose from true or false, multiple choice, fill in the blank, short answer, or any combination of formats you like. If you want to hear students' feelings and perceptions of your expectations, you will clearly learn more from a short answer quiz. If you are interested only in finding out whether students recall procedures as you taught them, then one of the simpler formats would work just fine.

2. *Determine the specific content you want to investigate.* Choose one or two activities and one or two transitions to be the focus of your quiz, targeting those for which you have the most complex expectations or that seem to be giving students the most difficulty. The questions on your quiz should deal with whether students can talk during an activity and what kind of movement is allowed, if any. Keep the quiz short enough that your students can complete it in ten minutes. In addition, you can quiz students on any of the policies and procedures from the syllabus you think are particularly important to review.

3. *Prepare your students to take the quiz.* Announce a few days in advance that you will be giving a quiz to help you identify whether the class understands your expectations, and explain why the material is important. Decide whether to grade the quiz, and then make that clear to your students. If it is to be graded, let students know that they cannot succeed academically without knowing how to function responsibly. If the quiz will not be graded, explain to your students that you still expect their best, and that if they do well on the quiz, they will likely be given more responsibility in the future. If you will be covering information from the syllabus, show students the portions they should study, and set aside some class time before the quiz for any questions your students may have. Exhibit 8.1 is a sample quiz on expectations.

If you find a significant number of errors on the quiz, continue the three-step process of teaching expectations, monitoring behavior, and providing positive and corrective feedback. If your procedures and expectations are understood, then you can begin to eliminate the teaching of expectations. Always remember to keep monitoring, however, by circulating and scanning, to keep students aware that you are observing their behavior.

Teaching expectations to new students. The first two weeks of school are the most important time for teaching behavioral expectations and classroom routines. However, most teachers will experience some degree of flux in student population over the course of the year. You are likely to have at least one student leave and at least one new student enter your class. Some schools have such high student mobility rates that fewer than half the students who are in a class at the beginning of the year are still there at the end.

When a new student enters your classroom, some form of orientation, similar to what you provide for all students during the first two weeks of school, is essential to get the student off to a successful start. You must have a plan for this. The higher you expect your student mobility rate to be, the more prepared you will need to be to teach your expectations to new students. There are three basic strategies for teaching your expectations to new students.

Teach the new student individually. The most common method of orienting a new student to your class is to spend some time with the student one on one, teaching her your expectations. To do this, you should speak with the student for a couple of minutes at the beginning of every activity and transition for several days, up to a week. While your other students do what is expected of them, tell the new student what is happening and explain your behavioral expectations for that activity or transition. If you have used CHAMPs or ACHIEVE sheets to

Exhibit 8.1
Sample Quiz on Expectations

Name _____   **Date** _____

Circle the letter for the best answer to each question.

1. When you enter the classroom and begin working on the challenge problem . . .

    a. you should be completely silent from the moment you enter the room.

    b. you can talk quietly as you enter, but must be silent when you take your seat.

    c. you can talk quietly about anything, but when the bell rings, you should be in your seat and then you can talk only about the challenge problem on the overhead projector.

    d. you can talk loudly about anything, but when the bell rings, you should get to your seat within two minutes and then get quiet.

2. During class, you can use the pencil sharpener . . .

    a. only before and after class.

    b. before and after class and during independent work periods.

    c. any time you need to.

    d. at no time without teacher permission.

3. When the teacher gives the attention signal and says, "Class, your attention please," you should . . .

    a. be silent and have your eyes on the teacher within five seconds.

    b. be silent and have your eyes on the teacher within ten seconds.

    c. be silent and have your eyes on the teacher within twenty seconds.

    d. loudly tell other students to be quiet and pay attention to the teacher.

4. During the time the teacher is speaking to the class, you may . . .

    a. talk quietly to someone near you and get out of your seat only to sharpen your pencil.

    b. talk quietly to someone near you and not get out of your seat for any reason.

    c. talk only if you have been called on by the teacher and get out of your seat only if you need a drink of water or supplies.

    d. talk only if you have been called on by the teacher. You may not get out of your seat without permission.

5. Active participation while the teacher is presenting lessons should look and sound a certain way. Circle any of the items that describe active participation. There are six correct answers.

    a. Sit up straight or lean forward.

    b. Raise your hand if you have something to say.

c. Answer questions when called on.

d. Write notes to your friends.

e. Write notes to keep in your binder that will help you study for tests.

f. Tell people who are talking that they need to be quiet and listen.

g. Have toys and things on your desk that will help entertain you during the lesson.

h. Keep your eyes on the person speaking or on the class notes you are writing.

i. Let your mind wander.

j. Talk while the teacher is talking.

k. Be respectful toward the teacher and other students in what you say and how you act.

l. Call out answers to questions.

m. Be vocal with your opinion.

n. Actively discuss the lesson.

6. When you return after an absence, you should . . .

a. ask the teacher, "Did I miss anything while I was gone?"

b. ask another student for his or her notes.

c. go to the file by the drinking fountain and find the folder for this class period and take the copied pages for the days you were absent.

d. go to the teacher's desk and open her plan book to the dates you missed, and copy all the important information.

7. In the parentheses after each of the following statements, put a **T** if the concept is true and an **F** if the concept is false about the weekly points you earn for behavior and effort.

a. Every student starts the week with 10 out of 20 possible points. (   )

b. Every reminder the teacher gives you about your behavior or effort in class costs 1 point. (   )

c. Every compliment the teacher gives you about your behavior or effort in class adds 1 point. (   )

d. These points are added into the grade book and are part of your academic grade. (   )

e. The teacher will take points away, without informing you about each incident. (   )

f. For severe misbehavior, you can have a choice between an office referral or a loss of points. (   )

g. You can make an appointment to discuss anything you do not understand or think is unfair about this system. (   )

prepare your expectations, you might give the student a copy. At the conclusion of the activity, let the student know how she did and orient her to the next transition and activity.

The advantage of this approach is that it generates frequent contact between you and the new student during her first week in class. The disadvantage is that it requires a great deal of your time, and your focus will be drawn away from your whole class at times. If you are likely to get between one and three new students during the year, pairing this approach with the next step of reteaching the entire class is probably the most effective. However, if you are likely to have many new students during the year, it will be impractical for you to take that much time with each new student.

Reteach the entire class. You can use the need to orient a new student as an opportunity to go over the CHAMPs expectations for all activities and transitions with the entire class. For one day, immediately before each activity and each major transition, ask students to volunteer some information about procedures and expected behaviors aloud for the benefit of the new student—for example, "Please raise your hand if you can tell Sandra one of the important expectations for independent work periods during math class." Call on students until all the important information has been reviewed. If students leave out something critical, review it in detail.

You should take only one day to review all expectations, but expect to spend a bit of time on this material in the next few days until your new student is as comfortable with your expectations as the rest of the class. Offer points to students who go out of their way to help the new student with notes, advice, or help during class if it is clear the new person does not know what is expected of him or her. This procedure has several advantages. The new student gets the essential information, and the information is reviewed and reinforced for the other students. Having students present the information communicates that the expectations are shared by the class, and not just the teacher. Finally, taking a couple of minutes to do this before each activity or transition makes a statement that you believe that student knowledge of the right way to do things is important enough to take the time to go over it.

The main disadvantage of this system is that if you have to do it more than once or twice, it will take time away from your class, and students may get weary of discussing the same expectations over and over. Therefore, if you get a new student soon after you've reviewed your expectations for another new student, use one of the other two methods.

The student mentor system. With this procedure, you will give individual class members the responsibility of orienting new students to the routines and procedures of your class—for example, "Paul, this is Rico. Rico is a student who really gets the procedures that will help him to be successful in this class. Rico will teach you what a class day will be like and tell you what is expected for each activity. Throughout the class period, you two have permission to quietly talk, even during times when you usually wouldn't be allowed to. Paul, if you have a question about how we do things, you can quietly ask Rico or me. Rico, any time during the next week that something is going on that may be new to Paul, please quietly explain to him what we are doing and why."

If you plan on using this procedure and are likely to have a lot of new students during the year, take time in the second or third week of school to talk to the entire class about how you may call on them individually to help orient a new student. Be sure not to use the same student as a mentor again and again. Have your class share the responsibility of teaching new students class expectations, and as new students become clear on your expectations, they can begin mentoring other newer students.

The advantage of this approach is that it takes pressure off you to spend instructional time with a new student. It also communicates your faith in your students to understand and implement your expectations fully. Be aware, however, of opportunities when you can have some good contact with the new student. You do not want her to feel disconnected with you, and you also want to make sure that she views you as the authority figure and not her student mentor. Make a point of interacting with the new student by helping her check her work, asking her if she's comfortable or has any questions.

Task 2: Mark on Your Planning Calendar Particular Times That You Will Reteach Your Expectations

At particular times of the year, student behavior may tend to deteriorate. If you reteach your expectations before these points, you may be able to reduce this predictable, but not inevitable, phenomenon (Wolf, Bixby, Glenn, & Gardner, 1990). To reteach your expectations during these times, implement the cycle as you did at the beginning of school. Implement step 1, and clarify your expectations before every activity. Then, following step 2, continue to monitor student behavior in a more obvious way than usual. Be more conspicuous with your observing, and move about the class more than you normally would. Finally, using step 3 of the process, provide feedback immediately after each activity and transition. If things go well, congratulate your students on their maturity and responsibility. If things do not go so well, let them know that you expect a higher level of independent management and cooperation from each of them. Briefly go over your expectations again, noting where your students met them and where they did not.

In addition to reteaching behavioral expectations, plan to reteach your Guidelines for Success. Pump up your students to strive to exhibit the traits outlined in the Guidelines for Success. Let students know that you will be striving to exhibit these traits yourself, and inform them that you have high expectations for them to do so as well.

For each of the times noted, put a reminder to yourself in your planning calendar to reteach expectations and include a note to yourself about why reteaching at this particular time may be important.

Thanksgiving break. Thanksgiving break may vary in your school district, but here it will be considered the three days before the holiday *and* the three days after it. Students often think that since the week is so short, not much will be going on in school. Remind students each day before the holiday that although the week is short, there will still be a lot of important work that needs to be done and you expect them to have the maturity to stay focused on it and behave in a responsible and self-disciplined manner. If things go well on Monday, then on Tuesday you do not need to completely reteach expectations, but simply give a quick reminder at the beginning of class about how well the students did before and that you expect the same today. On Wednesday, plan to reteach your expectations but maintain a high degree of normalcy. If it is your practice to give some extra free time on the day before a holiday, this should not stop you from doing so. The idea is simply to remind students that their time in class should not be affected by outside events.

Before winter break. Throughout December, plan to review your expectations one day each week and remind your students that your expectations in class will not change just because of the holiday season. Emphasize that by continuing with the established procedures and routines, they can concentrate their mental energy on mastering their academic objectives. If the routines and procedures break down, chaos will result, and nobody can learn or thrive in a chaotic classroom. During the last week before the winter break, plan to reteach your expectations at least twice that week, and every day if it becomes necessary.

After winter break. The days immediately after winter break are a time to begin again. Especially if this represents the start of a new semester, inform students that you are going to treat the first day or two back from vacation almost like the first day of school. Plan to go over the syllabus and pass out extra copies to any students who may have lost theirs. Put special emphasis on policies or procedures that may have been problematic during the first semester. Use the teaching expectations cycle for the first few days, emphasizing the *positive opposite* of any misbehaviors that begin to occur or that may not have been completely eliminated before the holiday. (*Positive opposite* refers to the positive behavior that a student should be engaged in instead of the misbehavior. For example, if students have been responding in disrespectful ways to comments made by other students during group discussions, the teacher could inform students of the problem and let them know that a respectful reaction would be to say nothing, to comment positively, or to disagree with the content of what the previous speaker said, but not "diss" the person making the comment.)

Before major tests. Two weeks prior to any major accountability testing like a midterm or a final exam, plan to reteach your expectations. Let students know that both teacher and students may feel a sense of pressure heading into any high-accountability situation. These stresses can lead to irritability, impatience, and hostility. The best way for the class to avoid such problems is for everyone to strive to do their best, treat everyone with respect, and generally make sure to continue following the Guidelines for Success and the class rules. In addition, at least once or twice a week as the testing approaches, reteach your expectations. Emphasize that everyone will do well on the test if the days before the test are well organized, orderly, and efficient rather than frantic and chaotic.

After major tests. Immediately after any major accountability testing, use the three-step cycle to review your expectations. Some students will assume that once testing is over, class is over and the rest of the year will be free time. Use the act of reteaching expectations to communicate that testing does not mark the end of anything. Emphasize that in your class, you use the entire year, and you expect them to take advantage of the opportunity this gives them.

Spring break. Immediately before and after spring break, reteach your expectations and the Guidelines for Success in much the same way you did before and after the winter break.

End of the school year. During the last three to four weeks of school, students will push limits and try to get you to let go of your structure. Return once more to the cycle to let your students know that your structure will stay in place until the last day of school. Let students know that when they have a job, employers do not want efficiency to go down just because a vacation is coming up. Reemphasize the Guidelines for Success and your expectations at least once each week during the last four weeks of school.

Task 3: Collect Objective Data About Classroom Behavior, and Adjust Your Management Plan Accordingly

When you monitor what is going on in your classroom, you will be able to make adjustments to your classroom management plan that will increase student success. Objective data can help you determine which aspects of your management plan should be maintained, which may need to be altered, and whether your level of structure is adequate.

To help you with your decisions about these issues, this book includes a variety of tools for collecting and evaluating objective information about your classroom. Without accurate information, your decisions are likely to be based on hunches, guesses, or whatever feels right at the moment (Brophy, 1983; Royer, Cisero, & Carlo, 1993). One of the requirements of professionalism is making informed decisions based on objective information. To use an example from the medical profession, when you go in for a routine physical examination, your physician gathers a variety of information: pulse, respiration, blood pressure, blood sugar, cholesterol levels, and so on. Then your doctor objectively evaluates the information she has gathered, along with your subjective reports about how you feel, and makes a judgment about your overall health. She may decide that you are just fine, or she may decide that additional information needs to be collected, or she may suggest that a treatment plan be implemented. Without the objective data, your physician would only be acting off your reports and would be much less able to assess your overall health accurately or make useful recommendations regarding your health care.

The appendixes at the back of this book contain the tools you can use to gather objective information about the overall health of your current classroom management plan. Following is a brief description of each of these tools. Reminding yourself to use them and periodically evaluate your strengths and areas for improvement is a powerful way to grow as a professional.

- *Appendix A: CHAMPs and ACHIEVE versus Daily Reality Rating Scales.* This tool allows you to look at each major activity and transition during your class and evaluate on a five-point scale how well students are meeting your CHAMPs expectations for that activity or transition. With that information, you will then be able to decide whether you need to reteach your CHAMPs expectations or modify the level of structure you have selected as most appropriate for your students. You should monitor this particular aspect of your classroom management plan (that is, the actual implementation of your CHAMPs expectations) several times per year. If you are using the ACHIEVE acronym and worksheet to define your expectations, there is a modified version of this tool within Appendix A.
- *Appendix B: Ratio of Interactions Monitoring Forms.* There are three versions of this tool for determining whether you have fallen into the criticism trap and are paying so much attention to misbehavior that you could be helping to perpetuate it yourself. The primary form documents your interactions with students during a particular class period. You can use the supplementary forms to document interactions with a specific student or to monitor your interactions with a specific behavior. You will then be able to see how much time you spend with particular students or working against particular misbehaviors. This will allow you to adjust your monitoring habits to be more effective in your classroom.
- *Appendix C: Misbehavior Recording Sheet.* Keeping a systematic record of your students' misbehavior for one day with all classes or for one week with one or two of your most problematic classes can help you determine whether you need to adjust your level of structure or whether your students would benefit from a targeted behavior management plan or classwide motivation system. There are four versions of this tool; choose the one that will allow you to most easily record any misbehavior that occurs in your classroom.
- *Appendix D: Grade Book Analysis Worksheet.* An up-to-date grade book has a wealth of data. This appendix shows you how to compile and analyze the data in your grade book to determine whether individual students are exhibiting chronic problems with absenteeism, tardiness,

work completion, or assignment failure. You can use the information from this analysis to make judgments about whether any student, or the class as a whole, would benefit from the implementation of a behavior management plan that targets one or more of these problems.

• *Appendix E: On-Task Behavior Observation Sheet.* This simple tool can be used to determine your class's average rate of on-task behavior during independent work times. If students are on task less than 80 percent of the time, you need to reteach your CHAMPs or ACHIEVE expectations for work periods or implement some form of classwide incentive system that will encourage students to use class work times more productively.

• *Appendix F: Opportunities to Respond Observation Sheet.* This tool can be used to examine the degree to which you actively engage students in your lesson. By making a videotape or by having a colleague observe you, you can determine how frequently students have the opportunity to respond, that is, to actually do something as opposed to being passive recipients of the lesson content. This provides one measure to help you evaluate the effectiveness of your instructional presentations and lesson design.

• *Appendix G: Student Satisfaction Survey.* Just as many businesses find it worthwhile to look at the satisfaction of their customers, you too can benefit from knowing how satisfied your students are with your classroom. This is a short survey that can be given to students at the end of the year or at the end of each semester. The information will help you identify any aspects of your classroom management plan that you need to communicate more clearly or present differently.

You are much more likely to use these tools if you build their implementation into your schedule. Therefore, write the prompts that follow into your calendar now. Each prompt should be as close to the suggested date as possible, allowing for scheduled events like class trips or testing.

As the year progresses and you come to a particular prompt on your calendar, go to the specified part of this book and follow the directions for collecting and analyzing your data. For now, simply familiarize yourself with the schedule and look at any of the tools that you think you will use. You will not need to be overly familiar with any of them at this time. When it is time to use a tool, plan on carefully reviewing it before implementing it.

Here is a possible schedule:

Week 3	Student Interviews or Quiz (Chapter Eight, Task 1)
Week 4 or 5	CHAMPs versus Daily Reality Rating (Appendix A)
Second month (early)	Ratio of Interactions Monitoring (Appendix B)
Second month (late)	Self-Evaluation of Teacher-Directed Instruction (Appendix F)
Third month (early)	Misbehavior Recording Sheet (Appendix C)
Third month (late)	Grade Book Analysis (Appendix D)
Fourth month	On-Task Behavior Observation (Appendix E)
End of semester	Student Satisfaction Survey (Appendix G)
January (early)	CHAMPs versus Daily Reality Rating (Appendix A)
January (late)	Misbehavior Recording Sheet (Appendix C)

February (early)	Ratio of Interactions Monitoring (Appendix B)
February (late)	On-Task Behavior Observation (Appendix E)
March (early)	Grade Book Analysis (Appendix D)
April (after spring break)	Self-Evaluation of Teacher-Directed Instruction (Appendix F)
End of semester	Student Satisfaction Survey (Appendix B)

Even if you have started implementing this book during the school year, you can still use this time line. From today's date, identify the next recommended evaluation activity. Write it on your planning calendar along with all the activities suggested for the remainder of the year. Implement those activities at the appropriate times.

In Conclusion

Even the most carefully thought out classroom management plan needs to be monitored and adjusted based on the needs of any particular class. How fast or slow to fade the teaching of expectations should be based on how well the class demonstrates knowledge and mastery of the classroom expectations, procedures, and routines. Problematic times of the year may require more structure and reteaching. Finally, by using a variety of methods to collect data on student behavior at different times of the year, you can metaphorically take the temperature and pulse of the class and make decisions about the "health" of your management plan. If you find the plan working well, carry on—after all, if it isn't broken, don't fix it. However, if you find areas that need improvement, you can tweak any number of variables to facilitate more responsible student behavior.

Implementation Self-Assessment Checklist

Use this worksheet to identify which parts of the tasks described in this chapter you have completed. For any item that has not been completed, note what needs to be done to complete it. Then transfer your notes to your planning calendar in the form of specific actions you need to take (for example, "November 18, Reteach expectations").

✔	Task	Notes and Implementation Ideas
☐	*Gradually decrease the amount of time spent teaching expectations, procedures, and routines.* I understand that teaching expectations on just the first day is not sufficient. I will continue to use the three-step communication for a couple of weeks, but gradually decrease the amount of time I spend communicating expectations. However, I will: 1. Verify that my students understand what is expected of them. 2. Teach my expectations to new students.	
☐	*Mark on your planning calendar particular times when you will reteach your expectations.* I understand that behavior may deteriorate at particular times of year; therefore, I will reteach my expectations before these times: • Thanksgiving break • Before and after winter break • Before and after major tests • Before and after spring break • Near the end of school	
☐	*Mark on your planning calendar times to collect objective data about classroom behavior using the tools in the appendixes and adjust your management plan accordingly.* I understand the importance of knowing what is going on in my classroom and that objective data can help me determine which aspects of my management plan should be maintained, which may need to be altered, and whether my level of structure is adequate. The tools in the appendixes can help me obtain objective data about my classroom management plan.	

Implementation Peer Study Worksheet

With one or more of your colleagues, work through the following discussion topics and activities related to the tasks in Chapter Eight. If necessary, refer back to the text to get additional ideas or for clarification. (See the Vision Peer Study Worksheet in Chapter One for suggestions on structuring effective discussion sessions.)

Task 1: Gradually Decrease the Amount of Time Spent Teaching Expectations, Procedures, and Routines

A. Have group members share perceptions of the efficacy of teaching expectations. For experienced teachers, compare the amount of teaching of expectations you did with this year's students to those in previous years. Is there a benefit in improved student behavior? If student behavior is going well, do you think it is time to fade the teaching of expectations? If behavior still needs improvement, does it make sense to continue teaching expectations until there is improvement?

B. Have individual group members share any quizzes and interview protocols they have developed to verify student understanding of behavioral expectations. Group members should give each other feedback. If applicable, work in pairs and arrange to interview each other's students.

Task 2: Mark on Your Planning Calendar Particular Times That You Will Reteach Your Expectations

A. Discuss group members' perceptions about the times that were suggested for reteaching. Do these times make sense, or are they potentially problematic? Are there other times of year or specific events within the school that may make reteaching appropriate?

Task 3: Collect Objective Data About Classroom Behavior, and Adjust Your Management Plan Accordingly

A. If there is a group consensus, divide the appendixes among the group members so that each member studies one appendix and the tools within that appendix to share with the group at your next meeting. Discuss the appendixes and the potential utility of the information that might be gathered.

B. Discuss group members' comfort levels with having another group member come into their room to collect data for some of the tools in the appendixes. For group members who wish to do so, make specific arrangements as to who observes what and when.

After implementing any of the tools, whether it was peer observation or self-implemented, plan to get together as a group and discuss what was learned and what classroom management adaptations, if any, group members made based on this information.

Chapter Nine

Proactive Planning for Chronic Misbehavior

No matter how well organized your classroom may be and no matter how effectively you have communicated your behavioral expectations to your students, a certain amount of misbehavior is still bound to occur. Although the rates of misbehavior will be much less if you have applied the techniques from this book, some misbehavior is inevitable. If an occasional misbehavior occurs but does not become repetitive, then there is no need for a systematic plan. However, once a misbehavior becomes chronic, intervention is necessary to break the pattern. Unfortunately, many teachers have a tendency to react to chronic student misbehavior in ways that actually lead to more, rather than less, inappropriate behavior (Chance, 1998; Lalli et al., 1999). This chapter is designed to help you view misbehavior as an opportunity to continue to educate your students about appropriate versus inappropriate behavior and then respond appropriately.

If you have several large classes per day, realistically, you will be able to design individualized behavior plans for only one or two situations at a time. As you read this chapter, keep one situation involving a specific chronic misbehavior in mind that you would like to improve. This could be a problem with an individual student or a group. If the problem is the behavior of the entire class, go through the other chapters of this book again to identify variables you can manipulate to have a positive impact on the entire class. In particular, pay attention to Chapters Two through Six.

The tasks in the chapter are designed to help you correct several severities of misbehavior using four different levels of intervention. Before reviewing them, it is useful to understand two basic concepts about correcting misbehavior that will help you respond to it in an intellectual and planned manner, not in an emotional way.

First, it is vital that you have a plan on how you will deal with student misbehavior ahead of time. When teachers know in advance how they will respond to misbehavior, they are less likely to get frustrated and more likely to be effective (see Chapter Five; Lovitt, 1978; McLeod, Fisher, & Hoover, 2003). By having consequences preplanned for rule infractions, you will know exactly what to do whenever a rule is violated. This chapter will help you learn how to deal with those misbehaviors that persist in spite of rules and consequences.

Second, correction procedures can be considered effective *only* if they reduce the occurrence of the misbehavior they address in the long term (O'Neill et al., 1997). This is a key point because it is not uncommon for a teacher to deal with an inappropriate behavior in a way that may resolve the problem at the moment but make the situation worse in the long run. In Chapter Six, the notion of the criticism trap was introduced: that students who are starved for attention may be encouraged to misbehave as a result of the repeated attention they get when the teacher corrects them. Although the student may stop a particular behavior for the moment, he will know that if he ever feels the need for attention, he can demonstrate the behavior and get it immediately.

The concept of evaluating the effectiveness of correctional procedures based on their impact on students' long-term behavior applies to situations other than those involving attention-seeking misbehaviors. For example, a teacher who sends an extremely disruptive student out of class may feel that he has solved the problem. However, if the student continues to misbehave, the student clearly does not feel that being sent out of class is a negative consequence. This is why observation and gathering information is such a vital part of this process. Analyzing and understanding the way your students view the consequences you assign them is key to gauging their effectiveness (Horner, Vaughn, Day, & Ard, 1996).

Finally, because most chronic misbehavior serves a purpose for the individual who demonstrates it and because there are many different reasons for misbehavior, correction efforts for specific misbehaviors will be more effective if they address the underlying causes of those behaviors (O'Neill et al., 1997). Students may misbehave for any number of reasons, including not knowing what the teacher expects, being unaware of demonstrating a behavior, not knowing the appropriate behavior, being starved for attention, or feeling a sense of power by being able to exert some kind of control over events around them. Some students even misbehave because being sent out of class or given a corrective assignment means they might not have to do course work they don't understand.

There are five tasks in this chapter:

Task 1: Implement basic interventions first, moving to more complex interventions only when necessary.

Task 2: Develop an intervention plan for awareness-type misbehaviors.

Task 3: Develop an intervention plan for ability-type misbehaviors.

Task 4: Develop an intervention plan for attention-seeking misbehaviors.

Task 5: Develop an intervention plan for habitual and purposeful types of misbehaviors.

Because of the depth of information presented, Task 1 is longer and more involved than any other in this book. It presents the four levels of intervention, ways to collect data on misbehavior, the four types of misbehavior, and steps to implement in cases of chronic misbehavior. Tasks 2 through 5 are targeted at the different types of misbehavior. Use the distinctions provided in Task 1 to direct you to those tasks relevant to your own classroom situation.

At the end of this chapter are the Self-Assessment Checklist and Peer Study Worksheet. Review the Peer Study Worksheet with a colleague, and, if possible, arrange to observe each other's classrooms. This will allow you to help one another fine-tune and implement your plan to intervene with any particular chronic misbehavior.

Task 1: Implement Basic Interventions First, Moving to More Complex Interventions Only When Necessary

Always try the easiest intervention strategies first. If they don't work, you can always implement more complex strategies to correct misbehavior.

First-Level Intervention

If you have read earlier chapters of this book, then you have already learned the strategy that should comprise your first attempt to intervene with any chronic problem: clarify expectations, increase attention to positive behavior, and respond consistently and calmly to the misbehavior (Mendler & Curwin, 1999). In this chapter, such a strategy is referred to as a *first-level intervention*.

Clarify the positive expectations you want the student to exhibit. If the problem is with an individual student, meet with the student privately to review your expectations. If the problem involves a small group or the whole class, clarify the positive expectations with this group. You may think this unnecessary, but reviewing your expectations and explaining the benefits of following them is always worth doing (Alberto & Troutman, 2003). Good dentists know that patients won't retain every piece of advice on achieving good oral hygiene from one visit; wedding planners know that the families of the bride and groom won't remember every instruction pertaining to the ceremony even after several rehearsals. And coaches know that you don't just tell the team what to do and expect them to reach mastery on their own; you clarify, inspire, and drill or practice. (Review Chapter Four for information on how to do this.)

Increase the ratio of attention to positive behavior to attention to negative behavior. Increase the amount of noncontingent attention you give the student when the student is not engaged in misbehavior (Ridley & Walther, 1995). This includes greeting the student, asking if she needs assistance, and making eye contact while you present lessons. Also, increase the frequency of descriptive and contingent positive feedback. In Chapter Six, it was suggested that teachers should strive for a three-to-one ratio. Try to achieve at least a *six*-to-one ratio of positive to negative attention. Since you are trying to *change* (not just maintain) a behavior, a significant increase in the ratio is a strong strategy.

Ensure that your reaction to misbehavior is briefer, calmer, more consistent, and more immediate than it has been previously. Your goal should be to minimize the amount and intensity of attention you give to negative behavior. If you have been reprimanding and implementing consequences in a lengthy or emotional manner, try to make those interactions briefer and more neutral (Orange, 2005). Mentally rehearse how you will respond to the misbehavior so that when it occurs, you can correct it and then immediately get back into the flow of instruction. (These concepts were discussed in Chapter Five.) As an intervention to correct chronic misbehavior, strive to use these strategies even more deliberately and consistently.

Try the first-level intervention strategy for at least two weeks. If the situation does not seem to be improving after two weeks, move on to the second-level intervention.

Second-Level Intervention

The second-level intervention strategy consists of all three first-level procedures with the addition of systematically collecting data on the misbehavior. This will help you make decisions about what to do next based on objective data, not your instinct (Hintze, Volpe, & Shapiro, 2002; Sugai & Tindal, 1993).

Data can be systematic, clear, and concise, but data can also be unsystematic, unclear, and of little use. In order to make sure you collect relevant, useful data, use the following most common methods of data collection (included are some suggestions on how to use them). The information below is adapted from *Project RIDE* (Beck, 1997).

Frequency data record the number of occurrences of a given behavior within a specific time period. (For example, use of obscenity can be recorded as the total times profanity is used within a class period.) Frequency data can be recorded using a variety of techniques:

- A tally sheet kept on a clipboard or an index card. Make a mark each time the target behavior occurs. If you are tracking several behaviors, you can divide the card into sections. For example, you could have a card with the name Joshua and two other headings on it: one for disruptive noises and one for negative comments.

- A wrist or golf counter. Each time the target behavior occurs, advance the counter. The counter can easily be kept in a pocket if you want to be unobtrusive.

- Paper clips in a pocket. Keep a supply of small objects (beads, beans, paper clips, buttons) in one pocket. Each time the target behavior occurs, move one of the objects to another pocket or a container. The number of objects collected at the end of the time period is the number to record. This technique will let you track only one behavior at a time, but it is effective and simple to use.

Once tallied, frequency data can be displayed on a simple chart like the one shown in Figure 9.1.

Duration data express the total amount of time a student engages in a given behavior. For example, off-task behavior can be expressed as the number of minutes a student is off task within a fifty-minute class period. This information can be useful when a student engages in a behavior for extended periods of time. A student may technically have been off-task only one time during the class—for the entire length of the class. You can see how tracking the total number of incidents would not be useful here. To record duration, you need a stopwatch. Start the watch when the target behavior begins and stop it when the target behavior stops. Start it

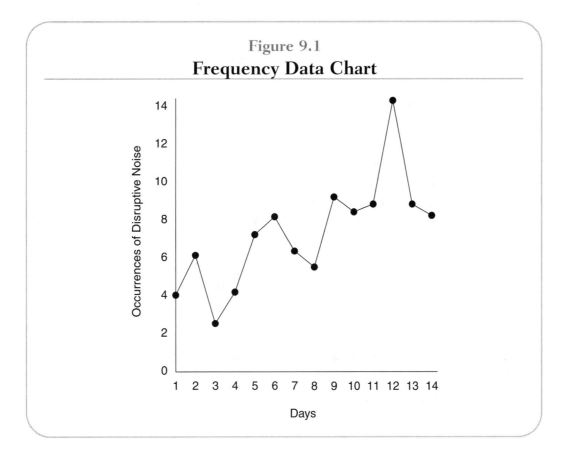

Figure 9.1
Frequency Data Chart

again if necessary. The total minutes on the watch when class is over tells you how much time the student spent misbehaving. This can then be recorded on a chart like the one shown in Figure 9.2.

Latency data express how much time passes between a directive and the student's response. This information is almost always used in the context of tracking compliance and direction following. To track this information on a student who is frequently noncompliant, you will need a stopwatch. Each time you give a direction, start the timer. Stop it when your instructions are carried out. If you do this during the entire class, you will have a latency total by the end of the class. Figure 9.3 shows an example of a latency chart.

Rating magnitude or quality is a way to record data that rate a student's behavior during a specified time period using a scale, say, from 1 to 5. At the end of each class period, for example, you and the target student rate the degree of cooperation and respect the student demonstrated toward you. A rating of 1 means that the student was disrespectful and uncooperative the entire time, while a rating of 5 represents that the student was respectful and cooperative during the entire class period.

Although this is subjective, discussing and determining the rating standards with the student beforehand can make this an accurate and helpful way of recording data. Because each rating is a numerical value, this information can be charted easily for quick reference. You can also track information on more than one student at a time. See Figure 9.4 for an example.

Figure 9.2
Duration Data Chart

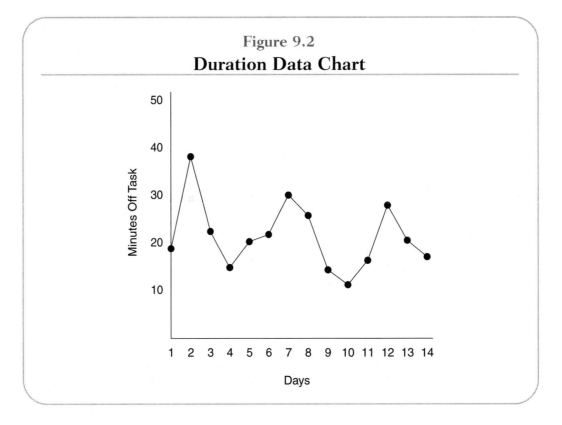

Figure 9.3
Latency Chart

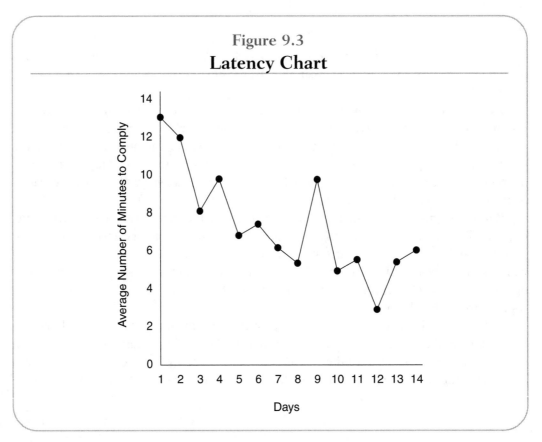

Meet with the student you plan to track before you begin collecting data. Inform him of your plan, and emphasize that you are collecting this information in order to determine if there is a problem. Then meet with the student for a few minutes each week to discuss the data on your chart.

The act of collecting data in a systematic way often serves to improve a problem situation in and of itself. This may be because the student is more aware you are serious about the problem. It may be because of the increased attention the student receives from you. It may be because in collecting the data, you are communicating that you value the student enough to have expectations that the situation will improve. It may simply be the placebo effect. Regardless of the reason, the phenomenon is frequent enough that regular data collection and debriefing with the student are reasonable to try when a simple first-level intervention was not sufficient.

In addition, the data will help you decide if the situation is improving, staying the same, or getting worse. Without data, your subjective perceptions about progress, or lack thereof, may be inaccurate. For example, let's say that by collecting data on the frequency of a student's sarcastic or disrespectful comments toward you, you find that the situation has gone from averaging ten comments per week to six per week over the three weeks you have been collecting data. Without the data, it is very likely that the six comments per week could be so aggravating that you might think the situation is not improving. However, a 40 percent reduction in the frequency of the problem indicates a successful intervention that needs no modification. Conversely, if you find over four weeks that the comments are continuing to average about ten per week, you would know with confidence that the second-level intervention is not sufficient and a more carefully planned third-level intervention is warranted.

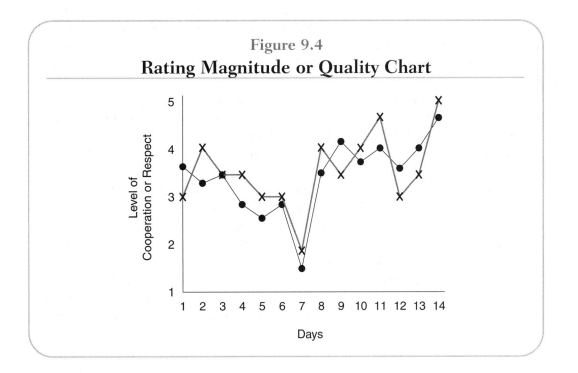

Figure 9.4
Rating Magnitude or Quality Chart

Third-Level Interventions

If the targeted behavior has not improved with the data collection and weekly debriefing, analyze the nature of the behavior. Then develop and implement a comprehensive intervention plan. These four steps represent the overall approach for any misbehavior that you identify as chronic:

Step 1: Analyze

Step 2: Plan

Step 3: Discuss

Step 4: Implement and monitor

Step 1: Analyze the nature of the target behavior. Collect data if you have not already done so. When you are concerned about a particular misbehavior but do not have any data to support your concern, collect information on it before you develop an intervention plan (O'Neill et al., 1997; Sterling-Turner, Robinson, & Wilczynski, 2001). The objective data you collect will help you define the problem more precisely and will give you a baseline from which you will be able to make judgments about the effectiveness of any intervention plan you implement.

If the target problem is unclear or you are disrupted or troubled by the behavior but unsure why, keep anecdotal records for a few days. Write down brief descriptions of specific situations that trouble you. Once you have notes from several incidents over a few days, you should be able to clarify the nature of the problem behavior. You can then collect more objective data on its frequency or duration over another few days (Marzano, 2003).

The next part of your analysis is to determine the cause or purpose of the misbehavior. Understanding the cause will help you understand the best way to deal with it. If a student is misbehaving because she wants attention, doling out corrective consequences each time she misbehaves may be giving her what she wants and will most likely be ineffective. But if a student continually fidgets severely enough that it is distracting to other students because she does not realize that her behavior is inappropriate or she is not aware of her behavior, you will have to intervene by helping the student to become aware each time she is exhibiting the problem behavior.

Chronic misbehavior can be divided into four subcategories: *awareness-type* misbehaviors, *ability-type* misbehaviors, *attention-seeking* misbehaviors, and *purposeful and habitual* misbehaviors. They are listed here with brief notes on how to deal with each. More specific instructions on intervening to correct each type of misbehavior are addressed in depth in the remainder of the tasks in this chapter.

Awareness-type misbehaviors. Sometimes a student may seem to be willfully misbehaving when in fact he is unaware of the behavior he is exhibiting. An example of an awareness-type misbehavior would be a student who always responds argumentatively to corrective feedback. He does this at school when he is given feedback for behavioral and academic performance, and, according to his mother, he shows the same behavior at home. The teacher first tries the early-stage correction strategy of discussing the problem with the student but sees no improvement in his behavior. Since this student responds negatively every time he is given corrective feedback and since initial efforts to correct the behavior with information have been ineffective, it is reasonable to assume that the student may not be aware of how negatively he behaves when he is given corrective feedback. Task 2 has information on developing an intervention plan for this type of misbehavior.

Ability-type misbehaviors. Sometimes a student who exhibits a misbehavior does so because he does not know how, or is unable, to exhibit the desired behavior. A student may have never learned how to stay focused during a class or may have a disability that makes it impossible to stay focused for extended periods of time. Such a student is exhibiting an ability-type misbehavior. He may want to behave, but it may be beyond his capabilities. Task 3 addresses how to intervene effectively with these types of misbehaviors.

Attention-seeking misbehaviors. A student may be behaving in a way that, consciously or unconsciously, seeks attention. This can also occur when the student is not misbehaving. Chronic blurting out, excessive helplessness, tattling, disruptions, and offering answers to every question are examples of behaviors that may be attention seeking in nature. Information on developing an intervention plan for attention-seeking misbehaviors is presented in Task 4.

Purposeful or habitual misbehaviors. When chronic misbehavior does not stem from a student's lack of awareness or ability and is not being exhibited because the student wants attention, then it must be serving some other purpose for the student. For example, some students misbehave to escape from something, like not doing homework they believe they will fail. Other students use misbehavior to gain a sense of power and control, such as when a student defies authority to show off for or gain respect from other students. There are some students for whom misbehavior has become so habitual that the original purpose of the misbehavior is lost. A student who has successfully engaged in attention-seeking behaviors for years will continue to do so for some time, even though she no longer gets attention from that misbehavior.

With behavior that is truly purposeful or habitual, you will need to include the use of corrective consequences as part of your intervention plan. Task 5 in this chapter provides information on developing an effective intervention plan for this type of misbehavior, including guidelines for using corrective consequences and a menu of specific consequences that you can use.

Step 2: Develop a preliminary intervention plan based on your analysis. Once you think you understand why the target behavior is occurring, review the decision-making chart shown in Figure 9.5. Think about the targeted misbehavior as you examine the chart. Then go to the information in this chapter that pertains to that misbehavior. Use Figure 9.5 to guide you to the procedures that fit the nature of the targeted problem.

Use the suggestions in the appropriate task to develop a preliminary plan for improving the target behavior. Although the specific procedures for each subcategory of chronic misbehavior (awareness, ability, attention seeking, and purposeful) are different, two fundamental steps must be part of all intervention plans. First, you need to encourage the positive opposite of the misbehavior. Always explain the proper way to do something after it has been done incorrectly. Second, your plan needs to specify exactly how you will respond to instances of the misbehavior while staying calm, consistent, and brief. Once you have a preliminary plan, you can continue with the remaining planning steps.

Step 3: Discuss your preliminary intervention plan with the student and, if necessary, the student's family. Prior to implementing an intervention plan for any chronic misbehavior, schedule a time to discuss your concerns and your proposed plan with the student. Just as you would take the time to go over a problem that the whole class was having, you should

Figure 9.5
Decision-Making Chart

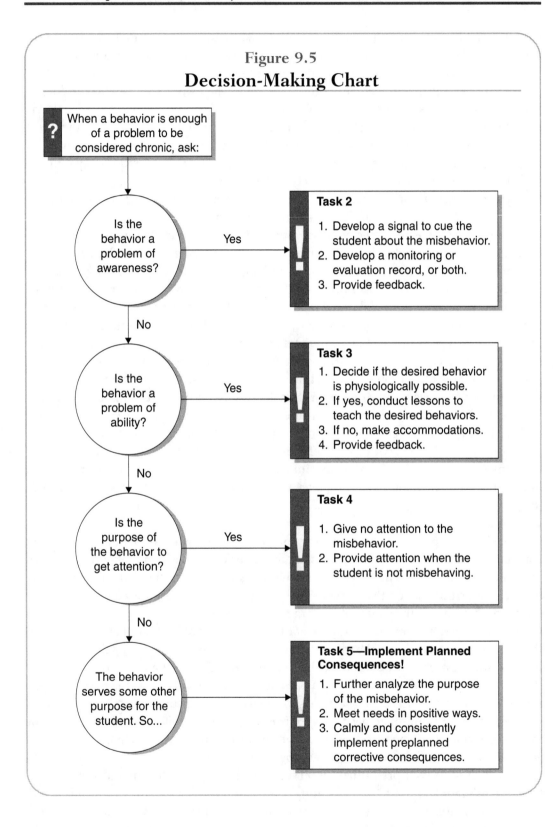

? When a behavior is enough of a problem to be considered chronic, ask:

Is the behavior a problem of awareness?

Yes →

Task 2
1. Develop a signal to cue the student about the misbehavior.
2. Develop a monitoring or evaluation record, or both.
3. Provide feedback.

No ↓

Is the behavior a problem of ability?

Yes →

Task 3
1. Decide if the desired behavior is physiologically possible.
2. If yes, conduct lessons to teach the desired behaviors.
3. If no, make accommodations.
4. Provide feedback.

No ↓

Is the purpose of the behavior to get attention?

Yes →

Task 4
1. Give no attention to the misbehavior.
2. Provide attention when the student is not misbehaving.

No ↓

The behavior serves some other purpose for the student. So...

Task 5—Implement Planned Consequences!
1. Further analyze the purpose of the misbehavior.
2. Meet needs in positive ways.
3. Calmly and consistently implement preplanned corrective consequences.

take the time to discuss problems with individual students. You also need to decide whether to include the student's family in the discussion. If the behavior is quite serious, like being abusive or violent, then involving the family may be requisite. If the misbehavior is relatively minor, you may elect to deal with the student directly. If you find you are on the fence, err on the side of caution and include the family.

During the discussion, define the target behavior as clearly as you can. Describe the behavior in observable terms, and share any objective data about the behavior that you have collected—for example: "Troy, you made sarcastic, disrespectful comments in class eight times in the last two days." Avoid making statements that imply judgments: "Troy, you are a smart-aleck all the time. Something has to be done."

After explaining the nature of the problem, present your proposed plan. Make sure the student (and the family, if present) understands all aspects of the proposal. Then invite ideas from the student for improving the plan. Incorporating reasonable suggestions from the student will give him a sense of ownership and will demonstrate that you want him to be an active partner in the effort to improve his behavior.

Step 4: Implement the intervention plan for at least two weeks, and monitor student behavior so you can evaluate the plan's effectiveness. Once you have analyzed the target behavior, developed a preliminary plan, and had a discussion with the student, you are ready to implement the plan. Keep this plan in effect for at least two weeks. During that time, continue to collect objective data on the behavior so that you can determine whether there is improvement (Alberto & Troutman, 2003). Do not be alarmed if the behavior gets worse at the beginning. This can happen even with a plan that will eventually be successful. For example, when you begin ignoring an attention-getting behavior, the student is likely to try even harder to get attention by misbehaving more frequently (O'Neill et al., 1997). If you persist, however, the student will eventually learn that responsible behavior leads to more attention than misbehavior.

After two weeks, evaluate the situation. If the behavior is improving, continue with your plan. It is very important to remember that most successful behavior changes occur gradually, slowly getting better over time. If you have seen no behavioral improvement after two weeks, try modifying one or more aspects of your plan. You might even ask the student for ideas on what would make the plan more effective. Whenever you make a change in your intervention plan, implement the new plan for the same minimum of two weeks and continue to evaluate its effectiveness by collecting and analyzing data.

Fourth-Level Interventions

If all other avenues have been exhausted, you may have to refer the situation to an individual or group that can help you. You might turn to others for their thoughts or suggestions, or you may have to look into different placement for your student. Where applicable, you may refer your student to a group that specializes in situations like yours (called many things in different districts, for example, CARE Teams, S Teams, SST Teams, or TAT Teams). If no such team exists in your district, consider referring the student to a school counselor, psychologist, or district specialist. One of the first things you will be asked after referring a student to someone else is what data you have. You will then be able to refer to all the data you have gathered through the first three intervention levels to show not only exactly what the problem is but what you have already tried.

Using the Levels

Always try the easy thing first. First-level intervention involves teaching expectations, increasing attention to positive behavior, and ensuring that your responses to misbehavior are immediate, calm, brief, and consistent. Second-level intervention adds data collection and debriefing the student to the first-level intervention. Third-level intervention requires you to think about the function the misbehavior serves and intervene accordingly. If the previous interventions are still unsuccessful, you may have to move to fourth-level intervention, asking for help or beginning the process of arranging for evaluation of need for special education services.

Task 2: Develop an Intervention Plan for Awareness-Type Misbehaviors

When a student misbehaves because she isn't aware of when or how often she is engaging in an irresponsible behavior, your intervention plan should focus on increasing the student's awareness of her behavior. It is not appropriate to use traditional corrective consequences, in the form of punishment, in this situation. When a student lacks awareness of her misbehavior, you first need to make sure that the student understands how she is supposed to behave; only then can you help her learn to recognize when she is misbehaving.

If you determine that a student's misbehavior stems from a lack of awareness, develop and implement this four-step intervention plan:

Step 1: Make sure the student knows what behavior you expect her to exhibit and what kind of behavior she is currently exhibiting. When you meet with your student to discuss the situation, be sure to explain the behavior you want her to demonstrate. Emphasize the benefit to the student of demonstrating this new behavior. Be prepared to identify actions you will take to help her learn this new behavior. Consider writing the behavioral goal into an informal contract, following the suggested goal contract form shown in Exhibit 9.1.

Step 2: Respond to instances of the misbehavior in a manner that lets the student know that she is not meeting the goal. Do not forget that students should not be punished for behavioral mistakes that are related to a lack of awareness or ability. Instead, each time an error occurs, give the student information about the inappropriate behavior and what she should be doing instead. Following are descriptions of several information-based correction strategies. Choose one or more that you can use to provide the student with information that will help her be more successful in the future. Remember that a student who is learning a new behavior may make frequent errors and need to be corrected each time:

• *Gentle verbal reprimands.* Effective reprimands are brief, quick, respectful, clear, and reasonably covert. Provide a verbal description of what the student should be doing. (Reprimands were discussed in detail in Chapter Five.)

• *Redirection.* Redirection involves turning a student's attention back to what she should be doing. Instead of verbally reminding the student, you will literally direct the student to the desired activity.

Exhibit 9.1
Goal Contract

Student _____

Class _____

Description of problem _____
_____

Goal _____
_____

Student responsibilities for achieving the goal _____
_____
_____
_____

Teacher support responsibilities _____
_____
_____
_____

Evaluation procedures _____
_____
_____
_____

Date of goal evaluation _____

Student's signature _____

Teacher's signature _____

• *Signal.* If a student seems truly unaware of when she is misbehaving, it can be helpful to use a verbal or nonverbal cue to signal the student. For example, if you have a student who hums while doing seatwork, the signal might be to say her name to get her attention and give your head a small shake. As long as you have discussed this with the student in advance, she will know the meaning of this signal and should stop humming any time she receives this signal. It may be effective to consult with the student beforehand to determine the most appropriate or effective signal.

• *Precorrection.* When you can determine that a student is likely to exhibit misbehavior in a particular situation, you can correct him before he actually misbehaves. This will preempt the misbehavior and thus help break habitual misbehavior. If a student has trouble accepting corrective feedback, you could use something like the following precorrection just before you return papers: "Sheila, I have some graded papers here for you. You solved most of the problems correctly, but you did make a couple of errors. Think about your reaction to this, and think of a way to keep it responsible, as we discussed."

Step 3: Monitor the student's behavior so that you and the student will have an objective basis for discussing progress. A student who is unaware he is misbehaving may have difficulty recognizing when he is engaging in the positive opposite of that behavior. By keeping records of positive and negative behavior, you will have an excellent way to demonstrate his progress. You can chart each day's positive and negative behavior totals and arrange to review the chart with the student periodically. In some cases, it can be beneficial to give the student a recording sheet and have him record the incidents himself (Alberto & Troutman, 2003). With a student who has a particularly difficult time recognizing his own behavior, this may not be beneficial, but if he is able to recognize his behavior once he is made aware of it, it may be very useful for him to track the information himself. If the student is unlikely to keep an accurate record or would be embarrassed to record his behavior in front of peers, you should do the recording. Arrange to meet with the student periodically (even every day if the issue occurs frequently) to chart the incidents and discuss progress. (For more ideas on this type of recording and for a sample of a recording sheet, see Chapter Two, Task 3.)

When a student's behavior problems involve more qualitative than quantitative issues (how well rather than how much), it can be useful to have the student use a self-evaluation monitoring form. He can rate the quality of his behavior at specific times during the class, or just at the end (see Exhibit 9.2).

Exhibit 9.2
Self-Evaluation Form

Name _____   Class Period _____
Problem Behavior _____

Directions:
At the end of the period, use the scale to rate the quality of behavior during the period. Record the rating in the boxes.

RATING	BEHAVIOR
0	Poor through the entire period
1	Good a little bit of the period
2	Good about half of the period
3	Good for most of the period
4	Good the entire period

M	T	W	TH	F

Step 4: Provide positive feedback when the student improves. If positive feedback doesn't seem sufficient to motivate the student to cease the misbehavior, consider using incentives. Throughout the day, as the student demonstrates success or takes steps toward success, provide positive verbal feedback. Increasing the student's awareness will require that she know when she is doing well. Without positive feedback, the student may get discouraged by the corrective feedback you provide when she makes an error (Sponder, 1993).

If you do not see progress in the form of a decrease in the misbehavior within a couple of weeks, consider establishing a simple system of incentives. A student who is learning to reduce the frequency of disruptive fidgeting (pencil tapping or drumming on desk, for example) could earn a point for each day of the week when the number of times you needed to signal a reminder to stop the noise was below an agreed-on level. When the student accumulates 8 points, he could earn a "get out of one homework assignment" ticket to be used for a short task of his choosing (not a term paper!).

Task 3: Develop an Intervention Plan for Ability-Type Misbehaviors

Sometimes a student misbehaves because he is physiologically unable to exhibit the appropriate behavior or does not know how to do so. The most effective intervention plans in these situations address the underlying cause of the situation. If a student is physically or neurologically unable to exhibit the desired behavior, then your intervention must involve making modifications to the student's environment or adjusting your expectations. If the student is capable of the behavior but does not know how to exhibit it, your intervention must teach the student how to exhibit the desired behavior. This is frequently called *teaching a replacement behavior*. If the student is physiologically unable to exhibit the desired behavior or does not know how, implementing corrective consequences is entirely inappropriate. Consequences will not help the student learn the new behavior and will only make the student feel at fault for something he has no control over.

An example to consider would be a student in your class who suffers from Tourette's syndrome. When reviewing this student's records, you see the notation that teachers are supposed to ignore "outbursts such as barking, snorting, or swearing" from this student in class. Your first thought might be that such a recommendation is ridiculous. However, the only way a student with Tourette's syndrome can control these kinds of behaviors or tics is through medication, and this works only for

> **Note**
>
> Unlike individuals with Tourette's syndrome, children who have been identified as having attention-deficit disorder—with or without hyperactivity—can learn to control their behavior. Although a student with this diagnosis may have some ability-type problems, those problems can be treated using some of the strategies outlined here.

some. In such a situation you will have to adjust your expectation that there will not be interruptions in your class. You may have to adjust the expectations of the other students in your class as well. If you are unsure whether a desired behavior is within a student's physiological capability, you will need to check with your special education staff, school psychologist, or the student's physician.

This task presents a four-step process for helping students who exhibit misbehavior that is related to a lack of ability but who can demonstrate the desired behavior:

Step 1: At a neutral time, have a discussion, and provide information that teaches the replacement behavior. At least three days a week, conduct private lessons with the student. Use these lessons to describe the desired behavior and have the student practice it. Keep in mind that when a student lacks the ability to demonstrate a particular behavior, just talking about it may not be enough for the student to grasp it (Marzano, 2003). Coaches know this. The basketball coach who would have her team excel in free-throw shooting not only provides step-by-step instructions and demonstration, but has the players practice the skill by taking free throws—lots of them. She provides repetition and daily practice across a period of weeks.

If you do not think you can provide the instruction yourself, talk to your administrator. Perhaps a school counselor could conduct the lessons with the student. In fact, if several students in your school have similar ability-type problems, the counselor might be able to run a small-group session.

Step 2: Correct errors in a manner that provides instruction. Punishing students for exhibiting inappropriate behavior when they have not yet learned to exhibit the behavior is inane and potentially cruel. On top of that, it's not likely to work. It is far more likely that the misbehavior will improve if you respond with a correction strategy such as proximity, gentle reprimands, a signal, or redirection (all of which were described in Task 2 in this chapter). For example, if you have a student who has been labeled with attention-deficit disorder and tends to drum on his desk, you might arrange to give him a signal each time he starts to drum. Teach him that when he sees you give the signal, he needs to stop drumming. This would be far more effective and appropriate than imposing a consequence.

Step 3: Make accommodations to increase the student's chance of succeeding. Determine whether there are modifications you might make in terms of daily schedule, class structure, behavioral expectations, your classroom's physical arrangement, or your classroom interactions that would make it easier for the student to be successful (Alberto & Troutman, 2003).

Step 4: Provide positive feedback when the student is successful or improves. Set up incentives if simple positive feedback seems insufficient to motivate the student. As the student demonstrates success or takes steps toward success, give her positive verbal feedback. Students who exhibit ability-type misbehaviors need information that lets them know when and what they are doing well. Without this positive feedback, these students may feel overwhelmed or discouraged by the corrective feedback they receive when they make errors (Hamre & Pianta, 2001). If the student fails to make progress within a week or two, consider establishing a simple incentive system. For example, if you have a student who has difficulty sitting still, for every specific period of time she is able to sit still, give her points toward a reward that she can look forward to.

Task 4: Develop an Intervention Plan for Attention-Seeking Misbehaviors

An attention-seeking misbehavior is a behavior that a student knows is unacceptable but engages in anyway to get teacher or peer attention. When a student is seeking attention through misbehavior, responding with a corrective strategy or consequence will give the student the attention he is looking for and therefore reinforce the misbehavior (Horner, Vaughn, Day, & Ard, 1996). The strategy that is most likely to correct this kind of misbehavior is planned ignoring. However, this strategy is not appropriate for early-stage attention-seeking misbehavior because ignoring the misbehavior in the early stages may lead the target student, and perhaps other students who observe the situation, to assume that the behavior is acceptable since you are not addressing the problem. In the early stages, provide verbal reprimands or other gentle corrective actions to communicate that you are serious about your expectations. Should you determine that ignoring is appropriate, when you meet with the student to inform her that the behavior is still unacceptable, communicate that from this point forward, you are going to deal with the problem by letting the student handle it without your intervention. This lets the student know that your ignoring is a planned action to help the student take responsibility for herself, not just that you don't notice the problem or that you have let go of your classroom expectations for responsible behavior.

With planned ignoring, you can substantially reduce the attention a student receives for misbehaving. At the same time, you need to give the student frequent attention when he or she is *not* misbehaving (Chance, 1998). The goal with this strategy is for the student to learn that using misbehavior to get attention is ineffective and that behaving responsibly results in frequent and satisfying attention. Planned ignoring is not the same as tolerating a student's misbehavior. Tolerating misbehavior implies that one has given up expecting a change and has decided to live with the misbehavior. Planned ignoring is a conscious strategy applied in an effort to change the misbehavior.

Following are suggested steps for implementing planned ignoring as part of an intervention plan designed to help a student learn to get his or her attention needs met without engaging in misbehavior:

Step 1: Ascertain whether ignoring is an appropriate response. To determine if ignoring is the best strategy for the problem behavior, ask yourself some questions:

Is this misbehavior really attention seeking in nature? If the student's misbehavior is a function of lack of ability or awareness, ignoring will not work and will encourage the behavior to continue. Not paying attention to a misbehavior caused by lack of awareness or ability is as inappropriate as ignoring math mistakes that students make. Without correction, students will assume they are doing things correctly. If a student thinks he is being helpful to you by coming and telling you about the misbehavior of others he has observed (tattling), then he needs lessons and feedback about the difference between tattling and social responsibility. But if the student fully understands that a behavior is not acceptable yet uses the misbehavior as a way to seek or demand attention from teacher or peers, then planned ignoring is likely to be effective.

Is the actual problem the frequency of the behavior, not the behavior itself? Sometimes the issue with attention-seeking behavior is not that the behavior itself is inappropriate, but rather that the frequency or duration with which the student engages in the behavior is problematic. Say you have a student who asks lots of questions and is always seeking teacher assistance. Although you do not want to discourage the student from asking questions or seeking assistance, if he asks for help more than is necessary, he has learned that displaying helplessness will get him attention.

You cannot ignore a student's questions or requests for assistance. You would not be able to justify such an action to the student, his family, or your principal. What you can do with the problem of excess, though, is specify what a reasonable amount of the behavior would be. As with other examples in this chapter, your role is part detective as you collect and use data. You should first determine how much this student asks for help compared to other students of similar intellectual ability. For a couple of days, keep a record of how many times the student asks for help and how many times one or two similar students ask for help. At the end of the second day, you might have a record that looks something like this:

> Mark [attention-seeking student]: Monday, 7 times; Tuesday, 9 times
> Olivia [student of similar ability]: Monday, 1 time; Tuesday, 2 times
> Rose [student of similar ability]: Monday, 3 times; Tuesday, 0 times

This objective information shows that your concern is warranted. It also lets you know that your goal should be to get Mark to the point where he asks for help no more than three or four times during a day.

Is the misbehavior so severe that ignoring it is inappropriate? Sometimes a behavior that is attention seeking in nature is so severe that you cannot responsibly ignore it. For example, if a student is hitting other students, you must intervene. Or if a student's disruptive behavior is so severe that lessons cannot continue, you must intervene. When an attention-getting misbehavior is that severe, you need to treat it as purposeful and habitual misbehavior and include the use of corrective consequences (see Task 5). Remember, though, that the student wants attention, so when you assign a consequence, make every effort to do so in a manner that gives the student as little attention as possible. In addition, continue to make a concerted effort to give the student frequent attention when he is not engaged in misbehavior. The goal is for the student to learn that although he will get attention for misbehavior, it is less satisfying than what he can easily get for behaving responsibly.

Will you ignore such behavior from all students or just from the target student? If the behavior is exhibited chronically by one or two students and intermittently by several others, you should ignore any student who exhibits it. If blurting out an answer without raising a hand is a problem for quite a few students, make a classwide announcement that you are going to ignore blurting out and only call on students who remember to raise their hands. If the behavior is exhibited primarily by one student, plan to ignore that student when she engages in the misbehavior, and give verbal reprimands to any other student who exhibits the misbehavior.

Once you determine that a behavior is attention seeking and that ignoring is an appropriate correction strategy, the next step is to develop an intervention that includes using planned ignoring. To develop an effective plan, you need to give careful thought to exactly which behaviors you will ignore. Determine which behaviors you will assign corrective consequences for and which you will encourage. For example, you might end up with a list like the following:

Behavior to Ignore	Behavior to Assign Consequences For	Behavior to Encourage
Blurting out	Bothering other students	Raising hand
Noises	Hitting	Hands/feet to self
Tapping his pencil	Kicking	Working quietly
		On task
		Getting immediately to work
		Following directions

Step 2: Discuss the proposed plan with the student. When the problem involves only one student, arrange to meet with that student and, when appropriate, his family. During the meeting, describe the problem behavior and your proposed solution to ignore it. Be sure to make clear that your intent is not to ignore the student as a person, but only the behavior the student is using to draw attention to himself. Explain that because you have such high expectations for the student's ability to manage this behavior, you are not going to give reminders or assign consequences. Inform the student that if he engages in more severe misbehaviors that cannot be ignored, like violent behavior in class, you *will* assign corrective consequences. Finally, let the student know that you will be looking for opportunities to give him your time and attention when he is behaving responsibly.

If the situation involves a behavior that many students exhibit, inform the entire class that you will use ignoring as a strategy. Emphasize that ignoring does not mean the behavior is acceptable. Rather, explain that you are using ignoring because this particular behavior is so clearly unacceptable that you should not have to take valuable time to tell students not to do something they already know they should not be doing. Keep the tone of this discussion positive, not accusatory, and remember to communicate your high expectations.

Step 3: When the misbehavior occurs, continue what you are doing, and provide positive feedback to other students. Once you have informed the student of your plan to ignore, give no attention to the misbehavior. Some teachers feel a need to tell the student each time, "I am ignoring you now." This is not ignoring and will undermine your strategy. Pay *no* attention at the time of the misbehavior. Do not shrug, sigh, or act exasperated. Simply continue to teach. Give your attention to students who are behaving responsibly at that moment. If other students pay attention to the student engaged in misbehavior, give a gentle verbal reprimand: "Chloe, please finish your math problems." If another student laughs at the student, simply remind him to focus on his own work.

During the first several days of using planned ignoring, the behavior may get worse before it begins to get better (Alberto & Troutman, 2003; Chance, 1998). In fact, that a behavior is getting worse is a sign your strategy is working. Remember that the student has received attention for exhibiting this behavior in the past, and that attention has been satisfying. Now when she exhibits the behavior, she does not get attention. The student's logical response, then, is to try harder to get your attention using the behavior that has been so successful in the past. If you continue to ignore her, eventually the student will learn that if she really wants attention, she needs to behave responsibly.

You must be consistent. Ignoring intermittently is worse than not ignoring at all. If you have decided to ignore blurting out, ignore *all* blurting out. If you ignore it the first five times it happens and then get frustrated and assign a consequence the sixth time, you simply teach the student to be more persistent.

A common question is, "What if I am ignoring a student's noises and blurting out, and he exhibits a severe misbehavior like hitting someone?" The answer is that you would follow through on school policy for a behavior of this severity, which in all probability will be writing a disciplinary referral.

Step 4: When the attention-seeking misbehavior ceases, give the student attention. You need to demonstrate to the student that responsible behavior results in attention. Therefore, shortly after the student begins behaving responsibly (within five minutes or so), give the student attention. Either praise the student for the responsible behavior or just go over and talk to the student for a few moments: "James, you are working so quietly, I thought I would come over and see if you had any questions or needed any help. You're doing a great job."

Step 5: Maintain frequent interactions with the student when he is not misbehaving. Chapter Six outlined the importance of providing at least three times more attention to positive behavior than negative behavior. This is essential whenever you are using planned ignoring. If the student does not experience lots of attention when behaving responsibly, he will simply increase his misbehavior until you are forced to acknowledge him. You must praise this student frequently and give him lots of noncontingent attention.

Step 6: Monitor the student's behavior to determine whether progress is being made. Continue whatever form of monitoring and data collection you established during the second-level intervention. After two weeks of using planned ignoring with the target behavior, evaluate whether the situation is improving. If it is not, continue ignoring the misbehavior and increase the amount and intensity of attention you provide when the student is not misbehaving. If there is still no improvement after another two weeks, abandon planned ignoring as a strategy, and treat this misbehavior as purposeful or habitual (see Task 5).

Task 5: Develop an Intervention Plan for Habitual and Purposeful Types of Misbehaviors

Chronic misbehavior may occur for reasons other than a lack of awareness or ability or a need for attention. Chronic misbehavior may help a student avoid something aversive or achieve a sense of power and control. Sometimes the original goal of a student's misbehavior has been long lost, and the student misbehaves just because the inappropriate behaviors have become firmly established in her behavioral repertoire (Sterling-Turner, Robinson, & Wilczynski, 2001).

When ongoing misbehavior is truly purposeful or habitual, it will probably be necessary to use corrective consequences to help the student learn that the misbehavior has negative costs. The use of corrective consequences alone, however, is not likely to be sufficient. Therefore, your intervention plan also needs to include removing any reinforcing aspects of the misbehavior and demonstrating to the student that positive behavior leads to positive results (O'Neill et al., 1997).

The remainder of this task describes guidelines for planning an intervention for purposeful and habitual misbehavior. This task addresses the important components of an intervention plan for this type of misbehavior:

Step 1: Remove any positive or satisfying aspects of demonstrating the misbehavior. Remember that the misbehavior you want to change has served a purpose for the student at some point. A student may misbehave in order to escape doing the academic work, or a student may not participate in class because he enjoys reading a book or listening to music more than paying attention to the lesson. As you develop your intervention plan, you need to ensure that the student will no longer get whatever it is that he has been getting from the misbehavior. If a student has gotten power by engaging in arguments with you, your plan will need to address how you will avoid engaging in arguments with this student. If a student has been using misbehavior to escape from doing his work, you will need to ensure that the corrective consequence you use does not let the student get out of his work. If a student enjoys hurting other people's feelings with mean comments, you will need to train yourself and the other students not to take his critical comments personally.

Step 2: Continually demonstrate to the student that positive behavior leads to positive results. In addition to making sure that the student will not benefit from the misbehavior, your intervention plan should specifically address how you can continually demonstrate to your students that responsible behavior is worthwhile (Hamre & Pianta, 2001). This can include an effort to meet the student's needs in positive ways and an effort to increase the student's motivation to behave responsibly.

Meet the student's needs in a positive way. Once you identify what purpose the misbehavior is serving, you need to find a positive way of satisfying that purpose. For example, if a student talks back as a means of seeking power, you might ask the student if he would be willing to be a positive help around the school. You could give the student a choice among several different jobs, such as tutoring a younger student or helping in the computer lab by learning to be a technician assistant to the computer teacher. Using appropriate corrective consequences along with giving the student a positive position of power can solve this kind of problem behavior much sooner than consequences alone.

If a student is seeking to escape academic work, you need to determine whether the student is capable of doing the work successfully. If not, modify his assignments or your expectations, or get some kind of help for the student so he will begin to experience success.

When a misbehavior involves competing reinforcement (for example, another activity that student enjoys), you can arrange for the student to have access to the desired reinforcement when he has met your expectations. If a student would rather read a novel than do his work, you might set it up so that he can read when his other work is completed. In addition, you might occasionally give the student an alternative assignment that involves reading a novel and giving a report to the class.

Increase the student's motivation to behave responsibly. For some students, a change in the type or frequency of positive feedback may be sufficient to increase their motivation to behave responsibly (see Chapter Six). In other cases, it may be necessary to establish some form of positive feedback system, like a system in which the student earns rewards for exhibiting positive behavior. (For ideas on individual contracts and systems, see Sprick & Howard, 1995.) An example of an individual system for increasing homework completion is shown in Exhibit 9.3.

Step 3: Implement corrective consequences that are appropriate for the problem behavior. When misbehavior is purposeful or habitual, you need to carefully plan how you will respond to specific instances of that behavior. If you do not preplan what your response will be, there is a high probability that you may inadvertently reinforce the misbehavior. The following suggestions can help you choose and implement an effective corrective consequence, one that will help the student learn that engaging in misbehavior has a logical cost associated with it.

Implement the corrective consequence consistently. If corrective consequences are going to reduce or eliminate purposeful or habitual misbehavior, they must be implemented consistently (O'Neill et al., 1997). When you implement a corrective consequence only some of the time, the consequence (no matter how severe) is not likely to change the behavior. In fact, it may even make things worse than if there was no consequence at all. When a student is able to engage in a misbehavior and not receive the designated consequence, he is likely to feel a great sense of satisfaction. Getting away with it can be so reinforcing that it can undo many corrections.

Teachers tend to implement corrective consequences based on an accumulation of misbehavior. Thus, what ends up controlling the use of consequences is teacher emotion. The teacher doesn't implement a consequence until he finally gets fed up with the misbehavior. This leads to grossly inconsistent responses. To change purposeful or habitual misbehavior, you need to define specific behaviors that are unacceptable and then implement corrective consequences for those behaviors *each* time, regardless of how you feel about the behavior at the time.

Exhibit 9.3

Individual Motivation System (Less Disruptive)

When a student is not concerned about the designated consequences of failing to turn in completed homework or does not value the sense of satisfaction that comes with completing and turning in required work, you may need to implement a system of external incentives (that is, rewards and consequences) to motivate him to turn in completed homework on time. If possible, involve the student's parent or guardian in developing this plan. If the family is supportive, it is quite probable that the rewards and consequences will be more powerful than you could provide at school.

1. **Establish a structured system for reinforcing the appropriate behavior and providing a consequence for the inappropriate behavior.**

   a. With the student, create a list of rewards he would like to earn. The rewards may need to be relatively high in perceived value in order to create a powerful incentive to motivate the student to get his homework completed on a regular basis. To get some ideas for the list, watch what the student does during a less structured time in class when he has choices. You can ask the student his preferences and, if the parents are involved, ask for their ideas on activities, privileges, or other rewards that the student might like to earn.

   b. Assign "prices" (in points) for each of the rewards on the list, and have the student select the reward he would like to earn first. The prices should be based on the instructional, personnel, or monetary cost of the items. Monetary cost is clear: the more expensive the item, the more points are required to earn it. Instructional cost refers to the amount of instructional time lost or interfered with by a particular reward. Thus, an activity that causes the student to miss part of academic instruction should require more points than one the student can do on his own free time. Personnel cost involves the time required by you or other staff to fulfill the reinforcer. Having lunch with the principal therefore would cost more points than spending five minutes of free time with a friend. The prices must be low enough that the student will think, for example, "You mean all I have to do is ＿＿＿＿＿＿, and I can earn ＿＿＿＿＿＿!" If the desired reinforcers are priced too high and would take the student too long to earn (from his perspective), he may not be any more motivated to complete his homework than he was without the system.

   c. Develop a homework completion self-monitoring form, and establish a system to translate each successfully filled-in space into points. For example, the student might earn 1 point each for accurately recording the assignment, the due date, and the necessary materials (3 points total). When the assignment is completed and turned in, the student might earn another 5 points, making each homework assignment worth 8 points.

   Larger assignments or projects, such as writing a report, could be broken down into steps, each with its own line and due date on the monitoring form. For example, the outline, the note cards, the rough draft, and the final draft could be treated as separate assignments, each worth 8 points—making the whole report worth a possible 32 reinforcement points.

   d. When the student has accumulated enough points to earn the reward he has chosen, he "spends" the points necessary, and the system begins again. That is, he selects another reward to earn and begins with zero points.

2. **Respond consistently to the inappropriate behavior.**

   a. Gently correct the student when he fails to turn in his homework.

   b. Establish consequences (in addition to any predetermined classwide consequences) for not being responsible for his homework. The most obvious consequence would be that if the student does not turn in the work, he fails that assignment. However, that consequence alone may be too abstract and delayed to affect the student's behavior in the short run. A more immediate consequence will probably be necessary (for example, the student is assigned after-school detention until the work is caught up).

   If the parents are working with you on the reinforcement portion of the plan, you can consider asking them to implement a consequence at home as well, such as grounding the student until he has caught up with his work. However, this is appropriate only if the parents are also reinforcing the student; the parental role should never be only punitive.

   c. When neither home-based nor school-based consequences are possible for whatever reason, there is more pressure on the positive aspects of the intervention to ensure that the plan is powerful enough to motivate the student to complete his homework, despite the lack of consequences for not turning it in.

3. **Use reinforcement to encourage appropriate behavior.**

   a. Give the student extra praise and attention for turning in completed homework on time.

   In addition, show interest and enthusiasm about how the student is doing on the system: "Salvador, every day this week you have earned all 8 points for every assignment. Congratulations! You should be very proud of your organizational skill."

Your goal should be to develop clear expectations of what behaviors are unacceptable so that you can be consistent. If you are concerned about disruptions, specify the precise behaviors you consider disruptive and identify examples of behaviors that are not disruptive. If your concern is a student who is disrespectful, describe specific ways the student has been disrespectful and ways the student could have behaved in the same situation that would have been respectful. Creating a T-chart that specifies responsible and irresponsible examples of behavior can help. Use the chart when discussing your expectations and consequences with the student. Exhibit 9.4 is a sample T-chart for a student who makes disruptive noises. You may need to give concrete examples of behaviors that have small differences (for example, making noise by wadding up paper as opposed to the minimal noise created by quietly placing a sheet of paper in the trash can).

Exhibit 9.4
T-Chart Sample for Disruptive Behaviors

Responsible Noise:	Irresponsible Noise:
• Putting paper in the trash	• Wadding up paper
• Getting paper out	• Tearing up paper
• Quietly opening and closing notebook rings	• Snapping open and closed notebook rings or slamming notebook on desk
• Writing, sharpening pencil at breaks	• Tapping pencil
• Raising hand, waiting to be called on, using an appropriate volume level	• Blurting out without raising hand or waiting to be called on
• Working quietly	• Humming, making clicking noises with tongue
• Once or twice a work period, asking a neighbor a work-related question	• Talking about anything other than work during work periods

Once you have developed a T-chart and discussed what constitutes responsible and irresponsible behavior with the student, be sure to implement the designated corrective consequence consistently.

Make sure the corrective consequence fits the severity and frequency of the misbehavior.
When deciding on the corrective consequence that you will implement, choose one that matches the severity of the problem (Mendler & Curwin, 1999). Start by examining the irresponsible behaviors listed on your T-chart. Choose a consequence that fits even the mildest example of the unacceptable behavior. All too often, teachers pick a consequence that is so harsh they are unwilling to implement it when the occasion arises, such as detention for a small infraction. This leads to inconsistency. You want a consequence that is mild enough that you will be comfortable implementing it every time the student exhibits irresponsible behaviors. As you think about your choice of a consequence, look at each example of a misbehavior listed on your T-chart. If the consequence seems too harsh for any of the examples of that behavior, you may need to select a milder consequence. When determining the severity of consequences, always err on the side of making consequences too mild. You can always give out more.

Whatever corrective consequences you choose, plan to implement the consequence in the same way for all of the misbehaviors. In other words, if you have decided to use demerits, all disruptive acts should result in 1 demerit. Do not create a situation in which some disruptive acts get more demerits than others. If you decide to use time owed as a consequence for a student who tends to be disrespectful, have each infraction equal the same amount of time owed.

In addition to matching the corrective consequence to severity of the infraction, consider the frequency of the infraction. For example, at first glance, it might seem reasonable to say that every time a student is disruptive, the student will be assigned an after-school detention. However, if the student is likely to be disruptive three to four times in a class period, that student will end up not paying for most of his infractions. Once you have assigned a detention for the first infraction, what can you then do with the second infraction and the third? If you did assign a detention for every infraction, the student might justifiably decide by the middle of the week that there is no reason to even bother to behave; she already has detentions stacked up for the next week and a half. Furthermore, when consequence severity does not match misbehavior frequency, you might be more inclined to be inconsistent with implementation. For example, by the second infraction, you might start thinking that you'll let some of the behaviors go by because you don't want the student to rack up too many detentions too quickly. Overly harsh consequences make consistency difficult for most teachers. The basic consequence should be only fifteen seconds owed immediately after class for each infraction. By taking into account the frequency, and establishing a consequence that can realistically be implemented for every infraction, you ensure that you can implement your consequence for every instance of the misbehavior. When it comes to correcting chronic misbehavior, what you use as a consequence is less important than that you do something consistently.

Plan to implement the consequence unemotionally. With purposeful or habitual misbehavior, there is a high probability that the student has learned that she can make adults frustrated, hurt, or angry. If you get angry when correcting the student, that response may actually reinforce the student's misbehavior. When a student feels hostility toward adults, seeing an adult get angry can be highly satisfying. For a student who feels powerless, getting an adult upset on a regular basis can provide a huge sense of power and control. You need to strive to implement corrective consequences unemotionally so your reactions do not give the student the idea that misbehavior is a way to achieve power over you.

Plan to interact with the student briefly at the time of the misbehavior. Never argue. When a student misbehaves, your interaction with that student should last less than five seconds. Simply state the misbehavior and state the consequence. A common mistake is to explain and justify. Resist this impulse. All explanations should be done in your initial discussion with the student or in a regularly scheduled follow-up meeting.

If you think the student will have a tendency to argue or deny that he exhibited the misbehavior, tell the student during your initial discussion that at the time of an incident, you will not argue or negotiate and that you will ignore any attempts on his part to do so. At the same time, let the student know that if he ever wants to speak to you about something he thinks is unfair, he can make an appointment to see you before or after school. Once you have made this clear, if the student continues to try to argue, simply remind him that he can make an appointment to see you. Then resume teaching.

Although keeping interactions brief may be a difficult habit to get into, it allows you to keep your focus where it belongs: on teaching and providing positive feedback to all students when they are meeting your expectations. Think about the consequence you are planning to use for the targeted misbehavior. If you cannot imagine implementing that consequence without lengthy explanations or negotiations at the time of the misbehavior, you should select a different consequence or plan to conduct a more thorough explanation of the plan during your initial meeting with the student.

Step 4: Implement the three-component plan. Once you have the behaviors (both positive and negative) and consequences well defined, ask yourself some what-if questions. *What if the student objects? What if the parents object? Will my administrator support me if there are objections? What if the behavior increases for a few days? Can I still follow through with this consequence? Do I need to explain this consequence to the entire class? Will I apply the consequence to anyone who exhibits this behavior or just to the target student?* The more issues you can identify and address, the greater the likelihood is that your intervention plan will be effective in reducing and eliminating the misbehavior. Discuss any what-if questions you cannot answer yourself with a school administrator or counselor. Do not implement any intervention plan until you know you can follow through on all aspects of it. Remember that your plan needs to address how you will eliminate positive benefits the student receives from engaging in the misbehavior and how you will see that the student experiences positive benefits from exhibiting responsible behavior.

Once all aspects of your plan have been developed and all potential difficulties have been resolved, meet with the student to explain what will happen each time she engages in the misbehavior. Make sure the student knows the cost of choosing to exhibit the misbehavior in the future. Keep the tone of this discussion positive. Remember that you should implement an intervention plan consistently for at least two weeks. In your role as detective, collect data on the behavior during this two-week period to determine whether the behavior is getting better or worse. Even if things seem to get worse for a few days, do not switch to a different consequence right away. After two weeks, if the behavior is about the same or getting worse, go through the planning steps again and make any necessary modifications. Monitor the behavior for another two weeks. If the behavior improves, continue what you are doing. If the behavior still has not improved, consider implementing a motivation system to encourage the student to improve his or her behavior in addition to trying a new corrective consequence.

In Conclusion

With any chronic misbehavior, always try the easy thing first. First-level interventions make minor modifications to your current management strategies. Second-level interventions use systematic data collection and regular debriefing with the student. If either of these levels of intervention is ineffective, continue data collection. Meaningful data will be useful in all subsequent interventions. Third-level interventions involve figuring out what the purpose of the behavior might be (what is the student getting out of exhibiting this misbehavior?) and developing an intervention plan that addresses that purpose. An intervention will be fundamentally different depending on whether the problem is one of awareness, ability, attention seeking, or habitual or purposeful.

If the third-level intervention is not successful after several weeks, try to determine if there are obvious weaknesses in the plan. You could even bring the student into this discussion. If there are changes that might have a reasonable chance of improving the behavior, make those changes and continue to implement the revised plan for several more weeks. If improvement occurs, continue the successful intervention.

If the third-level plan is not working and there are no obvious gaps or holes in the plan, it may be time to refer the problem for outside assistance—that is, thinking of this problem as needing fourth-level intervention. Depending on your school, this may be referral of the problem to a school counselor, professional problem-solving group, or school psychologist. Regardless of what other professionals you involve, be sure to let them know that you have implemented three other levels of intervention and that you have weeks of data that document the problem. This information will be invaluable as you and they explore the next directions designed to help this student.

Proactive Planning for Chronic Misbehavior Self-Assessment Checklist

Use this worksheet to identify which parts of the tasks described in this chapter you have completed. For any item that has not been completed, note what needs to be done to complete it. Then transfer your notes to your planning calendar in the form of specific actions you need to take (for example, "October 3, meet with Jonathan to discuss why I will begin keeping a frequency count of his disrespectful behavior").

✔	Task	Notes and Implementation Ideas
☐	*Implement basic interventions first, moving to more complex interventions only when necessary.* I understand that it's best to start with a simple plan when addressing misbehavior and move to more complex strategies only if necessary. I will first address misbehavior with a first-level intervention consisting of: • Clarifying the positive expectations I want my student to exhibit; • Increasing the ratio of attention to positive behavior to attention to negative behavior; and • Ensuring that my reaction to misbehavior is even more brief, calm, consistent, and immediate than it has been previously. If the first-level intervention doesn't work, I will move to a second-level intervention and add data collection and weekly debriefings with my target student to the plan. I will collect information on: • The frequency of the misbehavior • The duration of the misbehavior • How quickly my student responds to my directive • The degree of cooperation and respect my student demonstrates If necessary, I will then move to a third-level intervention, which has four steps: 1. Analyzing the nature of my student's behavior and collecting data if I have not done so already. 2. Developing a preliminary plan based on my analysis of the student's behavior. 3. Discussing my preliminary plan with the student and, if necessary, the student's family. 4. Implementing the intervention plan for at least two weeks and monitoring the student's behavior so I can evaluate my plan's effectiveness.	

Proactive Planning for Chronic Misbehavior Self-Assessment Checklist (*continued*)

☐

If the first three levels of intervention don't work, I will seek assistance from others or consider different placement for my student.

Developing an intervention plan for awareness-type misbehaviors.

I understand that with misbehaviors that stem from a student's lack of awareness of when (or how much) he or she is engaging in a misbehavior, I should use the following steps:

- Make sure the student knows the behavior I expect (the goal behavior).

- Respond to instances of the misbehavior in a way that lets the student know that he or she is not meeting the goal.

- Monitor the student's misbehavior so that I will have an objective basis for discussing progress with the student (and family).

- Give the student positive feedback when he or she is successful, and consider some type of incentive system if necessary.

☐

Developing an intervention plan for ability-type misbehaviors.

I understand that with ability-type misbehaviors, the first thing I need to do is ascertain whether the student is physiologically capable of exhibiting the goal behavior. If the student is not capable, then I must modify the environment or adjust my expectations, or both. I understand that if a student misbehaves due to a lack of knowledge, I should use the following steps:

- At a neutral time, have a discussion or provide lessons about the goal behavior.

- Respond to instances of misbehavior in a way that provides instruction to the student.

- Make accommodations to increase the student's chance of success.

- Provide positive feedback when the student is successful, and set up an incentive system if necessary.

☐

Developing an intervention plan for attention-seeking misbehaviors.

If a student exhibits a mild ongoing misbehavior that seems to stem from a need for attention, I will first ask myself the following questions to ascertain whether ignoring is the best strategy:

- Is the misbehavior really attention seeking in nature?

Proactive Planning for Chronic Misbehavior Self-Assessment Checklist (*continued*)

- Is the actual problem the frequency of the behavior, not the behavior itself?
- Is the misbehavior so severe that ignoring it is inappropriate?
- Will I ignore such behavior from all students or just from the target student?

After determining whether ignoring is an appropriate response, I will implement the following steps:

1. Discuss my proposed plan with my student.
2. Continue what I'm doing when the student misbehaves and provide positive feedback to other students.
3. When the student stops the attention-seeking behavior, I give the student attention.
4. Maintain frequent interactions with the student when he is not misbehaving.
5. Monitor the student's behavior to determine whether progress is being made.

Developing an intervention plan for habitual or purposeful-type misbehaviors.

1. For chronic misbehavior that does not stem from a lack of awareness or ability or a need for attention, I will develop and implement a comprehensive intervention that:
2. Removes any positive or satisfying aspects of demonstrating the misbehavior
3. Continually demonstrates to the student that positive behavior leads to positive results by:
   - Meeting the student's needs in a positive way
   - Working to increase the student's motivation to behave responsibly
4. Has corrective consequences that are appropriate for the problem behavior by:
   - Implementing the corrective consequence consistently
   - Making sure the consequence fits the severity and frequency of the misbehavior
   - Implementing the consequence unemotionally
   - Interacting with the student only briefly at the time of the misbehavior (I never argue)

Proactive Planning for Chronic Misbehavior
Peer Study Worksheet

With one or more of your colleagues, work through the following discussion topics and activities related to the tasks in Chapter Nine. If necessary, refer back to the text to get additional ideas or for clarification. See the Vision Peer Study Worksheet in Chapter One for suggestions on structuring effective discussion sessions.

Task 1: Implement Basic Interventions First, Moving to More Complex Interventions Only When Necessary

A. Discuss the four-level model presented. Do group members agree or disagree with this as a way of thinking about, and intervening with, chronic misbehavior? If there is disagreement, discuss alternatives.

B. Discuss the potential efficacy of the level 1 intervention: (1) clarify, (2) increase positive attention, and (3) react to misbehavior calmly and immediately. Should there be other standard procedures at this level? If so, what?

C. Discuss why in level 2 intervention, there should be objective data collected. Discuss why, in many cases, the act of collecting data and making the students aware you are doing so may be enough to begin to improve the problem situation.

Tasks 2 to 5: Developing Intervention Plans for Awareness, Ability, Attention Seeking, and Purposeful and Habitual Misbehaviors

A. Have each group member bring a case study of a chronic problem on which they have tried level 1 and level 2 interventions without success. Choose one of those problems, collectively analyze the type of misbehavior, and brainstorm a level 3 intervention plan. As time permits, get to as many of these problems as possible.

Appendix A: CHAMPs and ACHIEVE versus Daily Reality Rating Scales

The information in this appendix will help you determine the degree to which student behavior matches your expectations during daily activities and transitions.

Why
- To help you decide whether you need to reteach expectations
- To help you decide whether your current level of structure fits the needs of your class
- To help you decide whether you might need a classwide system to increase students' motivation

When
- During the fourth or fifth week of school
- Shortly after winter break

How
1. Make copies of the appropriate forms shown in Exhibits A.2, A.3, A.5, and A.6.
2. Choose one or more class periods in which student behavior tends to be the most problematic.

3. Identify the major activities and transitions that occur during the class period, and write each activity and transition on the "Activity" line in one of the form's rating boxes (see Exhibit A.1).

   If you plan to do this for several classes, you may want to spread your analysis across more than one day. For example, one day you might evaluate the first and third periods and the next day the fifth and seventh periods.

4. Before each activity or transition, briefly review your expectations with students. Immediately after completing the activity or transition, rate the degree to which students met your expectations, using the following rating scale:

   5 = All students met expectations

   4 = All but one or two students met expectations

   3 = Most students met expectations

   2 = About half the class met expectations

   1 = Most students did not meet expectations

Exhibit A.1
Samples from CHAMPs Rating Scale

Conversation	1 2 3 4 5
Help (Teacher Attention)	1 2 3 4 5
Activity: *Before the bell*	
Movement	1 2 3 4 5
Participation	1 2 3 4 5

Conversation	1 2 3 4 5
Help (Teacher Attention)	1 2 3 4 5
Activity: *Opening/Attendance*	
Movement	1 2 3 4 5
Participation	1 2 3 4 5

Conversation	1 2 3 4 5
Help (Teacher Attention)	1 2 3 4 5
Activity: *Teacher Directed*	
Movement	1 2 3 4 5
Participation	1 2 3 4 5

Conversation	1 2 3 4 5
Help (Teacher Attention)	1 2 3 4 5
Activity: *Independent Work*	
Movement	1 2 3 4 5
Participation	1 2 3 4 5

If you are using the ACHIEVE planning sheets to design your expectations, you may wish to use the evaluation forms in Exhibits A.5 and A.6 in place of the CHAMPs forms.

5. Review the data you have collected, and determine which activities or transitions may require reteaching of expectations. Exhibit A.4 has a sample completed form and conclusions. In addition, consider the following information as you interpret your data:

    If all activities and transitions rated a 4 or 5, you should not have to change your class's level of structure. If you have one or two students whose behavior concerns you, you may need to consider using one of the individual behavior management plans in Chapter Nine.

    If only 70 percent of activities and transitions rated a 4 or 5, it may be a good idea to reteach expectations for those activities that are not consistently going well over the next few days. See Chapter Eight, Task 1 for ideas. Again, if you have one or two students who seem to be having trouble with the structure of the class, consult Chapter Nine for some ideas.

    If less than 70 percent of activities and transitions rated 4 or 5, reteach your expectations and the policies and procedures outlined in your syllabus. See Chapter Eight, Task 1 for ideas. In addition, consider increasing the structure of your class. Review the tasks in Chapter Three to determine which aspects of your current classroom management plan might benefit from higher structure levels.

    If fewer than 50 percent of activities and transitions rated a 4 or 5, implement one of the classwide systems suggested in Chapter Nine. In addition, reteach your expectations and the policies and procedures outlined in your syllabus. See Chapter Eight, Task 1 for ideas. Finally, consider increasing the structure of your class. Review the tasks in Chapter Three to determine which aspects of your current classroom management plan might be implemented in a more structured manner.

> ### Note
> Some teachers may want to involve students in the rating process. If you choose to do this, explain the purpose and procedures ahead of time. Be sure to make clear that their input should not refer to individual students who did not meet expectations. A reproducible master of an enlarged rating form is provided in Exhibit A.3. It can be used as an overhead transparency if you plan to involve your class in the rating process.

CHAMPs versus Daily Reality Rating Scale:
Reproducible Form

Teacher Name: _____

Class Period: _____ Date: _____

RATINGS
   5 = All students met expectations
   4 = All but one or two students met expectations
   3 = Most students met expectations
   2 = About half the class met expectations
   1 = Most students did not meet expectations

Conversation 1 2 3 4 5 **H**elp (Teacher Attention) 1 2 3 4 5 **A**ctivity: **M**ovement 1 2 3 4 5 **P**articipation 1 2 3 4 5	**C**onversation 1 2 3 4 5 **H**elp (Teacher Attention) 1 2 3 4 5 **A**ctivity: **M**ovement 1 2 3 4 5 **P**articipation 1 2 3 4 5
Conversation 1 2 3 4 5 **H**elp (Teacher Attention) 1 2 3 4 5 **A**ctivity: **M**ovement 1 2 3 4 5 **P**articipation 1 2 3 4 5	**C**onversation 1 2 3 4 5 **H**elp (Teacher Attention) 1 2 3 4 5 **A**ctivity: **M**ovement 1 2 3 4 5 **P**articipation 1 2 3 4 5
Conversation 1 2 3 4 5 **H**elp (Teacher Attention) 1 2 3 4 5 **A**ctivity: **M**ovement 1 2 3 4 5 **P**articipation 1 2 3 4 5	**C**onversation 1 2 3 4 5 **H**elp (Teacher Attention) 1 2 3 4 5 **A**ctivity: **M**ovement 1 2 3 4 5 **P**articipation 1 2 3 4 5
Conversation 1 2 3 4 5 **H**elp (Teacher Attention) 1 2 3 4 5 **A**ctivity: **M**ovement 1 2 3 4 5 **P**articipation 1 2 3 4 5	**C**onversation 1 2 3 4 5 **H**elp (Teacher Attention) 1 2 3 4 5 **A**ctivity: **M**ovement 1 2 3 4 5 **P**articipation 1 2 3 4 5
Conversation 1 2 3 4 5 **H**elp (Teacher Attention) 1 2 3 4 5 **A**ctivity: **M**ovement 1 2 3 4 5 **P**articipation 1 2 3 4 5	**C**onversation 1 2 3 4 5 **H**elp (Teacher Attention) 1 2 3 4 5 **A**ctivity: **M**ovement 1 2 3 4 5 **P**articipation 1 2 3 4 5

CHAMPs versus Daily Reality Rating Scale: Reproducible Form

RATINGS
- 5 = All students met expectations
- 4 = All but one or two students met expectations
- 3 = Most students met expectations
- 2 = About half the class met expectations
- 1 = Most students did not meet expectations

Conversation	1	2	3	4	5
Help (Teacher Attention)	1	2	3	4	5
Activity:					
Movement	1	2	3	4	5
Participation	1	2	3	4	5

Conversation	1	2	3	4	5
Help (Teacher Attention)	1	2	3	4	5
Activity:					
Movement	1	2	3	4	5
Participation	1	2	3	4	5

Conversation	1	2	3	4	5
Help (Teacher Attention)	1	2	3	4	5
Activity:					
Movement	1	2	3	4	5
Participation	1	2	3	4	5

CHAMPs versus Daily Reality Rating Scale:
Completed Sample

Teacher Name: _Julie Howard_

Class Period: _____ Date:_____

RATINGS

    5 = All students met expectations

    4 = All but one or two students met expectations

    3 = Most students met expectations

    2 = About half the class met expectations

    1 = Most students did not meet expectations

Conversation 1 2 3 4 ⑤ **H**elp (Teacher Attention) 1 2 3 4 ⑤ **A**ctivity: *Before the Bell* **M**ovement 1 2 3 4 ⑤ **P**articipation 1 2 3 4 ⑤	**C**onversation 1 ② 3 4 5 **H**elp (Teacher Attention) 1 2 3 4 ⑤ **A**ctivity: *Cooperative Groups* **M**ovement 1 2 3 4 ⑤ **P**articipation 1 2 3 ④ 5
Conversation 1 2 3 ④ 5 **H**elp (Teacher Attention) 1 2 3 4 ⑤ **A**ctivity: *Attendance/Opening* **M**ovement 1 2 3 ④ 5 **P**articipation 1 2 3 4 ⑤	**C**onversation 1 2 3 4 ⑤ **H**elp (Teacher Attention) 1 2 3 4 ⑤ **A**ctivity: *Getting ready for Ind. Work* ◯ **M**ovement 1 2 3 4 ⑤
Conversation 1 2 3 4 ⑤ **H**elp (Teacher Attention) 1 2 3 4 ⑤ **A**ctivity: *Teacher-directed Instruction-Math* ◯ **M**ovement 1 2 3 ④ 5	**C**onversation 1 2 3 4 ⑤ **H**elp (Teacher Attention) 1 2 3 ④ 5 **A**ctivity: *Independent Work* **M**ovement 1 2 3 ④ 5 **P**articipation 1 2 3 4 ⑤
Conversation 1 2 ③ 4 5 **H**elp (Teacher Attention) 1 2 3 4 ⑤ **A**ctivity: *Getting into Cooperative Group (T)* ◯ **M**ovement 1 2 3 ④ 5	**C**onversation 1 2 3 4 ⑤ **H**elp (Teacher Attention) 1 2 3 4 ⑤ **A**ctivity: *Wrap-up/Closing* **M**ovement 1 2 3 4 ⑤ **P**articipation 1 2 3 4 ⑤

Analysis

In this sample, only one activity (Cooperative Groups) and one transition (Getting into Cooperative Groups) have ratings that are less than 4 and 5. The ratings indicate that the main problem is that students are talking too loudly so the noise level in the room is excessive. Therefore, the teacher decides to leave the classroom level at a low level of structure. However, she plans to reteach her behavioral expectations, with a special emphasis on how students in each cooperative group can monitor and manage the voice levels within their own groups.

ACHIEVE versus Daily Reality Rating Scale:
Reproducible Form

Teacher Name: _____

Class Period: _____ Date:_____

RATINGS

    5 = All students met expectations

    4 = All but one or two students met expectations

    3 = Most students met expectations

    2 = About half the class met expectations

    1 = Most students did not meet expectations

Activity:	
Conversation	1 2 3 4 5
Help	1 2 3 4 5
Integrity	1 2 3 4 5
Effort	1 2 3 4 5
Value	1 2 3 4 5
Efficiency	1 2 3 4 5

Activity:	
Conversation	1 2 3 4 5
Help	1 2 3 4 5
Integrity	1 2 3 4 5
Effort	1 2 3 4 5
Value	1 2 3 4 5
Efficiency	1 2 3 4 5

Activity:	
Conversation	1 2 3 4 5
Help	1 2 3 4 5
Integrity	1 2 3 4 5
Effort	1 2 3 4 5
Value	1 2 3 4 5
Efficiency	1 2 3 4 5

Activity:	
Conversation	1 2 3 4 5
Help	1 2 3 4 5
Integrity	1 2 3 4 5
Effort	1 2 3 4 5
Value	1 2 3 4 5
Efficiency	1 2 3 4 5

Activity:	
Conversation	1 2 3 4 5
Help	1 2 3 4 5
Integrity	1 2 3 4 5
Effort	1 2 3 4 5
Value	1 2 3 4 5
Efficiency	1 2 3 4 5

Activity:	
Conversation	1 2 3 4 5
Help	1 2 3 4 5
Integrity	1 2 3 4 5
Effort	1 2 3 4 5
Value	1 2 3 4 5
Efficiency	1 2 3 4 5

Transition 1:

Transition 2:

Transition 3:

ACHIEVE versus Daily Reality Rating Scale:
Reproducible Form

RATINGS

5 = All students met expectations

4 = All but one or two students met expectations

3 = Most students met expectations

2 = About half the class met expectations

1 = Most students did not meet expectations

Activity:

Conversation	1	2	3	4	5
Help	1	2	3	4	5
Integrity	1	2	3	4	5
Effort	1	2	3	4	5
Value	1	2	3	4	5
Efficiency	1	2	3	4	5

Activity:

Conversation	1	2	3	4	5
Help	1	2	3	4	5
Integrity	1	2	3	4	5
Effort	1	2	3	4	5
Value	1	2	3	4	5
Efficiency	1	2	3	4	5

Activity:

Conversation	1	2	3	4	5
Help	1	2	3	4	5
Integrity	1	2	3	4	5
Effort	1	2	3	4	5
Value	1	2	3	4	5
Efficiency	1	2	3	4	5

ACHIEVE versus Daily Reality Rating Scale:
Reproducible Form (*continued*)

Transition 1:

Transition 2:

Transition 3:

Appendix B: Ratio of Interactions Monitoring Forms

The information in this appendix will help you to determine whether you are interacting with students at least three times more when they are behaving responsibly than when they are misbehaving.

Why

- To help you evaluate whether you have fallen into the criticism trap—responding to misbehavior so frequently that although the misbehavior stops in the short run, it will actually increase over time
- To help you decide whether you need to increase the number of interactions you have with students when they are behaving appropriately

When

- During the second month of school
- In early to mid-February

How

1. Make a copy (or copies) of the appropriate reproducible forms in Exhibits B.1, B.2, and B.3.
2. Make sure you thoroughly understand the difference between positive interactions with students and negative interactions with students. Review the following:

Student behavior generates the interaction but should never dictate the tone of the interaction. Even negative interactions should not have a negative tone.

When you interact with a student who is engaging in appropriate or desirable behavior, the interaction would be counted as "Attention to Positive."

Examples

Praise	"Owen, you have been using this work time very efficiently and have accomplished a great deal."
Noncontingent attention	"Charlene, how are you today?"
Implementing a positive system	"Theresa and Josh each earned a marble in the jar for the class. They worked out a disagreement without needing my help."

Note that the comment under "Implementing a positive system" would be counted as two positive interactions because the teacher gave attention to two different students.

When you interact with a student who is engaging in inappropriate or undesirable behavior, the interaction should be recorded as "Attention to Negative."

Examples

Reminders	"Cody, you need to get back to work."
Reprimands	"Hanna, you know that you should be keeping your hands to yourself."
Corrections	"Ty, I don't think you need to tell me about that because I think you can handle that on your own."
Warnings	"Jennifer, if I have to speak to you again about talking in class, I will have to call your mother."
Consequences	"Priya, that is disruptive. You owe one minute off recess."

3. Determine the class periods during which you seem to have the most trouble being positive with students, and record (using audio- or videotape) those periods for one day.

4. Listen to (or watch) the recording, and mark your interactions on the Ratio of Interactions Monitoring Form. To do this, make a tally mark under "Attention to Positive" for each interaction you had with a student or the class when the behavior was responsible. Make a tally mark under "Attention to Negative" for each interaction you had with a student or the class when the behavior was irresponsible. Do not mark instructions to the group, like what page to turn to, or instructions on an activity at all. You should, however, count an instruction to an individual student like, "Beth, please turn out the lights" as positive or negative based on how the student was behaving at the time of the instruction.

5. Calculate your ratio of positive interactions to negative interactions with students. If you coded your interactions as above, you can further analyze them by type of attention, gender, and so on.

6. Analyze your performance.

Evaluate whether you achieved an overall three-to-one ratio of positives to negatives.

Evaluate whether your ratio of positives to negatives varies by category (for example, your ratio is lower with females than males).

Evaluate the overall style of your interactions, noting your tone of voice, sincerity, and intensity, and determine whether you are satisfied with it.

> **Note**
>
> If you wish to get more detailed information, consider using codes instead of simple tally marks for each interaction. For example:
>
> M or F: Brief attention to an individual male or female student
> C: Brief attention to the class or a group
> F/15: Attention to an individual female lasting approximately 15 seconds
> NC: Noncontingent attention to a student (for example, "Good morning")
> NV: Nonverbal attention (that is, a reassuring smile or a threatening look)

Evaluate the contingency of the positive feedback you give to individual students.

Evaluate whether one or two individuals received most of the negative interactions. If so, plan to use the Ratios of Interactions with a Particular Student form.

Evaluate if you had to correct a particular category of behavior (for example, off-task talking) more frequently than other problems. If so, use the Ratio of Interactions Monitoring Form with a Particular Behavior.

7. Plan a course of action.

If your overall interactions, or any subset of interactions, do not reflect a three-to-one positive to negative ratio, use the strategies at the end of this appendix and make an effort to decrease attention to negative behavior and increase attention to positive behavior. After approximately two weeks, monitor your interactions again to see if you have achieved the desired three-to-one ratio.

Once you have successfully achieved a three-to-one ratio, check for an improvement in student behavior. If students are behaving better, congratulate yourself and keep up the good work. If they are not, reread Chapter Six to see if there are any variables regarding student motivation that you have not implemented. In addition, read Chapter Nine to determine whether a motivation system might be appropriate.

Following the blank reproducible monitoring interactions forms, Exhibit B.4 shows a completed sample form with a brief analysis of its results.

Increasing Positive Interactions

As necessary, implement one or more of the following strategies:

1. Each time you have a negative interaction, remind yourself that you "owe" three positives.

2. Identify specific times during each day that you will give individual students, or the whole class, positive feedback on some aspect of their behavior or class performance. For example, at the beginning of the math lesson, you might compliment five or six students who are doing well or are paying attention.

3. Use individual conference times to compliment individual students on their performance.

4. Frequently scan the room for behaviors you can reinforce.

5. Identify particular events that occur during the day (for example, a student getting a drink of water) that will serve as a prompt to observe the class and identify a behavior to reinforce.

6. Reduce the amount of attention (time and intensity) the student receives for misbehavior. Increase the amount of attention (time and intensity) the student receives when not engaged in misbehavior.

7. Mentally tell yourself that each time you attend to a negative behavior, you "owe" that student three positive interactions when she or he is not engaged in misbehavior.

8. Interact with the student frequently with noncontingent positives.

Decreasing Negative Interactions

As necessary, implement one or more of the following strategies:

1. Identify whether there are aspects of the physical setting, schedule, organization, or something else that you might modify to reduce the probability that students will misbehave. For example, if some students push others in the rush to get out the door, excuse the students by rows or table groups.

2. Try "precorrecting" misbehavior. For example, if you anticipate that students will push each other while leaving the classroom, give a prompt like, "Remember to keep your hands and feet to yourself as you are leaving the room when I excuse the class."

3. Try praising someone for doing it the "right way" and intervene only if the misbehaving student does not change the behavior.

Your goal here is *not* to eliminate all negative interactions. Some are essential. For example, if a student does not know that a particular behavior is unacceptable, a gentle correction is the most direct and efficient way to provide the information the student needs to be successful. Or if you have a preestablished corrective consequence for a particular behavior, you must intervene anytime a student exhibits that behavior in order to maintain consistency.

Ratio of Interactions Monitoring Form During a
Particular Time of Day: Reproducible Form

Teacher: _____   Date: _____

Student's Name: _____

Coding System:

Attention to Positive	Attention to Negative

Analysis and Plan of Action:

Ratio of Interactions Monitoring Form
with a Particular Student: Reproducible Form

Teacher: _____ Date: _____

Student's Name: _____

Coding System:

Note *every* interaction you have with the student.

Attention to Positive	Attention to Negative

Analysis and Plan of Action:

Ratio of Interactions Monitoring Form
with a Particular Behavior: Reproducible Form

Teacher: _____   Date: _____

Student's Name: _____

Coding System:

Label the positive and negative behavior that will be monitored (e.g., Attention to Respect & to Disrespect).

Attention to Positive	Attention to Negative
_____	_____
(behavior label)	(behavior label)

NOTE: Decide if you will post this data for the class to see or if you wish to keep a less obtrusive record, like marks on a clipboard.

Analysis and Plan of Action:

Exhibit B.4

Ratio of Interactions Monitoring Form During a Particular Time of Day: Completed Sample

Teacher: _Mrs. Hammond_   Date: _October   12, 2006_

Behavior: _____

Coding System:

> M = Male
> F = Female
> N = Nick
> C = Class (as a whole)

Attention to Positive	Attention to Negative
M, M, M, F, M, F F, C, F, N, F, M C, M, M, N, F, M	N, N, M, N, F, F, N N, C, M, M, N

Analysis and Plan of Action:

My overall ratio is 1.5:1, so I need to decrease negatives and increase positives to get to 3:1 ratios. (If Nick's data are pulled out, I am almost at 3:1!!)

My interactions with Nick are 1:3 (negative), so I should work on this and monitor my interactions with Nick in a week.

Appendix C: Misbehavior Recording Sheet

The information in this appendix will help you determine whether you will require an intervention plan to deal with specific types of student misbehavior. If you are using behavior and effort grading (see Chapter Two), you probably already have a very good record of the frequency and kind of misbehaviors occurring in your class.

Why
- To help you identify how often and why you are intervening with students regarding their inappropriate behaviors
- To help you detect any patterns in your students' misbehavior (for example, time of day, day of the week, individual students)
- To give you specific and objective information about individual student behavior that you can share with the student and his or her family, when necessary
- To help you decide whether you need a classwide system to increase students' motivation to behave responsibly

When
- During the early part of the third month of school
- And in mid- to late January

How
1. Determine how you will track misbehavior in your class.

   Choose one of the two reproducible forms shown in Exhibits C.1 and C.2 and make copies. If you wish to design your own form, you can certainly do so, but you should look to those in this appendix for the essentials. Exhibit C.1 is a weekly record of misbehavior, by day, organized by student name. This form is designed for one class, so if you plan to monitor multiple classes, use a separate copy for each.

The second form is for teachers who find it easier to use a seating chart to record data rather than an alphabetical listing. Exhibit C.2 provides weekly records of misbehavior organized by student seating, with a square representing each desk. Use the form weekly, with one form per class. Use the horizontal lines within the square to track the days of the week. If the desks in your classroom are arranged in clusters or a U-shape, you will have to create your form.

Decide whether to monitor misbehavior in one, two, or all of your classes. Try it initially with only one class for a week. You should probably start with the class with the most misbehavior. If you find the information useful, you can then decide whether to use the form with the rest of your classes.

2. Put the appropriate misbehavior recording sheet on a clipboard, and plan to keep the clipboard close by for a week of the classes you have decided to monitor.

3. Explain to students that for the next five classes, you will be recording any time you have to speak to them about inappropriate behavior.

4. Whenever you speak to a student about a misbehavior, note the specific misbehavior on the form, using a coding system such as the following:

   o = Off-task

   h = Hands/feet/objects bothering others

   t = Talking

   d = Disruption

   s = Out of seat

   a = Arguing

   It is essential that your code consist of easy-to-remember letters to represent each major type of misbehavior you are likely to deal with.

5. Analyze the data and determine a plan of action.

   You may find that the behavior of some students improves simply because you are keeping records. If so, consider using the misbehavior recording sheet on an ongoing basis, although if you do so, you may wish to build in a positive component as well (see Chapter Two, Task 2).

   Make a subjective decision regarding your level of concern about the amount of misbehavior in your class. If you are not particularly concerned, do not bother making any changes.

   If you *are* concerned about the amount of misbehavior in your class, analyze the data from the misbehavior record sheet further. First, determine how much of the misbehavior is exhibited by just a few students. Identify the two or three students who had the most frequent incidents of misbehavior, and calculate the percentage of the total class misbehavior that could be attributed to them. To find this number, divide the total number of misbehaviors exhibited by the two or three students by the total number of misbehaviors exhibited by the entire class. For example, if the three students' total for two days was 45 and the total for the rest of the students was 16, you would divide 45 by the misbehavior total of 61 (45 + 16) to get a percentage of 74.

Once you have identified the percentage of misbehavior exhibited by the top two or three misbehaving students, use the following criteria to determine the most appropriate action:

- If more than 90 percent of the total classroom misbehavior can be attributed to the particular individual students, keep your level of structure and procedures as they are. For the individuals with the most misbehavior, consider implementing individual behavior management plans.

> ### Note
> It may seem to you right now that you will spend all your time recording information. However, remember that you are only going to mark one letter each time you have to speak to a student about misbehavior, which takes only a second or two. The hardest part of this task is not the time but remembering to keep the form near you when you are teaching and while you are circulating throughout the room.

- If 60 to 89 percent of the total classroom misbehavior can be attributed to the two or three individuals, plan to reteach your expectations for a few days, and then once per week for another month. (See Chapter Eight, Task 1.) In addition, consider individual behavior management plans for the students whose behavior is the most problematic. (See Chapter Nine.)

- If less than 60 percent of the misbehavior can be attributed to the two or three individuals, then your problem is classwide, and you should review and implement all the suggestions for high structure within Chapter Three. Also, plan to reteach your expectations for a few days and then once a week for another month. (See Chapter Eight, Task 1.) Also consider implementing one or more of the classwide systems discussed in Chapter Nine.

Following the reproducible forms, Exhibit C.3 shows a completed sample misbehavior recording sheet, including a brief analysis of its results.

Exhibit C.1
Misbehavior Recording Sheet: Student Name

Date _____ Reminders _____

Class Period _____

Name	Mon.	Tues.	Wed.	Thurs.	Fri.	Total

Codes:

Exhibit C.2
Misbehavior Recording Sheet: Seating Chart

(Weekly)

Date _____   Reminders _____

Class Period _____   _____

Name _____	Name _____	Name _____	Name _____	Name _____
Name _____	Name _____	Name _____	Name _____	Name _____
Name _____	Name _____	Name _____	Name _____	Name _____
Name _____	Name _____	Name _____	Name _____	Name _____
Name _____	Name _____	Name _____	Name _____	Name _____
Name _____	Name _____	Name _____	Name _____	Name _____
Name _____	Name _____	Name _____	Name _____	Name _____

Codes:

Exhibit C.3

Misbehavior Recording Sheet—Daily by Name: Example

Date _11/3/06_

Reminders _On Wed. remind about Fri. test_

Class Period _2_

Name	Mon.	Tues.	Wed.	Thurs.	Fri.	Total
Anderson, Chantel				T		1
Bahena, Ruben						0
Bell, Justin						0
Carrouza, Melinda		T		T	T	3
Cummings, Teresa						0
Demalski, Lee			T			1
Diaz, Margo						0
Etienne, Jerry						0
Fujiyama, Kim						0
Grover, Matthew						0
Henry, Scott	DDT	DO		DT	T	8
Isaacson, Chris						0
Kaufman, Jamie				D		1
King, Mark						0
LaRouche, Janel				T		1
Morales, Maria Louisa				T		1
Narlin, Jenny						0
Neely, Jacob			O	O		2
Nguyen, Trang						0
Ogden, Todd	TTD	D	OO	T	TT	9
Pallant, Jared						0
Piercey, Dawn			T	O	T	3
Reaves, Myra						0
Thomason, Rahsaan	TT		T	T	TT	6
Vandever, Aaron						0
Wong, Charlene						0
Yamamota, James		T		OT		3

Codes: D = Disruption O = Off Task T = Talking

Analysis and Plan of Action:

Scott Henry, Todd Ogden, and Rahsaan Thomason are the students who misbehave the most. Together they had a total of 23 misbehaviors for the week. The class total including them was 36. That means the misbehaviors of these three students accounted for approximately 64% of the total class misbehavior! This suggests a medium level of structure is appropriate for the class, which is what I already have in place. I do not believe the class requires a motivation system, but I will instead reteach expectations until behavior improves.

Appendix D: Grade Book Analysis Worksheet

The information in this appendix will help you determine whether the rates of tardies, attendance, work completion, and work quality among your students are satisfactory.

Why
To help you decide whether you need to implement a plan to improve:
- Student punctuality rates
- Student attendance rates
- Student work completion rates
- The quality of student work

When
- During the third month of school
- And in early to mid-March

How
1. Make copies of the reproducible form shown in Exhibit D.1.
2. Calculate rates of punctuality, attendance, work completion, and work quality for each student in your class and then record them on a grade book analysis worksheet.

   To calculate the *punctuality rate* for each student, divide the actual number of days the student has been arriving on time to your class by the total number of days school has been in session.

   To calculate the *attendance rate* for each student, divide the actual number of days the student has been at school by the total number of days school has been in session.

   To calculate the *rate of work completion* for each student, divide the actual number of in-class and homework assignments the student has turned in by the total number of in-class assignments that have been due at the present date.

To calculate the *percentage of quality work,* first determine what you consider to be quality work. You can define quality as any assignment with a passing grade or above, or you may prefer to define quality as a particular grade. For each student, divide the number of assignments that meet your definition of quality by the total number of assignments given to date.

3. Calculate the overall grade status of each student in your class, and record the information on a grade book analysis worksheet.

> ## Note
> If you do not have a computer-based grade book that will compute this information, consider having a responsible student or parent volunteer assist you with tasks 2 and 3. If you do have someone other than yourself do these calculations, replace student names with numbers to protect your students' confidentiality. This can be done easily by making a photocopy of your grade book pages with the students' names covered, and then replacing the names with numbers.

To calculate the overall grade status, simply use your grade book to determine the current grade of each student.

For each area you are evaluating (for example, attendance, work quality), determine a cut-off percentage that indicates a cause for concern. For example, with punctuality, attendance, and work completion, it may be 95 percent; for work not meeting your quality standards, it may be 80 percent.

Analyze your results, and decide on a plan of action for each area. If only one or two individuals fall below the cut-off percentage in any area, examine any interrelating information in the data. For example, a student may be failing because she is not attending regularly and is therefore not completing work.

Consider implementing some kind of individual intervention. For example, you might:

- Arrange to discuss the problem with the student.
- Arrange to discuss the problem with the student and the student's family.
- Make sure the student is capable of doing assigned tasks independently.
- Establish an individualized motivational plan for the student.
- Discuss the problem with your school counselor, school psychologist, or behavior specialist.

If more than two or three individuals fall below the cut-off percentage in a particular area, consider implementing some kind of whole-class intervention. For example, you might:

- Revise or reteach your expectations for independent work periods. See Chapter Eight.
- Review and, if necessary, revise your procedures for managing work completion. See Chapter Three.
- Publicly post and discuss daily class percentages. See Chapter Nine.

Grade Book Analysis Worksheet

Teacher _____   Date _____

Student Name or Number	% Attendance	% Punctuality	% Work Completion	% Quality Work	Overall Grade Status

Appendix E:
On-Task Behavior
Observation Sheet

T he information in this appendix is to help you determine the degree to which your students are using their in-class independent work time effectively.

Why

- To help you decide whether you need to reteach your expectations for independent work periods

- To help you identify the possible cause of poor work completion rates and misbehavior during independent work periods

When

- During the fourth month of school

- And in mid- to late February

How

1. Make copies of the reproducible form shown in Exhibit E.1.

2. Identify the independent work periods that you wish to monitor. Target any class or classes that are having trouble completing their work or those with frequent misbehavior.

3. Determine whether you will be conducting your own observation or if you will ask a colleague to do it.

   Having a colleague collect the data for your class has several advantages. First, you will be available to do whatever you usually do during this work period, such as circulating and answering questions. In addition, a colleague is likely to be more objective. You may have an unconscious tendency to make students look better or worse than they really are. Finally, exchanging classroom observations with a colleague gives both of you an opportunity to share ideas about how to help students improve their overall rate of on-task behavior.

4. During the observation period, the person who is collecting data should use the instantaneous time sampling method of observation:

   The observer should be positioned away from high-traffic areas, in a place where she can easily see students working at their seats. She should have a blank on-task behavior observation sheet and a pen or a pencil.

   The observer should choose an observation pattern that allows her to observe each student in the class a minimum of three times. For example, if students are in rows, the observer might start with the student in the front row to the left. She would then look at the next front-row student to the right, and then the next, until she has observed each student in that row. Then the observer would watch the students in the second row, moving from left to right, then the third row, and so on. After observing the last student in the back row, she would repeat this pattern at least two more times. The pattern is important; it keeps the data much more accurate than simply taking a randomly viewed sample of the students.

   When observing an individual student, the observer should look at that student for only an instant. Then she would look down at the paper and ask herself whether the student was on- or off-task at the time of observation. If the student was on-task, the observer marks a plus sign, and if the student was off-task, she marks a minus sign. This should be repeated for every student, following the pattern established in the previous step. The idea is for the observer to set up a rhythm with a quick pace, spending no more than three to five seconds on each student. The observing party should view the student, react to his or her behavior, mark it down, and move on. It should take no longer to do than it does to read or describe. The mark should reflect what the student is doing at the moment of observation. It should *not* reflect what the student was doing immediately before or after.

   The observer should follow the pattern and take in the whole class at least three times. When finished, the observation sheet should look something like the example below, taken from a class with thirty students:

   $$+ + + - - + + + + + + + + + - + + + + + + + + + + - - + - +$$
   $$+ + - + + + + + + - + + + + + + + + + + + + - + + + + + - - -$$
   $$+ + + + + + + - - + + - + + + - + + - - - + + + - - + + +$$

   Notice that no effort is made to record which student was on- or off-task. That would defeat the purpose of looking for a class average.

5. Determine the percentage of on-task behavior by dividing the total number of on-task marks (pluses) by the total number of marks (pluses and minuses). In the sample shown, this would be 70 divided by 90, meaning that during the observation period, the class was on task approximately 78 percent of the time.

6. Analyze the data and, if necessary, determine a plan of action.

If your class had an on-task rate of 90 percent or higher, provide positive feedback to your class, including telling them how they did, and encourage them to keep up the good work. If you feel that the percentage does not accurately reflect their typical behavior, because they were behaving for the observer or some other reason, let them know that you are pleased with what they demonstrated they could do and that you want them to strive to behave the way they did for the observer every day. If you know that most or all of the off-task behavior was exhibited by one or two students, arrange a private discussion with those individuals. Use the time to set improvement goals for the students and, if necessary, to develop individualized management plans to help them learn to manage work times more responsibly.

> **Note**
>
> If the process of monitoring seemed to improve your students' behavior, take advantage of it. Consider teaching the students how to use the form, and periodically ask a student to observe the class and record their behavior. Give the class feedback at the end of the work period. Use this procedure once a week until the class is consistently 90 percent on task or better.

If the class had an on-task rate of between 80 and 89 percent, tell them how they did and let them know that although they did fairly well, there is room for improvement. Together with the students, identify strategies that individuals might use to monitor and improve their own on-task behavior. If you feel that the percentage does not accurately reflect their typical behavior, let them know that you are pleased with what they demonstrated they could do and that you want them to strive to behave the same way every day. If you know that most or all of the off-task behavior was exhibited by one or two students, arrange a private discussion with those individuals. Use the time to set improvement goals for the students and, if necessary, develop individualized management plans to help then learn to manage their work time more responsibly.

If the class had an on-task rate of less than 80 percent, tell them what their percentage was, and explain that they need to improve. Review your expectations for independent work periods, placing special emphasis on what constitutes appropriate participation (see Chapter Eight). At a later time, examine your grade book. If, despite their high rates of off-task behavior, the class has high rates of work completion (above 95 percent), consider the possibility that you are giving your students too much class time to do their assignments. If both on-task behavior and work completion are low, you may want to establish a classwide system such as public posting of work completion (see Chapter Nine). If your students are averaging on-task behavior less than 80 percent, you are losing valuable instructional time, and you need to intervene.

On-Task Behavior Observation Sheet: Reproducible Form

Teacher: _____   Date: _____

Observer: _____

Activity:

Analysis and Plan of Action

Appendix F: Opportunities to Respond Observation Sheet

The information in this appendix will help you determine the degree to which your students are engaged during the teacher-directed instruction parts of your class.

Why
- To help you decide whether you need to modify your instructional methods to create more active student involvement
- To help you identify the possible causes of poor work completion rates and misbehavior during teacher-directed lessons

When
- During the fourth month of school
- And in mid- to late February

How
1. Make copies of the reproducible form shown in Exhibit F.1.

2. Identify the teacher-directed lessons that you wish to monitor. Target any class or classes that are having trouble staying focused or those with frequent misbehavior during lessons.

3. Determine whether you will be conducting your own observation using videotape or having a colleague observe your lesson.

Analyzing your own lesson has several advantages. First, it will be less threatening to your students than having someone else watch you teach. In addition, you will learn a great deal about your own teaching by observing students during your lesson. The major disadvantage is that students may behave differently when you observe them than they would for a neutral party. Another disadvantage is that there may be restrictions on taping students without getting parental permission.

Having a colleague collect the data has several advantages. A colleague is more likely to be objective. You may have an unconscious tendency to make students look better or worse than they really are. Finally, exchanging classroom observations with a colleague gives the two of you an opportunity to share ideas about how to create lessons that facilitate your students' actively engaging.

4.   During the observation period, plan to focus on three or four specific students.

If you are videotaping, set the camera to the side of the room toward the back. Inform students that you are taping your teaching so you can improve the quality of your lessons. Focus the camera on a group of four students, preferably four who represent different ability levels, so you can see them making written or verbal responses.

If you are having a colleague observe, arrange for him to sit to one side of the room, toward the back, and have him observe four students of different ability levels.

Record the start time of the lesson. During the lesson, mark on the observation sheet each time any of the target students makes a verbal response with a "V." Mark each time any of the target students makes a written response with a "W."

At the end of the teacher-directed portion of the lesson, record the stop time and the length of the lesson. If you have an observer who is not available for the entire class period, have him or her record the length of the observation.

5.   Determine the average number of responses per minute.

Determine the average response rate for the four students by adding the total of V's and W's and dividing by four.

Divide the number of minutes by the average response rate. This figure is the average responses per minute.

6.   Analyze the data and, if necessary, determine a plan of action.

Preliminary research with younger students determined that learning was maximized when students were responding between four to six times per minute during instruction on new material with 80 percent accuracy and responding between nine and twelve times per minute during drill and practice work with 90 percent accuracy (Council for Exceptional Children, 1987; Gunter, Hummel, & Venn, 1998).

There is little research, however, on what represents optimal response rates with older students with more complex tasks and with different types of activities such as discussion and lecture. Therefore, you (and your colleague if you had an observer) need to determine if the number of student responses is optimal for your class. Recognize that the more students are doing something that engages them with the lesson content, the greater the chances will be that they are learning the essential content.

If students seemed overly passive during your lesson, explore with colleagues or instructional supervisors and department chairpersons how to get students to participate more actively. More active response methods could include whole group choral responses, whole group physical responses (for example, "Stand up if the statement is true, stay seated if false"), copying notes, and quick ungraded quizzes.

Opportunities to Respond Observation Sheet:
Reproducible Form

Teacher: _____ Date: _____

Observer: _____

Activity: _____

Lesson start time: _____ Lesson end time: _____

Duration of Observation (number of minutes): _____

Student 1	Student 2	Student 3	Student 4

Mark a V for each verbal response. Mark a W for each written response.

Total number of responses: _____ divided by 4 equals: _____
(average number of responses)

Number of minutes divided by average number of responses equals _____
(average responses per minute)

Notes on subjective perception of the degree of student engagement in the lesson:

Analysis and Plan of Action

Appendix G:
Student
Satisfaction Survey

The information in this appendix is to help you determine how your students perceive various logistic and organizational features of your classroom.

Why
- To help you identify those aspects of your classroom program that are working well and those that may need modification
- To help you identify whether there are aspects of your classroom program that you need to communicate more clearly to students and their families

When
- Last two weeks of school
- Midyear (optional)

How
1. Check with your administrator to make sure that there are no policies or procedures that giving a survey of this type would violate.

2. Make copies of the two-page reproducible form shown in Exhibit G.1. (The survey can and should be modified to reflect your classroom program and any areas of concern that you may have.)

3. Determine if you will have students complete this independently in class or if you will try to involve students' parents. Recognize that attempting to involve the parents reduces the probability that you will get surveys back from all students. If you plan to try to get these from parents, determine how you will let families know that the survey is coming and the logistics of how families will receive and return the survey. For example, you could send the surveys home with students and have them returned by students. Or, if your school can budget for postage, you could send the surveys by mail with preaddressed, postage-paid return envelopes enclosed.

4. If you are giving the survey in class, remind students that the surveys are anonymous, but you hope they will give honest and productive answers to help you become a more effective teacher. Let them know that you have a box by the door in which they can place the completed survey so you will never see who made particular responses.

5. When all surveys have been returned, analyze the results. Keep in mind that although the information is subjective opinion, it can help you identify aspects of your classroom that may require further review. For example, if 50 percent of the families respond that students did not have enough homework, you should carefully consider whether the amount of homework you assign is sufficient. On the other hand, if 60 percent say the amount of homework is about right, 20 percent say it's too much, and 20 percent say it's not enough, you can probably assume that the amount of homework matches the average family's perception of what is appropriate.

Giving a survey of this type can be unnerving for you. As you examine the results, remind yourself that you cannot take critical information personally. Rather, you are looking for patterns of information that will help you fine-tune your classroom program.

Student Satisfaction Survey: Reproducible Form

Dear Students,

   As we approach this point in the school year, I want to thank you all for your help and support. As a professional trying to meet the needs of all students, I am always looking for ways to improve. You can help by giving me feedback about the strengths and weaknesses you see in my program. Please take a few minutes to fill out the following survey.

   Note there is no place to put your name. I will not know who wrote what unless you wish to sign your name. Once you have completed the survey, fold it in half, and place it in the box by the door.

Sincerely,

Homework

1. The amount of homework assigned has been:

   ○ Way too much   ○ A bit too much   ○ About right   ○ Not enough

2. The difficulty of homework has been:

   ○ Way too hard   ○ A bit too hard   ○ About right   ○ Too easy

Assignments and Class Work

1. The amount of in-class work assigned has been:

   ○ Way too much   ○ A bit too much   ○ About right   ○ Not enough

2. The difficulty of in-class work has been:

   ○ Way too hard   ○ A bit too hard   ○ About right   ○ Too easy

3. Most of the time I felt that the work has been:

   ○ Stupid   ○ Boring   ○ Okay   ○ Interesting   ○ Fun

4. Describe one valuable thing you learned this year: _____

   _____

   _____

Student Satisfaction Survey: Reproducible Form
(*continued*)

5. Identify one type of activity there should be more of:

   ○ Lecture   ○ Discussion   ○ Cooperative groups   ○ Independent work   ○ Simulations

6. Identify one type of activity there should be less of:

   ○ Lecture   ○ Discussion   ○ Cooperative groups   ○ Independent work   ○ Simulations

....

Classroom Atmosphere

1. Most of the time, I have . . .

   ○ hated coming to this class   ○ felt that this class is okay   ○ looked forward to class

Please explain your answer:

_____
_____
_____

2. I think the teacher has treated me with respect . . .

   ○ not often   ○ most of the time   ○ all of the time

Please explain your answer:

_____
_____
_____

3. What might I have done differently to make this year a more pleasant and productive experience for you?

_____
_____
_____
_____
_____
_____

References

Alberto, P. A., & Troutman, A. C. (2003). *Applied behavior analysis for teachers* (6th ed.). Upper Saddle River, NJ: Merrill Prentice Hall.

Archer, A., & Gleason, M. (2003). *Advanced skills for school success: Modules 1 through 4.* North Billerica, MA: Curriculum Associates.

Archer, A., Gleason, M., & Vachon, V. (2005). *REWARDS (Reading excellence: Word attack and rate development strategies).* Longmont, CO: Sopris West.

Assor, A., & Connell, J. P. (1992). The validity of students' self-reports as measures of performance-affecting self-appraisals. In D. H. Schunk & J. Meece (Eds.), *Student perceptions in the classroom* (pp. 25–46). Mahwah, NJ: Erlbaum.

Baer, D. M. (1999). *How to plan for generalization.* Austin, TX: Pro-Ed.

Baron, E. B. (1992). *Discipline strategies for teachers.* Bloomington, IN: Phi Delta Kappa.

Beck, R. (1997). *Project RIDE: Responding to individual differences in education.* Longmont, CO: Sopris West.

Becker, W. C., & Engelmann, S. (1971). *Teaching: A course in applied psychology.* Columbus, OH: Science Research Associates.

Bell, K. (1998). In the beginning: Teacher created a positive learning environment. *Teaching Elementary Physical Education, 9,* 12–14.

Biglan, A. (1995). Translating what we know about the context of antisocial behavior into a lower prevalence of such behavior. *Journal of Applied Behavior Analysis, 28,* 479–492.

Brophy, J. (1983). Conceptualizing student motivation. *Educational Psychologist, 18,* 200–215.

Brophy, J. (1998). *Failure syndrome students.* Champaign, IL: University of Illinois, ERIC Clearinghouse on Elementary and Early Childhood Education. (ERIC Document Reproduction Service No. ED419625)

Brophy, J., & Good, T. L. (1986). Teacher behavior and student achievement. In M. C. Whitrock (Ed.), *Handbook of Research on Teaching* (3rd ed., pp. 328–375). New York: Macmillan.

Burnette, J. (1999). *Critical behaviors and strategies for teaching culturally diverse students.* Reston, VA: ERIC Clearinghouse on Disabilities and Gifted Education. (ERIC Document Reproduction Service No. ED435147)

Cameron, J., Banko, K. M., & Pierce, W. D. (2001). Pervasive negative effects of rewards on intrinsic motivation: The myth continues. *Behavior Analyst, 24,* 1–44.

Chance, P. (1998). *First course in applied behavior analysis.* Belmont, CA: Brooks/Cole.

Colvin, G., & Sugai, G. (1988). Proactive strategies for managing social behavior problems: An instructional approach. *Education and Treatment of Children, 11,* 341–348.

Cotton, K. (1999). *Research you can use to improve results* (4th ed.). Alexandra, VA: Association for Supervision and Curriculum Development.

Council for Exceptional Children. (1987). *Academy for effective instruction: Working with mildly handicapped students.* Reston, VA: Author.

Covington, M. (2000). Goal theory, motivation, and school achievement: An integrative review. *Annual Review of Psychology, 51,* 171–200.

Dawson-Rodrigues, K., Lavay, B., Butt, K., & Lacourse, M. (1997). A plan to reduce transition time in physical education. *Journal of Physical Education, Recreation and Dance, 68,* 30–34.

Deno, S. (1985). The importance of goal ambitiousness and goal mastery to student achievement. *Exceptional Children, 52,* 63–71.

Deno, S. L., Espin, C. A., & Fuchs, L. S. (2002). Evaluation strategies for preventing and remediating basic skill deficits. In M. R. Shinn, H. M. Walker, & G. Stoner (Eds.), *Interventions for academic and behavior problems II: Preventive and remedial approaches.* Bethesda, MD: National Association of School Psychologists.

Deshler, D. D., Schumaker, J. B., Lenz, B. K., Bulgren, J. A., Hock, M. F., Knight, J., & Ehren, B. J. (2001). Ensuring content-area learning by secondary students with learning disabilities. *Learning Disabilities Research and Practice, 16*(2), 96–108.

Detrich, R. (1999). Increasing treatment fidelity by matching interventions to contextual variables within the educational setting. *School Psychology Review, 28,* 608–620.

Emmer, E. T., Evertson, C. M., & Worsham, M. E. (2002). *Classroom management for secondary teachers* (6th ed.). Needham Heights, MA: Allyn & Bacon.

Feather, N. T. (Ed.). (1982). *Expectations and actions.* Mahwah, NJ: Erlbaum.

Fisher, C., Berliner, D., Filby, N., Marliave, R., Cahen, L., & Dishaw, M. (1980). Teaching behaviors, academic learning time, and student achievement: An overview. In C. Denham & A. Lieberman (Eds.), *Time to learn.* Washington, DC: National Institute of Education.

Gunter, P., Hummel, J., & Venn, M. (1998). Are effective academic practices used to teach students with behavior disorders? *Beyond Behavior, 9,* 5–11.

Hamre, B. K., & Pianta, R. C. (2001). Early teacher-child relationships and the trajectory of children's school outcomes through eighth grade. *Child Development, 72,* 652–638.

Harlan, J. C. (2002). *Behavior management strategies for teachers: Achieving instructional effectiveness, student success, and student motivation—every teacher and any student can!* Springfield, IL: Charles C Thomas.

Harniss, M. K., Stein, M., & Carnine, D. (2002). Promoting mathematics achievement. In M. R. Shinn, H. M. Walker, & G. Stoner (Eds.), *Interventions for academic and behavior problems II: Preventive and remedial approaches* (pp. 571–587). Bethesda, MD: National Association of School Psychologists.

Henderson, H. S., Jenson, W. R., & Erken, N. (1986). Variable internal reinforcement for increasing on-task behavior in classrooms. *Education and Treatment of Children, 9,* 250–263.

Hintze, J. M., Volpe, R. J., & Shapiro, E. S. (2002). Best practices in the systematic direct observation of student behavior. In A. Thomas & J. Grimes (Eds.), *Best practices in school psychology IV.* Washington, DC: National Association of School Psychologists.

Horner, R. H., Vaughn, B. J., Day, H. M., & Ard, W. R. (1996). The relationship between setting events and problem behavior: Expanding our understanding of behavioral support. In L. Koegel, R. L. Koegel, & G. Dunlap (Eds.), *Positive behavioral support: Including people with difficult behavior in the community* (pp. 381–402). Baltimore, MD: Paul Brookes.

Iwata, B. A., Smith, R. G., & Michael, J. (2000). Current research on the influence of establishing operations on behavior in applied settings. *Journal of Applied Behavior Analysis, 33,* 411–418.

Jones, V., & Jones, L. (2004). *Comprehensive classroom management: Creating positive learning environments and solving problems* (7th ed.). Needham Heights, MA: Allyn & Bacon.

Kame'enui, E. J., Carnine, D. W., Dixon, R. C., Simmons, D. C., & Coyne, M. D. (2002). Introduction. In *Effective teaching strategies that accommodate diverse learners* (2nd ed., pp. 203–215). Upper Saddle River, NJ: Merrill Prentice Hall.

Kame'enui, E. J., & Simmons, D. C. (1990). *Designing instructional strategies: The prevention of academic learning problems.* Columbus, OH: Merrill.

Lalli, J. S., Vollmer, T. R., Progar, P. R., Wright, C., Borrero, J., Daniel, D., Hoffner Bartohold, C., Tocco, K., & May, W. (1999). Competition between positive and negative reinforcement in the treatment of escape behavior. *Journal of Applied Behavior Analysis, 32,* 285–296.

Lam, T.C.M. (1995). *Fairness in performance assessment.* Greensboro, NC: ERIC Clearinghouse on Counseling and Student Services. (ERIC Document Reproduction Service No. ED391982)

Langland, S., Lewis-Palmer, T., & Sugai, G. (1998). Teaching respect in the classroom: An instructional approach. *Journal of Behavioral Education, 8,* 245–262.

Laraway, S., Snycerski, S., Michael, J., & Poling, A. (2003). Motivating operations and terms to describe them: Some further refinements. *Journal of Applied Behavior Analysis, 36,* 407–414.

Lewis, T. J., & Sugai, G. (1999). Effective behavior support: A systems approach to proactive schoolwide management. *Focus on Exceptional Children, 31*(6), 1–24.

Lovitt, T. C. (1978). *Managing inappropriate behaviors in the classroom.* Reston, VA: Council for Exceptional Children.

Lynn, S. K. (1994). Create an effective learning environment. *Strategies, 7,* 14–17.

Ma, X., & Willms, J. D. (2004). School disciplinary climate: Characteristics and effects on eighth grade achievement. *Alberta Journal of Educational Research, 50,* 169–188.

Malone, B. G., & Tietjens, C. L. (2000). Re-examination of classroom rules: The need for clarity and specified behavior. *Special Services in the Schools, 16,* 159–170.

Martens, B. K., Lochner, D. G., & Kelly, S. Q. (1992). The effects of variable-interval reinforcement on academic engagement: A demonstration of matching theory. *Journal of Applied Behavior Analysis, 25,* 143–151.

Martin, D. V. (1989). *Transition management: The student teacher's Achilles heel.* Paper presented at the annual meeting of the Association of Teacher Educators, St. Louis, MO.

Marzano, R. J. (2003). *Classroom management that works: Research-based strategies for every teacher.* Alexandria, VA: Association for Supervision and Curriculum Development.

McCloud, S. (2005). From chaos to consistency: When one urban elementary school changed its culture from rowdy to calm, student achievement fell into place. *Educational Leadership, 62*(5), 46–49.

McLean, E. (1993). Tips for beginners: Steps to better homework. *Mathematics Teacher, 86,* 212.

McLeod, J., Fisher, J., & Hoover, G. (2003). *The key elements of classroom management: Managing time and space, student behavior, and instructional strategies.* Alexandria, VA: Association for Supervision and Curriculum Development.

McNeely, C. A., Nonnemaker, J. A., & Blum, R. W. (2002). Promoting school connectedness: Evidence from the National Longitudinal Study of Adolescent Health. *Journal of School Health, 72*(4), 138–146.

Meece, J. L., Blumenfield, P. C., & Hoyle, R. H. (1988). Students' goal orientations and cognitive engagement in classroom activities. *Journal of Educational Psychology, 80,* 514–523.

Mendler, A. N., & Curwin, R. L. (1999). *Discipline with dignity for challenging youth.* Bloomington, IN: National Educational Service.

Metzger, M. (2002). Learning to discipline. *Phi Delta Kappan, 84,* 77–84.

Moran, C., Stobbe, J., Baron, W., Miller, J., & Moir, E. (2000). *Keys to the classroom: A teacher's guide to the first month of school.* Thousand Oaks, CA: Corwin Press.

National Research Council. (2000). *How people learn: Brain, mind, experience, and school.* Washington, DC: National Academy Press.

Nelson, R. (1996). Designing schools to meet the needs of students who exhibit disruptive behavior. *Journal of Emotional and Behavioral Disorders, 4,* 147–161.

O'Neill, R. E., Horner, R. H., Albin, R. W., Storey, K., Sprague, J. R., & Newton, J. S. (1997). *Functional assessment and program development for problem behavior: A practical handbook* (2nd ed.). Pacific Grove, CA: Brooks/Cole.

Orange, C. (2005). *Smart strategies for avoiding classroom mistakes.* Thousand Oaks, CA: Corwin Press.

Paine, S. C., Radicchi, J., Rosellini, L. C., Deutchman, L., & Darch, C. B. (1983). *Structuring your classroom for academic success.* Champaign, IL: Research Press.

Patrick, H., Turner, J. C., Meyer, D. K., & Midgley, C. (2003). How teachers establish psychological environments during the first days of school: Associations with avoidance in mathematics. *Teachers College Record, 105,* 1521–1558.

Reddy, R., Rhodes, J. E., & Mulhall, P. (2003). The influence of teacher support on student adjustment in the middle school years: A latent growth curve study. *Development and Psychopathology, 15,* 119–138.

Ridley, D. S., & Walther, B. (1995). *Creating responsible learners: The role of a positive classroom environment.* Washington, DC: American Psychological Association.

Rosenshine, B., & Stevens, R. (1986). Teacher behavior and student achievement. In M. C. Whitrock (Ed.), *Handbook of research on teaching* (3rd ed., pp. 376–391). New York: Macmillan.

Royer, J. M., Cisero, C. A., & Carlo, M. S. (1993). Techniques and procedures for assessing cognitive skills. *Review of Educational Research, 63,* 201–243.

Scarborough, H. S., & Parker, J. D. (2003). Matthew effects in children with learning disabilities: Development of reading, IQ, and psychosocial problems from grade 2 to grade 8. *Annals of Dyslexia, 53,* 47–71.

Schell, L. M., & Burden, P. R. (1985). Working with beginning teachers. *Small School Forum, 7,* 13–15.

Schumaker, J. B., Deshler, D. D., & McKnight, P. (2002). Ensuring success in the secondary general education curriculum through the use of teaching routines. In M. A. Shinn, H. M. Walker, & G. Stoner (Eds.), *Interventions for academic and behavior problems II: Preventive and remedial approaches* (pp. 791–823). Bethesda, MD: National Association of School Psychologists.

Silva, F. J., Yuille, R., & Peters, L. K. (2000). A method for illustrating the continuity of behavior during schedules of reinforcement. *Teaching of Psychology, 27,* 145–148.

Simola, R. (1996). *Teaching in the real world.* Englewood, CO: Teacher Ideas Press.

Skiba, R., & Peterson, R. (2003). Teaching the social curriculum: School discipline as instruction. *Preventing School Failure, 47,* 66–73.

Skinner, E. A., & Belmont, M. J. (1993). Motivation in the classroom: Reciprocal effects of teacher behavior and student engagement across the school year. *Journal of Educational Psychology, 85,* 571–581.

Spaulding, R. L. (1978). Control of deviancy in the classroom as a consequence of ego-enhancing behavior management techniques. *Journal of Research and Development in Education, 11,* 39–52.

Sponder, B. (1993). Twenty golden opportunities to enhance student learning: Use them or lose them. *Teaching and Learning, 15,* 18–24.

Sprick, R. S. (1994). *Cafeteria discipline: Positive techniques for lunchroom supervision* [Video program]. Eugene, OR: Pacific Northwest Publishing.

Sprick, R. S. (2004). *START on time! Safe transitions and reduced tardiness* [Multimedia program]. Eugene, OR: Pacific Northwest Publishing.

Sprick, R. S., Borgmeier, C., & Nolet, V. (2002). In M. A. Shinn, H. M. Walker, & G. Stoner (Eds.), *Interventions for academic and behavior problems II: Preventive and remedial approaches* (pp. 373–402). Bethesda, MD: National Association of School Psychologists.

Sprick, R. S., Garrison, M., & Howard, L. (1998). *CHAMPs: A proactive and positive approach to classroom management.* Eugene, OR: Pacific Northwest Publishing.

Sprick, R. S., & Howard, L. (1995). *The teacher's encyclopedia of behavior management: 100 problems, 500 plans.* Eugene, OR: Pacific Northwest Publishing.

Sprick, R. S., Howard, L., Wise, B. J., Marcum, K., & Haykin, M. (1998). *Administrator's desk reference of behavior management* (Vol. 1). Eugene, OR: Pacific Northwest Publishing.

Sprick, R. S., Sprick, M. S., & Garrison, M. (1993). *Interventions: Collaborative planning for high risk students.* Eugene, OR: Pacific Northwest Publishing.

Sprick, R. S., Sprick, M. S., & Garrison, M. (2002). *Foundations: Establishing positive discipline policies* [Video program]. Eugene, OR: Pacific Northwest Publishing,

Sterling-Turner, H. E., Robinson, S. L., & Wilczynski, S. M. (2001). Functional assessment of distracting and disruptive behaviors in the school setting. *School Psychology Review, 30,* 211–226.

Stone, R. (2002). *Best practices for high school classrooms: What award-winning secondary teachers do.* Thousand Oaks, CA: Corwin Press.

Stronge, J. H. (2002). *Qualities of effective teachers.* Alexandria, VA: Association for Supervision and Curriculum Development.

Sugai, G. M., & Tindal, G. A. (1993). *Effective school consultation: An interactive approach.* Pacific Grove, CA: Brooks/Cole.

Tanner, B. M., Bottoms, G., Caro, F., & Bearman, A. (2003). *Instructional strategies: How teachers teach matters.* Atlanta, GA: Southern Regional Educational Board.

Teachers favor standards, consequences . . . and a helping hand. (1996). *American Educator, 20,* 18–21.

Wolf, D., Bixby, J., Glenn, J., & Gardner, H. (1990). To use their minds well: Investigating new forms of student assessment. *Review of Research in Education, 17,* 31–74.

Wolfgang, C. H., & Glickman, C. D. (1986). *Solving discipline problems: Strategies for classroom teachers* (2nd ed.). Needham Heights, MA: Allyn & Bacon.

Woodward, J. (2001). Using grades to assess student performance. *Journal of School Improvement, 2,* 44–45.

Ysseldyke, J. E., & Christenson, S. L. (1987). Evaluating students' instructional environments. *RASE, 8,* 17–24.

Index